Successful
Credit Control

Successful Credit Control

Second Edition

Martin Posner

John Wiley & Sons

Chichester · New York · Weinheim · Brisbane · Singapore · Toronto

First published by BSP Professional Books, 1990

This edition copyright © 1998 by John Wiley & Sons Ltd,
Baffins Lane, Chichester,
West Sussex PO19 1UD, England

National   01243 779777
International   (+44) 1243 779777
e-mail (for orders and customer service enquiries):
cs-books@wiley.co.uk
Visit our Home Page on http://www.wiley.co.uk
or http://www.wiley.com

Other Wiley Editorial Offices

John Wiley & Sons, Inc., 605 Third Avenue,
New York, NY 10158-0012, USA

WILEY-VCH Verlag GmbH, Pappelallee 3,
D-69469 Weinheim, Germany

Jacaranda Wiley Ltd, 33 Park Road, Milton,
Queensland 4064, Australia

John Wiley & Sons (Asia) Pte Ltd, 2 Clementi Loop #02-01,
Jin Xing Distripark, Singapore 129809

John Wiley & Sons (Canada) Ltd, 22 Worcester Road,
Rexdale, Ontario M9W 1L1, Canada

Library of Congress Cataloging-in-Publication Data

Posner, Martin,
    Successful credit control / Martin Posner. — 2nd ed.
       p.   cm.
    Previously published: Oxford : BSP Professional Books, 1990.
    Includes index.
    ISBN 0-471-97526-5 (pbk.)
    1. Credit—Management. 2. Credit—Great Britain. I. Title.
HG3751.P67   1998
658.8'8—dc21   97–45614
                                              CIP

British Library Cataloguing in Publication Data

A catalogue record for this book is available from the British Library

ISBN 0-471-97526-5

Typeset in 10/12pt Times by Dorwyn Ltd, Rowlands Castle, Hants
Printed and bound in Great Britain by Redwood Books, Trowbridge, Wiltshire
This book is printed on acid-free paper responsibly manufactured from sustainable forestry, in which at least two trees are planted for each one used for paper production.

Contents

Foreword to the
First Edition

SIR KENNETH CORK, *GBE, DLitt, FCA, FICM*
President of the Institute of Credit Management

I have known Martin Posner for many years, through his membership of the Institute of Credit Management. Martin Posner has done a great deal of work in making the Institute of Credit Management the useful and influential organisation which it is. He is a Member of Council, and has served as Chairman of the Education Committee.

He has written this book, which I would prefer to call a bible, for the credit manager. It is clear and concise, and is the kind of book that, whichever problem a credit manager has, he will be able to open it at the relevant page, and almost certainly find the answer. Not only is there practical advice as to how a credit manager should set up his office and approach his job, but he has produced a list of organisations which are of help to credit managers with addresses, showing their specialist services. Anyone trading overseas will find similar information in relation to other countries.

Perhaps the most valuable part of this book is that containing the many working examples of how an approach should be made to the customer; any reader who has perused this section will realise that the debtor is also a customer. The credit manager, in assessing a risk, has also to see that the customer is not driven elsewhere by too unattractive an approach.

I think the reader will realise that this thoroughly detailed discipline would only be carried out with a limited number of customers, and therefore the system must, of its own volition, throw up the cases where particular care is needed.

I do not think I have ever read such a complete bible. It might even be possible, with diligence, for a complete beginner in the profession, with this book beside him, to act as a professional!

I recommend this book as compulsory reading to all aspiring credit managers.

Kenneth Cork

Foreword to the Second Edition

SIR ROGER CORK, *FCA, FICM, FIPA*
Lord Mayor of London,
Senior Vice President of the Institute of Credit Management

I was delighted to be asked by Martin to add the foreword to the second edition of his quite superb book. My father, Sir Kenneth Cork, wrote the foreword to the first edition when he was President of the Institute of Credit Management. He was extremely complimentary concerning Martin and his book and I can only echo those comments.

This second edition contains much updated information and is once again a book that is going to be extremely useful to credit managers whether they be of long standing or new into the profession.

As a past chairman of the Institute and presently a Vice President thereof, I am acutely aware of the many benefits of an excellent book like this one.

Martin has put his considerable expertise and knowledge into the revision of the first edition to make an even better second edition. I can thoroughly recommend it to everyone.

Roger Cork

Preface

This book is written for credit control and sales ledger staff who wish to develop their skills in assessment to increase profitable sales and organisation of the Sales Ledger and collection techniques to increase cash flow.

Credit managers, their staff and, especially, students and newcomers to credit will find that the many interviews with experts in the world of credit highlight how profitable sales can increase when research is carried out.

With the intense commercial pressure to pass orders, different types of business organisations are covered in some detail. UK and overseas research is emphasised so that workable systems can be planned and the anxiety of bad debts can be reduced.

To gain the greatest benefit readers should try to read a chapter in its entirety.

My sincere thanks to the many members of the Institute of Credit Management and other contributors including Chambers of Commerce, and Credit Insurers. I must especially thank Intrum Justitia for their generous sponsorship, Peter Brooker of Experian, Phillip Mellor of Dun & Bradstreet, Ken Redpath of Fletcher & Collins and Creditreform for their research; and Keith Lyward of Pritchard Joyce & Hinds and Jim Nolan of Nolan Macleod for their enormous contribution on debt recovery practices in England, Wales and Scotland. I also wish to thank NatWest Bank and HSBC Group and the many insolvency practitioners who have helped me, and NCM for their continuous support.

Finally I must thank my wife June for her support and for devoting an enormous amount of time at the computer and Sally Rosebery for her masterly redesigning of many of the illustrations and constant support for the novice computer operator.

Introduction

It is so easy to give away your product or service if no assessment is first made on the customer.

Credit granting can be defined as confidence, trust and belief in a customer's ability to pay at a definite date for goods or services supplied today. This confidence is gained by carefully assessing the character, history and background of the buyer. The objective, when receiving an order from an unknown customer, is to obtain enough information to reveal whether the customer is able to pay or not, and if they have a track record in the past of paying accounts on demand.

Many readers may see the credit control function as a collection routine. My philosophy is different. The offering of various credit-granting schemes acts as an inducement to buyers. This attitude helps to cement a relationship between the marketing and the finance wing of any trading organisation to increase sales. There is always a commercial risk when selling either in the home market or overseas. But risks can be reduced if the sales ledger/credit control/accounts function is administered in a professional way. By saying 'yes' to a sale, your business will have a bigger market share and the all-important profits will increase. All that is necessary is research.

Since 1990 when the first edition was written there has been a dramatic increase in the number of businesses operating in the UK. There are now about 3.8 million. This figure includes sole traders, partnerships and limited companies.

Creating customer care to sustain repeat business is essential. Computerisation and information technology now enable credit staff to assess credit requirements far more quickly. But due to mergers, re-engineering and management buy-outs the old pareto 80:20 sales ledger ratios have changed.

However, some aspects of credit control have not changed. David Coates, the Managing Director of Experian, confirmed that in 1997 only 20 per cent of UK businesses obtained credit reports on their customers. Nick Wilson, the ICM Professor of Credit Management, published a survey in 1995 which showed that 52% of all invoices were paid late. Businesses with fewer than 20 people often employ one person who carries out all the accounting tasks. But between 30–40 per cent of a business's net assets are represented by debtors. The new interviews with credit staff have been especially chosen to illustrate how smaller companies can apply the best practices on a smaller scale.

The Market

In the UK alone there are over 3.9 million operating businesses. Looking overseas, there are at least 240 countries who may be persuaded to buy a product or service because of design, quality or price. I will highlight the additional areas which an exporter must consider. These include the economic and political risks, plus government regulations, local customs and documentation.

The Risks

One of the greatest dangers to credit granters is not fully understanding the risks in supplying to different legal personalities, e.g. minors, sole traders and limited companies in the UK. In Chapter 1 I will list a number of business organisations that you may be selling to in the United Kingdom. This is the first key question, as each type of business has a different legal structure. The responsibility for payment and the financial structure of the businesses will all vary.

In this book I will try to guide readers through the maze of facts and information which, if assembled in order of priority, will help to create profitable sales. It is an enjoyable, exciting and fascinating pursuit, learning how to interpret bankers' opinions, traders' references, sales reports, company accounts and trade and newspaper reports.

It has always been my policy to emphasise the assessment side of credit-granting and professional management of the sales ledger. Research and planning is essential to increase profitable sales. Regrettably, if this work is not carried out, the credit control department may try to collect accounts which are uncollectable. Why do I highlight this point? In reviewing statistics for 1995 in England and Wales alone, there were over 2.2 million default summonses issued in the county courts. In 1996 there were nearly 14,000 limited company liquidations, and for the period 1986 there were 24,306 Orders issued for Bankruptcy Proceedings, covering England, Wales and Scotland. As a warning to those who are new to credit-granting, it is possible to purchase an 'off the shelf' limited company for under £200 which includes the two one pound shares which have to be issued under the Companies Act. Once the formalities of purchasing a limited company have been completed, a company can legally start trading.

Improving collection methods and planning cash flow techniques is definitely not difficult. Examples of successful schemes will be illustrated.

The object of amending this book is to help businesses to increase profitable sales so that their personnel will not go home at night thinking, 'Will I get paid?'.

The law is given in this book as stated at March 1997.

Martin Posner

1
The Basic Principles of Credit Assessment

WHAT DO YOU KNOW?

Before any assessment can take place I ask the question, 'What do you know about the new or existing customer or account?' (Debtors on the ledger can represent 40 per cent of the value of current assets in a business). To have confidence in advancing credit there must be information on which to access a risk.

My philosophy is to be flexible on credit-granting when selling. Saying 'no' to a customer may be an easy answer, but your competitors may gain a profitable sale. This is not the way to increase turnover and profit.

My description of credit is confidence, trust and belief in the ability of the customer to pay for goods or services supplied today at a defined, future date.

To be able to have this confidence you will need to obtain answers to a number of key questions. The first is, who is the customer?

Are they:

- Sole trader?
  Partnership?
  Limited company?
  Public limited company?
  Multinational company?
- A government ministry?
  A public authority?
  Privatised bodies?
  A local authority?
- An association or club?
  An institute?

- An individual consumer (adult)?
  A minor?

In groups one and three, the next question is, 'How long have they been established?' The answer to this point is not always conclusive as there may have been a change of ownership, or a management buyout (see Chapter 4). What is the experience of the directors, managers, proprietors or partners? Their background training, education, experience of working in other companies or fields, will often be a strong indication that you can have greater trust and confidence in them. The age of the managers, their lifestyle and personal character can often influence a credit application. With an ever-increasing number of divorces and one-parent families, creating a picture is helpful when assessing credit needs. Here is an example where further investigation will be required.

> A limited company which delivers building materials to the trade and has been established for 15 years, is sold to a young person. The only comment from the salesforce is that he has a black and gold Sierra and looks very prosperous. At this point the capital, assets and liabilities of the company are not known. The real ownership of the business needs to be checked, and whether the bank has a charge on the assets. It is possible that the actual name of the company will have been changed. There is no indication how the business has paid their accounts in the past, but a request has been received for 60 days credit!

THE NAME

My second key question is, 'Have you the correct name and address?' This is vitally important as there are approximately 900,000 limited companies that may be trading, and 3,000,000 sole traders and partnerships trading in the UK. New limited companies are being registered at a rate of about 3000 names per week. There are also some 46 million consumers (above age 16 who are financially active) registered on the voters' list. Surprisingly, there were over 13 million changes of address when the register of names was checked in March, 1997.

If the name or address is incorrect, the information gained at that reference point will be of little value. It may also mean that goods or services will not be correctly delivered, and the invoice and statement could be returned. A first class investment is to purchase a complete set of UK telephone directories and a set of *Yellow Pages* directories. This can often save the cost of contacting a credit bureau to obtain the same information.

The other reason why the cross-checking of a name and address is recommended, is that the individual business or company may be fraudulent. The checking of the telephone and fax number should be carried out for the same reason (see Chapter 4, Fraudulent Transactions – Long Firm Fraud).

New Business Form

When reviewing the administration for opening a new account it will make life far easier if a 'new business form' is designed, which incorporates all the facts and pieces of information that you need to make an estimation of the customer's requirements. This can include a credit limit.

I should like to guide readers through the new business form example which, of course, should be designed for your own individual business requirements.

The form should also be used as a marketing tool to assist the sales department to plan their potential sales and distribution programme.

The box for confirming where invoice/statement should be sent 'if different from heading address' is designed to save the many days or weeks it will take to redirect mail. The names of directors of the business are useful for future marketing and will create a cross-bearing when an independent report is studied (see Chapter 4). The names and private addresses of sole traders and partners will assist the credit bureaux to carry out credit checks on personal spending habits. A record of the person to contact for purchase or account queries will definitely save hours of wasted time in trying to find the right person – use of individual name will also create good will.

The bank and two trade reference boxes will enable a trader to apply for current financial and trading information. However, the application for a trade reference must be exceedingly well drafted and designed so that the maximum information is obtained. On this essential point I will go into far greater detail in Chapter 5.

The age of the business and number of employees will create a framework for assessment. I have always asked for the annual sales turnover. This is often a sensitive subject, and some companies may refuse to give it. Obtaining the figure will enable you to estimate the strength or weakness of the business in relation to all the other information which is being assembled. I have found that if a telephone call is made to the proprietor or director, phrased 'May I ask you what your turnover is?', for example, not only will this information be offered, but other interesting facts on the operation of the business will emerge (see Chapter 4, Personal Visits).

Market Conditions and Terms of Trading

Quite often an order will have been accepted on credit terms without any assessment having been made. This could be suicidal. It need not happen if there is a credit policy. Frequently the seller has one credit term without advising the buyer. The buyer pays when it suits them. Neither party knows each other's terms, so absolutely no payment terms have been agreed.

Name and address of business:	Address to which invoice / statement should be sent: (if different from business address)
Telephone number: Fax number: E-mail address:	
Please indicate main directors or owners of the business (If sole trader or partners, give private addresses):	Please list any parent, asssociate or subsidiary companies:
Who should be contacted: in respect of supply or purchase queries: in respect of account queries:	

Banker's name and address:	Please specify two trade references:	
	1.	2.
Sort code:	Credit limit authorised £	
Credit Manager's Authorisation:		Date:

It would be helpful if you would describe your business as below (please tick)

a) Type of firm
   Private Limited Company ☐
   Public Limited Company ☐
   Co. Registration Number: _____
   Partnership ☐
   Sole Ownership ☐
   Other (specify) ☐

VAT Registration number: _____

b) Trade

c) Age of business:
   Up to 1 year ☐
   1 to 3 years ☐
   3 to 6 years ☐
   6 to 10 years ☐
   10 or more years ☐

d) If possible please indicate approximate size of business in terms of:
   (i) Number of employees:
   (ii) Annual sales turnover (£000s)

e) Likely products to be purchased:

f) Are management accounts available to us
   on a confidential basis: Yes | No

g) What is the likely value of purchases:
   In 6 months' time
   In 1 year's time

Any additional remarks you may have concerning your business activities:

Signed: | Date:

Figure 1.1 A suggested design for an application form to open a credit account

To protect business profits the first principles of credit granting are:

1. Is there a credit policy?
2. Does everyone understand it?
3. Is it adhered to?
4. What is the cost of advancing credit?

Depending on the number of products or services and competitors, the credit policy can be varied to appeal to the maximum number of customers who can be sold to without reducing efficiency or service. Terms can be adapted to meet seasonal factors, e.g. the Christmas buying, high stock levels for seasonal trade or products which will have a limited shelf life.

To give a further example, the highest sales of lawnmowers will not normally be made between November and March in the northern hemisphere. However, I have seen brilliant marketing and credit plans where the manufacturers, in conjunction with the wholesalers and retailers, increased their sales by offering longer credit facilities. The traders had, however, taken considerable care in calculating their net profit margins after allowing for the cost of credit.

If the credit policy is to work, everyone from the managing director/proprietor down to the order clerk, delivery driver, salesman or woman, should use it as a tool to create more sales.

Credit terms should be advised to all employees verbally and confirmed in writing. I have seen sales forces drive a coach and horses through a credit scheme where the sales director was only interested in turnover.

The cost of credit will include any interest charges for borrowing finance to purchase in bulk, including the period when the stock is unsold and the period of credit given to the buyers. Insurance, storage and stock control maintenance can cost up to 15 per cent per annum of its value.

Reservation of Title

A Reservation of Title (RoT) clause is a minefield for the unwary. Basically, this is a fairly recent contractual term which suppliers add to their terms and conditions to keep title of the goods or machinery until their customer has paid for them. The original reservation case in English law was the *Romalpa* case in 1976, *Aluminium Industrie Vaasen BV* v. *Romalpa Aluminium Ltd.*

Reservation of title has been available for suppliers to use since the Sale of Goods Act 1893. Since the *Romalpa* case there have been seven cases which demonstrate a particular feature of RoT and a further 16 cases which are relevant to certain trades and suppliers.

Receivers and liquidators are able to reject many retention claims because the formalities of drawing the attention of the clause to the buyer have not been carried out. The terms must be communicated to the customer, and the seller must be able to demonstrate that their customer has seen and agreed to the terms. The customer's formal acknowledgment of RoT terms will be of great advantage if the customer becomes insolvent or bankrupt.

It is essential that a solicitor with specialist knowledge of RoT clauses actually draws up the reservation of title clauses which relate to the particular business.

COST OF BORROWING

At the time of writing, the cost of borrowing on overdraft through a High Street clearing bank could cost anything from 8.5 per cent to perhaps 14.5 per cent, depending on the history and background of the business who wanted to borrow funds. A banker would look at their trade, accounts and their experience and knowledge of their business. From this information the banker will decide whether the loan should be on a secured or unsecured basis.

Reviewing the base rates over the last 26 years demonstrates that rates can and do change quite dramatically.

Base Rate

Business loans for plant and machinery are available from clearing banks. Terms of between one and 30 years can be fixed and the loan period will, of course, depend on the life of the asset which is being considered. By using a business loan a company can use its overdraft facility to finance seasonal or fluctuating work in progress. The debtor ledger is supported, so that the fear of a cash flow shortage is safeguarded. A calculation to ascertain the cost of credit will also show whether the sale will generate sufficient profit to support the selling scheme.

gross profit − cost of finance = real profit margin

When reviewing these figures, the actual time it takes to collect the debt should be considered (see Chapter 5) as this will be the real cost of credit. Once the real profit margin is known, an evaluation can be made on competitors.

UNDERSTANDING THE MARKET CONDITIONS

The person responsible for authorising credit and who wishes their company to succeed must carry out extensive reading and research so that they are really *au fait* with present marketing conditions.

Effective Date	Rate (%)	Effective Date	Rate (%)	Effective Date	Rate (%)
16.9.71	5.00	15.6.79	14.00	15.10.86	11.00
26.11.71	4.50	14.11.79	15.50	10.3.87	10.50
9.6.72	5.00	19.11.79	17.00	19.3.87	10.00
30.6.72	6.00	7.7.80	16.00	29.4.87	9.50
21.7.72	7.00	25.11.80	14.00	11.5.87	9.00
12.12.72	7.50	11.3.81	12.00	7.8.87	10.00
9.1.73	8.25	16.9.81	14.00	26.10.87	9.50
25.1.73	8.50	1.10.81	16.00	5.11.87	9.00
14.2.73	9.50	14.10.81	15.50	4.12.87	8.50
4.4.73	9.00	9.11.81	15.00	2.2.88	9.00
22.5.73	8.50	4.12.81	14.50	17.3.88	8.50
15.6.73	8.00	25.1.82	14.00	11.4.88	8.00
2.8.73	10.00	25.2.82	13.50	18.5.88	7.50
23.8.73	11.00	12.3.82	13.00	3.6.88	8.00
14.11.73	13.00	8.6.82	12.50	7.6.88	8.50
11.4.74	12.50	14.7.82	12.00	22.6.88	9.00
23.5.74	12.00	2.8.82	11.50	28.6.88	9.50
21.1.75	11.50	18.8.82	11.00	4.7.88	10.00
6.3.75	11.00	31.8.82	10.50	18.7.88	10.50
20.3.75	10.50	7.10.82	10.00	8.8.88	11.00
22.4.75	9.50	14.10.82	9.50	25.8.88	12.00
6.8.75	10.00	5.11.82	9.00	25.11.88	13.00
7.10.75	11.00	29.11.82	10.00	24.5.89	14.00
13.1.76	10.50	12.1.83	11.00	5.10.89	15.00
2.2.76	10.00	16.3.83	10.50	8.10.90	14.00
9.2.76	9.50	15.4.83	10.00	13.2.91	13.50
25.5.76	11.00	15.6.83	9.50	27.2.91	13.00
14.6.76	10.50	4.10.83	9.00	22.3.91	12.50
14.9.76	12.00	15.3.84	8.50	12.4.91	12.00
11.10.76	13.50	10.5.84	9.00	24.5.91	11.50
26.10.76	14.00	27.6.84	9.25	12.7.91	11.00
26.1.77	13.00	9.7.84	10.00	4.9.91	10.50
4.2.77	12.50	12.7.84	12.00	5.5.92	10.00
18.2.77	11.50	9.8.84	11.50	16.9.92	12.00
14.3.77	10.50	10.8.84	11.00	17.9.92	10.00
31.3.77	9.50	20.8.84	10.50	22.9.92	9.00
26.4.77	9.00	7.11.84	10.00	6.10.92	8.00
3.5.77	8.50	23.11.84	9.50	13.11.92	7.00
9.8.77	8.00	11.1.85	10.50	26.1.93	6.00
13.9.77	7.00	14.1.85	12.00	23.11.93	5.50
17.10.77	6.00	28.1.85	14.00	8.2.94	5.25
29.11.77	7.50	21.3.85	13.50	12.9.94	5.75
9.1.78	6.50	29.3.85	13.00	7.12.94	6.25
20.4.78	7.50	19.4.85	12.50	2.2.95	6.75
10.5.78	9.00	16.7.85	12.00	13.12.95	6.50
12.6.78	10.00	30.7.85	11.50	18.1.96	6.25
6.11.78	11.50	9.1.86	12.50	8.3.96	6.00
14.11.78	12.50	19.3.86	11.50	6.6.96	5.75
14.2.79	13.50	8.4.86	11.00	30.10.96	6.00
6.3.79	13.00	21.4.86	10.50	6.5.97	6.25
6.4.79	12.00	23.5.86	10.00	6.6.97	6.50

Figure 1.2   Changes in base rate

Competition within any trade is always intense. Sources outside Europe can often manufacture and supply goods or a service at a fraction of the cost of the UK supplier. The reading of all trade journals, plus the early morning reading of the *Financial Times* is essential to monitor daily new items which can dramatically change a company's sales plan. Credit personnel, as a matter of course, must create the appropriate atmosphere, so that they are automatically invited to budget or sales meetings that affect business plans.

Regrettably, many people in business today still consider the credit controller, credit manager or sales ledger supervisor to be a desk-bound penpusher who says 'no' to the sales force. Here is an actual example of a positive response:

> A specialised label printing company (A) announce that they are targeted to increase credit sales by 15 per cent. They have been established for five and a half years. One extra person is to be recruited to the sales force. There is competition from a nearby company (C) who undercharge by 20 per cent and who have been in existence for two years. Their maximum credit terms are 30 days, but it is understood that they are slow in collecting their debts and customers have actually boasted that they get over 70 days credit! A second competitor (B) offers 60 days credit where the sales per month are in excess of £1000. It is known that their collection methods are thorough. In fact, they are so zealous that they have lost customers. Printing company A does not want to start a credit auction but, looking at companies B and C's credit and collection policies, there is much that the new salesperson in conjunction with the credit controller can do to gain more customers by varying credit terms.
>
> If the customers are financially viable there is no reason why company A cannot offer individual terms between 30 and 60 days, provided that the all-important profit margin has already been calculated when agreeing to the contract. A retrospective discount structure could be planned so that if sales of more than, say, £3000, £30,000, £300,000 per month or year are achieved, a cash discount or credit note could be issued. A discount for prompt payment could be offered, but this marketing scheme may not seem so attractive as a discount for ordering larger quantities. A cash discount of even 2½ per cent can create a heavy drain on profits if the operating profit margins are low.
>
> If company B only gives 60 day terms for orders over £1000, there is an opportunity to vary terms. A second tactic is for the credit controller, in conjunction with the salesman, to say that although the company's collection department is thorough, they are also a very pleasant group of people.
>
> Company C's product, price and service must be studied. Can they continue to undercut the market and not collect their outstanding debts? Can it be proved that company A's printing is of a higher quality, more speedily produced and with faster delivery and more generous credit terms?

One word of warning – companies anxious to increase the credit terms they receive from suppliers will often say that they already receive 60/90/120 terms from company X. Their statement may not be true, and therefore needs to be checked out through the credit or sales department. It is a ploy that can be difficult to correct and expensive on profits, if the statements are just accepted at face value.

Another way to enhance credit terms is to offer settlement on the 20th of the month after delivery, but make sure that the delivery or service is carried out very early in month one. The customer then gains 50 days credit. For a business that wishes to use credit to gain extra sales but cannot afford to give an excessive credit period, terms of, for instance, 15 or 30 days from invoice or despatch date can generate trade. These terms can only be used to increase sales provided that materials supplied, or services given, are immediately available.

SUMMARY

A major credit bureau estimated that there may be at least 3.8 million businesses operating in the UK as at December 1997. It is *essential* to confirm the exact trading name and address and to ascertain the legal status of the business so that a credit check can be carried out before extending credit. Ask yourself the following questions:

- Who is your customer?
- How long have they been established?
- Have they completed the new business form?
- Have payment terms been agreed?
- Have you got a credit granting policy administered via a definite route?

2
Creating Profitable Sales and Customer Care

In some companies, the conflict between sales and finance is so severe that the company actually loses sales and profits to their competitors. Both sales and credit personnel must understand basically how they can each contribute to create a profitable sale. Historically, selling has always had a higher profile than credit-granting. Little is known about the art of credit control as it is a relatively new profession. In fact, in the UK, the Institute of Credit Mangement was only formed in 1938, after Cuthbert Greig had visited the USA and seen their National Association (see Chapter 7, National Association of Credit Management). Credit management in the UK has not only caught up with North American practice but now may be edging ahead due to Professor Nick Wilson's research at the University of Bradford's Management Centre (see Chapter 7). In the 1950s and 1960s most UK literature and training programmes on credit-granting were based on North American practices.

It is the credit controller's responsibility to advise, train and educate their management in the reasons why a certain method of credit assessment should be taken. Professional credit staff do obtain an incredible amount of vital information about their company's customers and their competitors through their training and their grapevines. Provided that these sources of information and facts are kept absolutely confidential to the company, the sales staff will then begin to appreciate how, as a team, extra sales can be generated.

I have the utmost regard for a professional salesman or woman. Their job is never easy and, unless they are selling a unique product or service, there are always competitors on the horizon. This competition automatically compels any sales force to be aggressive and determined not only in obtaining new business, but also in holding on to existing customers. When the representative makes repeat calls they will also try to increase their market share and gain the maximum amount of information on their customers' activities.

Because of the high cost of physically calling on customers, telesales personnel and self-employed sales people are now carrying out these tasks as well
(see Chapter 4, Personal Visits).

While repeat customer contact is being made, marketing information is
being received which is vital for the supplying company's stock and work-in-
progress plans. Other snippets will greatly assist the credit control department
in assessment of present or future requirements (Chapter 4, Personal Visits).

HOW TO CREATE A GOOD WORKING RELATIONSHIP

The way to create a good working relationship between sales and credit is for
both parties to visit potential and existing customers together. They must first
discuss each customer's background before the visit takes place as they are
both ambassadors of their company. I have seen an absolutely perfect sale
collapse because credit personnel and sales had not prepared for their meeting with the customer. Without customers no-one has a job. Unfortunately, it
is still possible to lose a customer in 20 seconds, even when the relationship
may have taken 20 years to develop.

Sales and Credit Working Together

The message I preach is my firm belief that by offering a range of credit terms,
not only can a company's market share increase, but also the all-important
profit margin is protected as the trade risk has already been assessed. As a
credit manager, my first priority is to get the message across that I am determined to increase profitable sales. There are managing directors and chairmen of major concerns who still believe that credit control consists of sending
out demand letters.

When I meet a salesman or woman for the first time, I tell them that I want
to get to know their mode of operation, the customers in their area and their
problems. I am completely honest with them, telling them my strategy, suc-
cesses and failures. This informal chat, perhaps over lunch or at a pub, can
then develop into arranging to visit groups of customers. But before that
happens the customer briefing takes place.

As credit mangers and controllers have to have an operating knowledge of
the entire range of activities of their business, this is my way to open the initial
discussion and to create a partnership. Credit personnel also have a thorough
knowledge of accounting. Sales personnel often have problems in this area
and their initial training does not always cover the flow of an order through all
its documentation.

Here is an example of a discussion that actually took place when I went out with a keen salesman who had only been with the company for three months.

We arranged to meet at the branch office before visiting the customer so that any delivery problems were known to us both. I got into his company car and immediately noticed that the gear change was poor when pulling away. We started talking about car servicing and then it all came out. Our salesman was furious that since he had started with the company his car was always breaking down. There were 84,000 miles on the clock and the car should have been replaced many months earlier. He was getting behind in calling on customers as he was always at the garage, and consequently was losing orders.

I then started to hear about the other problems. His sales code number was not always noted on the invoices so he lost commission. He had listed a number of credit notes which were required by a customer taking advantage of a special offer. While driving to the customer I outlined what I would do to get these problems rectified.

My discussion afterwards with the sales and transport managers had an effect, and the salesman did in fact get a far better car. When we eventually returned to the accounts department I personally introduced him to all the staff who created the invoice and credit note flow. What had actually happened was that the official coding of the new salesman's area had not been notified. He also had not been given the customary tour of every section of the company. The administration manual covered these areas but someone had 'forgotten' to hand it over!

My relations with this salesman had developed from the discussion in the car and this was before we had even met his first customer.

You can never be certain how a customer will receive you on your first visit. Here is a note of an actual visit.

An Actual Visit

The customer had started his sports programmes printing business three months after leaving a major printers. He had taken a short lease on a single storey unit on a new industrial estate near Watford. He looked harassed; his business was growing but the cash for his first orders had not yet arrived. We discussed his problems, I mentioned that I was a specialist and enjoyed the collecting side of the business. He received about 15 minutes help on techniques of collecting, and was given my card in case he had need of further advice. Between the salesman and myself we gained a further order.

I agreed to allow a further 20 days credit period on the initial stock, provided that he kept me informed on the payment pattern of his major customers. He did not let me down and that account gradually increased from a mere £500 a month to £3500 by the end of the first year.

My philosophy is always to help customers. In 95 per cent of all these visits there were always at least three benefits. We got to know the customer far better, the collecting of the account in future would be easier and prospects for increasing sales were on the horizon as we already knew his plans for marketing for the next 20 months. Our visit had lasted just 45 minutes.

CASE STUDY OF A PROGRESSIVE DEPARTMENT

This is an update of a company that I reviewed in 1989. The company still believes in creating profitable business but they are now working even closer with their customers to create a real working partnership. The department title, Customer Financial Services, puts the customer first. The vision statement for the department is that they should be 'the most professional and effective Credit Management team dedicated to achieving success through co-operative partnership with all their businesses and customers.' To understand the philosophy of the company one only has to read part of the department's mission statement to realise how focused they are on achieving their goals. For example, apart from achieving financial targets they must be sensitive to business goals and market needs. At the same time the team must be receptive to manage high risk exposures. The team is also required to add value through professional communication and guidance to customers both internally and externally, and 'Grow themselves in order to attain the highest quality standards to maximise their contribution to the company's performance'. Although within a period of six years they have contracted their sales base, the company still has sales in excess of £500 million, but they are now putting more business through existing dealerships. Therefore some credit lines are now far larger so there is even more pressure on the department to monitor any deterioration in the payment patterns of their customers.

Developing Assessment Schemes

To show how credit granting is developing, apart from using CD Rom and on-line financial information, their credit analyst has designed and built a customised two-page risk analysis sheet which incorporates two Z scores. The analysis particularly highlights turnover and margins, which include gross and trading profit, and the vitally important 'where the money went'. All these figures cover three to four years and are in colour to show differences and trends. The company also liaise with Professor Nick Wilson, who occupies the Chair of Credit at the University of Bradford Management Centre, in the development of their credit assessment techniques.

Accounting and Monitoring

Turning to the marketplace, the company's products are sold to a wide range of commerce and industry.

You may think that assessment is all mechanical. This is not so, as any order over £5000 is personally vetted, account balances which are more than £20,000 are carefully monitored day by day, and any account which is more than £5000 on their aged debt analysis is constantly reviewed.

All these tasks are helped by on-line computer systems, but the credit staff are highly trained so that their credit assessment can be carried out in a more professional and competent manner. Credit Scoring is a further development which has taken place in the last three years. They are now developing a computerised accounting and information system which covers all their European operations, the in-house programme which will supply the same data in whichever country they are manufacturing and selling. There will also be a huge benefit as the query management system will be improved.

Customer Relationships

Finally, to illustrate how important they consider their relationship with their customers, the company operate a separate consultancy unit to help their customers to improve their efficiency and turnover, and enable them to do a better management job in selling the supplying company's range of products.

CREATING CUSTOMER CARE

The following interview with Honeywell Control Systems Ltd., a manufacturer of heating components and the management of computer systems, shows how credit and sales can work together. It illustrates how a company with many millions of pounds' worth of sales is focused on their customers, developing new assessment techniques, and is taking a proactive role in monitoring market conditions in the UK and overseas. It used to take up to three weeks to open an account, but today they can almost guarantee that if a salesman picks up an order he can get the credit account approved and the account set up within the same day.

HONEYWELL CONTROL SYSTEMS LTD

The biggest change in this company that has taken place is the amount of information that is available. They have more competition in the marketplace than five years ago, so they have to be far more proactive. The company does not necessarily win new customers because of the product any more, even if their product is the same as five or six other competitors on price and service. This company wins new business and extra orders on the quality of their after-sales service. Their advantage is in the *total* sales operation, which includes follow up with customers, and dealing with their technical queries as the end buyer needs a considerable amount of support. The company emphasise that in this area they can offer better payment terms and reaction to their customers' requirements.

Credit Staff's Expertise

An invoice could be up to several million pounds, with stage payments, and within the contract a bank guarantee may be required. These invoices may take many hours to draft, they are delivered by special post and a signature is obtained to confirm that the invoice has been accepted. The credit team of some twelve people make sure that they know about any queries, and if any items are found to be short delivered, a credit note is issued quickly.

When supplying highly technical products to companies whose management is more engineering based than financial, quite often help is given by the credit department when they have cash flow problems. When these situations occur the credit controllers pay personal visits to solve problems. Order patterns can be re-structured, stock holdings can be reduced, and extended credit terms can be negotiated. In the credit manager's words, 'It's all about being flexible, rather than saying OK, you're up to your credit limit, no more deliveries.' Credit appraisal and collection methods are targeted to meet market conditions. When their credit department is dealing with smaller companies, they often find that the accounts person does everything: he/she raises the invoices, pays the supplier, pays wages, and does all manner of accounting tasks. They are not usually very proficient, and they are nervous about chasing their customers for money.

Solving Customers' Financial Problems

Customers' visits often highlight problems, particularly with distributors. Their credit team tries to build relationships up front, so that the distributor advises the credit department when they have a problem. A typical example was of a company buying £100,000 of products monthly. Their order pattern was rescheduled so that there was less stock held in their warehouse, and extended terms were agreed. With another customer, because of a new market, a monthly direct debit was agreed for a set amount and every quarter the account was reconciled to make sure that the payments balanced actual deliveries.

New Developments

The case study company's accounting system is set up so that they can never lose a transaction. All their entries are stored in an optical disc storage system so that all invoices and other credit documents can be perfectly reproduced.

A 'Sales Importance Rating' is being developed so that on one side the profit margin, sales potential, and 'how easy to replace the customer' is measured. Alongside this rating there will be a credit rating and a payment or performance score so that if a customer becomes overdue, the score can be adjusted. For example, if an account is rated A10 it is of prime importance to the sales force, but if the payment score is poor, discussions will take place between sales and credit so that they can work together to solve the problems. This is an entirely different method of working from the old approach – when the original credit manager was first appointed, there was real antagonism between the credit and sales departments.

There are many ideas and actions such as these that the above company carry out which accounts staff in small companies would benefit from adapting.

HOW BRITVIC OPERATES PROACTIVELY

Soft drinks is a highly competitive business. Britvic have a simple philosophy: they want to trade with everybody who wants their products, providing of course that those customers have the ability to pay their bills and a willingness to pay to agreed credit terms. In an interview Ted Brown, the Receivables Manager of Britvic Soft Drinks Ltd, who was at the time of the interview National Chairman of the Institute of Credit Management, explained graphically how the entire operation had changed since 1990 when they were awarded the Pepsi franchise.

In January 1990 their turnover was £250 million and by June 1997 it was £600 million. The increase was due to Britvic's purchasing Robinsons Drinks, as well as organic growth. On the personnel side in January 1990 the credit staff numbered 101, whereas today there are just 58 in the team. The DSO's (days sales outstanding) were 70 days, whereas in 1997 the average was down to 33.8 days.

When Ted Brown was appointed he specified what type of computer system he wanted. Previously there had been brought forward statement balances to reconcile. A specification went out to tender, although ultimately the system was built by their own IT department. Every part of the system was tested by a user team which was headed by Judy Crowdy, who is now their Credit Manager, and six credit representatives. The testing team then became the user training team.

New Responsibilities

With the old system the staff was divided into clerks, senior clerks, supervisors, controllers, managers, and there were five different tasks – credit control, litigation, master file, queries and assessment which were separately carried out. Once the new accounting system was in operation, a new job description was created for a person to be called a credit representative. This person now carried out all the above tasks, and was also responsible for customer liaison, and within an agreed matrix they were authorised to open up accounts to the value of £2500. The credit representatives' duties included making sure that Britvic would get paid on time and, if necessary, recommending legal action. Their salary was raised from £8000 to £12,000 to reflect their new responsibilities. The credit staff are now responsible for their own training and development, and at their six-monthly appraisals they are asked what they want or need to develop.

Britvic's Four Objectives

The four key objectives which the entire company follows are:

- Customer Satisfaction
- Employee Motivation
- Return on Assets
- Market Share.

To show how this works, one of their service levels with a major supermarket is that 95% of their invoices are passed on their first submission.

Customer Care and Profits

Because their customers like to see people, Britvic employ an army of soft drink advisors. In the old days a sales representative would call every four weeks on every customer, a method now far too expensive to carry out. Now, at the bottom end of the market their telesales team make the contacts. The major change that has taken place, however, is that where the sales force used to be targeted on volume and turnover, they are now targeted on profits.

Opening Accounts

In their new account procedure they have only two criteria for assessing customers. *Can* they pay, and *will* they pay? A few years ago accounts took weeks to open, now an account can be open within 48 hours, provided that the form is filled in correctly (they have in-house links with Dun & Bradstreet and Equifax). If a representative is with a customer and they agree to sign a direct debit, and the sum is under £2500, drinks are delivered the next day – sometimes even the same day!

The Collection Cycle

Britvic are fairly tight on their collection cycle. Their customers are invoiced within 48 hours of delivery, the invoice is triggered by the delivery note being returned to the depot. Products supplied within the month are due to be paid on the 21st of the following month. If the customer has not paid by this date, credit control run off a default list. If there is no known reason why payment has not been made, their customers are placed on stop immediately. Future deliveries are controlled at the depots, and the next day's call list will exclude all 'on stop' customers.

If customers default regularly, the credit representative will ring them up and say that 'their willingness to pay to their credit terms is in doubt'. The customers will either pay or be placed on direct debit. This procedure has the total support of the Britvic Board.

Monitoring

Each month Judy Crowdy and her team review every account in the ledger and estimate which accounts will not be paid to terms. A monthly bad debt provision is then made. The main job of a credit representative is to have a good rapport with their customers so that they get paid on time. Judy Crowdy attends at least two sales meetings a month and will visit a number of customers each month.

One member of staff summarised their decision making by saying that 'You have to take risks now and again as it could be big business for many years to come, or you could close the door and they go elsewhere. With credit granting you just try and do the best you can, some customers will fail and we realise that.'

Conclusion

My visit to this department proved that a credit representative could be a multi-skilled person, they were all thoroughly enjoying their work, their ledger balances were definitely not the usual 20/80 Pareto ratios. They were all proactive in their approach to their work, perhaps due to their training, where each person is developing their skills so that they gain promotion.

CASE STUDY OF A COMPANY WITH LITTLE CREDIT CONTROL

The business sells industrial products, their turnover is about £200,000 a year, they have just two employees and they have been established just over two years. Their office and warehouse is spotlessly neat and tidy. If they have time to organise it, a new business form is filled in by new customers which states the terms are 14 days. Their computer system is well over 10 years old, and customers are not always advised on what the payment terms are. The company does not appear to carry out any credit checks, and they already have one substantial bad debt. In reviewing the earlier case studies, what could this small business learn from them? They all have a business plan, and they carefully monitor targets. All their accounts are assessed and reassessed to create maximum sales and profits. Every account is important to them and they are constantly trying to improve every management system.

SUMMARY

Provided that a new customer has been assessed for credit (or an existing customer reassessed), it is then possible to negotiate a range of credit terms which will retain the customer and create a profit for your business.

- Are Sales and Credit working together to create profitable sales?
- Can you make enough time to visit your key customers?
- Can you make more time to talk to your sales force?
- Can you convert any of the ideas in the three major case studies discussed above, to improve your sales and profits and minimise bad debts?
- Are all incoming orders vetted before despatch?

3
Types of Business

THE NAME

There is nothing more vital than to check the exact name of the business with whom you intend to trade.

Under the new Business Names Act 1985, which consolidated certain details of the Companies Act 1981, any business carried on under a name other than that of the owner or owners is required to disclose certain trading details. This Act affects sole traders, individuals, partnerships and limited companies if they use a business name other than the full corporate name of the company. Unlike the old Registration of Business Names Act 1916, which required registration at Companies Registration Office (now called Companies House), the Business Names Act 1985 only requires that a notice be displayed prominently where it can be read where the business is carried on.

The business name must be shown legibly on all business letters, written orders, invoices and receipts and written demands for payment of debts which arise in the course of business. The disadvantage with this system is that Companies House is not required to keep an index. At the time of writing there may be 3,000,000 sole traders and partnerships operating in the UK. In the 1996 voter's list there were over 13 million changes of address that affected individual private householders.

Limited Company Names

As at March 1997 there were at least 900,000 active private and PLC companies trading in the UK. When registering a company name, the proposers must be absolutely certain that the name they propose to use is not in use already. If the name is very similar it could cause no end of problems such as being invoiced or charged for goods or services which were the responsibility of the 'similarly named' company. Companies House will not give approval for a name if it already appears in their Index of Companies.

If, in the opinion of the Secretary of State, the name is offensive, approval may not be given. There is also a fairly extensive list of words or expressions which may not be used. The Department of Trade and Industry also reserves the right to seek advice from relevant bodies to confirm that the said proposers of the company are legitimate. For example: Architect, Pharmacist, Bank. The Secretary of State will check words in a title which imply national or international pre-eminence, for example 'International' or 'Scottish'. There are over 50 other words which imply specific objects or functions which will be examined before the Registrar of Companies will give approval. There are 14 other words or expressions such as 'Royal' or 'University' where the relevant body or department has to be contacted with the registration documents before the formalities of approval can be given.

There are over 30 most useful 'Notes for Guidance' booklets issued by Companies House, of which four are listed here:

1. New Companies
2. Choosing a Company Name
3. Companies Act 1985 Sensitive Words and Expressions
4. Change of Company Name.

For the address of Companies House see Chapter 4.

The Company Registration Number

Although the directors of a limited company can agree to a change of name for the company, the original registered number of the company never changes. Tables 3.1, 3.2 and 3.3 list the company registration numbers which were issued for limited companies in England and Wales from 1856 to 1996, Scotland from 1860 to 1996 and Northern Ireland from 1921 to 1996.

A SOLE TRADER

A sole trader is totally responsible for the debts of his or her business. Again the full name of the proprietor should be checked against the consumer credit data files of one of the major credit bureaux and the business trading style checked against the commercial information file for trading history (see Chapter 4).

When transacting with a sole trader on a credit basis it is again essential to consider:

Table 3.1 Last company number registered for each year – England and Wales

Year	Number	Year	Number	Year	Number
1856	676	1910	113484	1965	867954
1857	1108	1911	119448	1966	895085
1858	1412	1912	126250	1967	925272
1859	1715	1913	133125	1968	945100
1860	2095	1914	138836	1969	969352
1861	2534	1915	142591	1970	998618
1862	2920	1916	145673	1971	1036747
	152C	1917	149276	1972	1089028
1863	876C	1918	152445	1973	1154108
1864	1790C	1919	162272	1974	1195179
1865	2726C	1920	172367	1975	1239101
1866	3402	1921	178772	1976	1293229
1867	3837	1922	186771	1977	1346436
1868	4248	1923	194785	1978	1407229
1869	4679	1924	202765	1979	1470412
1870	5220	1925	210804	1980	1536863
1871	5920	1926	218609	1981	1606313
1872	6862	1927	227015	1982	1689701
1873	7951	1928	236041	1983	1781527
1874	9075	1929	244720	1984	1874887
1875	10153	1930	253138	1985	1974498
1876	11094	1931	261534	1986	2086548
1877	11940	1932	271756	1987	2209435
1878	12718	1933	283169	1988	2328615
1879	13641	1934	295660	1989	2453983
1880	14803	1935	308786	1990	2570949
1881	16251	1936	322550	1991	2675035
1882	17727	1937	333298	1992	2776655
1883	19260	1938	347934	1993	2885358
1884	20630	1939	358528	1994	3005271
1885	21974	1940	364624	1995	3142524
1886	23712	1941	371610	1996	3298232
1887	25605	1942	378088	1997	
1888	27953	1943	384666	1998	
1889	30533	1944	392186	1999	
1890	33075	1945	402532	2000	
1891	35522	1946	426602		
1892	37893	1947	447312		
1893	40226	1948	462968		
1894	42895	1949	476742		
1895	46432	1950	490034		
1896	50723	1951	502976		
1897	55475	1952	514749		
1898	60128	1953	527520		
1899	64661	1954	542795		
1900	69174	1955	559525		
1901	72319	1956	576476		
1902	75922	1957	596398		
1903	79620	1958	617877		
1904	83101	1959	646027		
1905	87070	1960	679264		
1906	91473	1961	711828		
1907	96288	1962	745608		
1908	100935	1963	786388		
1909	106771	1964	832957		

Table 3.2   Last company number registered for each year – Scotland

Year		Number	Year		Number	Year		Number	Year		Number
1860	SC	53	1900	SC	4781	1940	SC	21607	1980	SC	73602
1861	SC		1901	SC	4982	1941	SC	21945	1981	SC	77096
1862	SC		1902	SC	5239	1942	SC	22263	1982	SC	81341
1863	SC	151	1903	SC	5504	1943	SC	22634	1983	SC	86104
1864	SC		1904	SC	5740	1944	SC	23067	1984	SC	91119
1865	SC	194	1905	SC	6027	1945	SC	23699	1985	SC	96610
1866	SC	255	1906	SC	6373	1946	SC	24924	1986	SC	102635
1867	SC	266	1907	SC	6710	1947	SC	26013	1987	SC	108521
1868			1908	SC	6979	1948	SC	26763	1988	SC	115419
1869	SC	317	1909	SC	7479	1949	SC	27457	1989	SC	122204
1870	SC	328	1910	SC	7754	1950	SC	28084	1990	SC	129174
1871	SC	378	1911	SC	8105	1951	SC	28680	1991	SC	135827
1872	SC		1912	SC	8495	1952	SC	29209	1992	SC	141943
1873	SC		1913	SC	8894	1953	SC	29801	1993	SC	148271
1874	SC	578	1914	SC	9292	1954	SC	30498	1994	SC	155261
1875	SC	610	1915	SC	9514	1955	SC	31236	1995	SC	162439
1876	SC	699	1916	SC	9731	1956	SC	31931	1996	SC	171156
1877	SC	792	1917	SC	9957	1957	SC	32763	1997	SC	
1878	SC	848	1918	SC	10182	1958	SC	33557	1998	SC	
1879	SC	926	1919	SC	10868	1959	SC	34728	1999	SC	
1880	SC	986	1920	SC	11539	1960	SC	35987	2000	SC	
1881	SC	1054	1921	SC	11975	1961	SC	37132			
1882	SC	1150	1922	SC	12503	1962	SC	38289			
1883	SC	1310	1923	SC	12954	1963	SC	39742			
1884	SC	1422	1924	SC	13450	1964	SC	41578			
1885	SC	1491	1925	SC	13939	1965	SC	42981			
1886	SC	1584	1926	SC	14430	1966	SC	44179			
1887	SC	1670	1927	SC	14870	1967	SC	45346			
1888	SC	1783	1928	SC	15383	1968	SC	46221			
1889	SC	1909	1929	SC	15814	1969	SC	47158			
1890	SC	2101	1930	SC	16265	1970	SC	48261			
1891	SC	2240	1931	SC	16676	1971	SC	49716			
1892	SC	2409	1932	SC	17103	1972	SC	52116			
1893	SC	2577	1933	SC	17647	1973	SC	54788			
1894	SC	2816	1934	SC	18236	1974	SC	56914			
1895	SC	3050	1935	SC	18863	1975	SC	59161			
1896	SC	3377	1936	SC	19506	1976	SC	61439			
1897	SC	3715	1937	SC	20119	1977	SC	63793			
1898	SC	4109	1938	SC	20764	1978	SC	66775			
1899	SC	4430	1939	SC	21278	1979	SC	70311			

1. the person's experience in the trade
2. their character and age
3. the financial strength and age of the business (see Chapter 5, Assessment)

Under the partnerships section I mentioned that taking bankruptcy proceedings was one way of trying to recover an outstanding debt. Taking this type of action with a sole trader can be even more difficult, as you are relying on just one person's ability to generate enough business for the enterprise to be profitable. Remember, at the time of writing, only a debt of more than £750

Table 3.3   Last company number registered for each year – Northern Ireland

Year	Numbers	Year	Numbers
1921	NI00001–NI00016	1961	NI04775–NI05128
1922	NI00017–NI00067	1962	NI05129–NI05446
1923	NI00068–NI00144	1963	NI05447–NI05808
1924	NI00145–NI00232	1964	NI05809–NI06227
1925	NI00233–NI00299	1965	NI06228–NI06594
1926	NI00300–NI00375	1966	NI06595–NI06848
1927	NI00367–NI00456	1967	NI06849–NI07153
1928	NI00457–NI00520	1968	NI07154–NI07495
1929	NI00521–NI00597	1969	NI07496–NI07791
1930	NI00598–NI00660	1970	NI07792–NI08131
1931	NI00661–NI00723	1971	NI08132–NI08515
1932	NI00724–NI00809	1972	NI08516–NI09205
1933	NI00810–NI00882	1973	NI09206–NI09926
1934	NI00883–NI00950	1974	NI09927–NI10519
1935	NI00951–NI01029	1975	NI10520–NI11093
1936	NI01030–NI01114	1976	NI11094–NI11720
1937	NI01115–NI01202	1977	NI11721–NI12474
1938	NI01203–NI01316	1978	NI12475–NI13293
1939	NI01317–NI01424	1979	NI13294–NI14043
1940	NI01425–NI01464	1980	NI14044–NI14667
1941	NI01465–NI01539	1981	NI14668–NI15323
1942	NI01540–NI01636	1982	NI15324–NI16344
1943	NI01637–NI01741	1983	NI16345–NI17167
1944	NI01742–NI01844	1984	NI17168–NI18080
1945	NI01845–NI01992	1985	NI18081–NI19045
1946	NI01993–NI02243	1986	NI19046–NI20088
1947	NI02244–NI02438	1987	NI20089–NI21185
1948	NI02439–NI02619	1988	NI21186–NI22281
1949	NI02620–NI02765	1989	NI22282–NI24017
1950	NI02766–NI02910	1990	NI24018–NI25165
1951	NI02911–NI03053	1991	NI25166–NI26192
1952	NI03054–NI03186	1992	NI26193–NI27137
1953	NI03187–NI03295	1993	NI27138–NI28056
1954	NI03296–NI03459	1994	NI28057–NI29080
1955	NI03460–NI03622	1995	NI29081–NI30307
1956	NI03623–NI03811	1996	NI30308–NI31786
1957	NI03812–NI03988	1997	
1958	NI03989–NI04195	1998	
1959	NI04196–NI04465	1999	
1960	NI04466–NI04774	2000	

owed by an individual can be used in evidence for bankruptcy proceedings. Two creditors with debts that amount to £750 or more can combine. Unfortunately there is a stumbling block. The cost of taking proceedings can range between £450 to £700.

WHAT IS A PARTNERSHIP? – RESPONSIBILITY FOR PAYMENT

A partnership is governed by the Partnership Act of 1890. Regrettably, even in this modern world, I have come across partnerships where no formal agreement has ever been raised. The danger here is that if the partnership is made up of just two members, if one becomes ill or they have a serious disagreement, the partnership can collapse. Many partnerships are absolutely solid and have first class reputations, but a commercial disagreement, which could be brought about by, for example, one of the partners getting a divorce, can cause vast problems. It is difficult to take proceedings and if there are few personal assets it may take considerable time and effort to confirm whether or not it is financially viable to make the partners bankrupt.

The rule yet again is to carry out thorough assessments. Once the number of partners reaches more than 20 members they have to apply for limited company incorporation under the Companies Act 1985. The only exception is under Section 716 of the Act where accountants, solicitors and members of the Stock Exchange may form partnerships of numbers greater than 20.

WHAT IS A PRIVATE LIMITED COMPANY?

It is a fallacy to believe that if you are supplying a private limited company that the company is liable and able to pay your debts. A private limited company has an artificial legal identity. It is regarded in law as a person who can own land and property and transact contracts. The actual directors are not personally responsible for paying the debts of their company. It is only when wrongful or fraudulent trading can be proved that not just the directors but also managers, shareholders and shadow directors may be personally liable under the Insolvency Act 1986. The wording of the Act states 'Directors and even managers who exercise some control over the company may risk disqualification and personal liability for the debts of the company in the event of failure.' The legislation in the Insolvency Act 1986 and Company Directors Disqualification Act 1986, may appear to strengthen the law. Pre-assessment before any credit transaction is far safer than trying to petition to wind up a company which may have no assets whatsoever (see Chapters 9 and 11).

Directors' and Managers' Responsibilities

Although the original Companies Act was passed in 1855 and many amendments have since been passed to regulate the administration of a private limited company, there is remarkably little to define the responsibilities and duties of a director. Under the Companies Act 1985, Section 741, the title of director or shadow director is defined as 'including any person occupying the position of director, by whatever name called.' Under subsection (2) a 'shadow director means a person in accordance with whose directions or instructions the directors of the company are accustomed to act'. This clause is vitally important if a company becomes insolvent. To quote Grant Thornton's booklet, *Directors and the Insolvency Act*:

> It is clear that in the event of failure a person who exercises a measure of control may risk disqualification and personal liability for the debts of the company, even though he is not called a director.

In theory, this may assist creditors, but in practical terms it could be a long and expensive operation to try and recover liquid funds or assets from an individual who has already been seen to be irresponsible when managing a company. It is also possible for the director to gain personal indemnity against this type of action.

Two recent cases illustrate the strengths of these new Acts. A director was disqualified for five years as he had acted irresponsibly. The companies were insolvent and accounts had not been prepared for many years. In another case, a non-director was disqualified for not paying Crown debts. So it can be seen that anyone who takes part in the management of a company could be liable.

Formation of a Private Limited Company

To illustrate how quickly a private limited company can be formed, at the time of writing it is possible to purchase an 'off the shelf' limited company for £180 including VAT. A same day Limited Company Registration can be arranged for £285 inclusive of VAT provided that the forms 288a and 287 are filled in correctly before 2.00 pm (as at July 1997) by ICC Legal and Commercial Services Ltd, Crwys House, 33 Crwys Road, Cardiff CF2 4Y. The formalities can be concluded within 15 minutes. Provided that the director and the company secretary of that company do not require a name change and they have in their possession the Certificate of Incorporation, they can trade. The legal liability of the limited company is that the director and/or shareholders actually pay for a minimum of two one-pound shares. This is their liability.

Readers should not be confused between authorised and issued share capital. Authorised capital is the maximum amount of share capital that may be raised; whereas the issued share capital is the actual number of shares that have been allotted and paid for.

In Section 1(1) of the Companies Act 1985 it states that 'Any two or more persons associated for a lawful purpose may, by subscribing their names to a memorandum of association', form a company. The ICC registration company can arrange to change the name for £45, but the new name cannot be used for trading until a new Certificate of Incorporation is issued by Companies House, which takes about two weeks. If anyone wishes to cut costs even further it is possible to purchase a company direct from Companies House, Cardiff. It does, however, entail purchasing from a law stationers a set of articles and memorandum of association.

As an indication of the number of private limited companies which are formed in this way, ICC in July 1997 were selling 'off the shelf' companies at the rate of between 10 and 15 per day. The total number of new private limited companies which were registered in 1996 was 165,903.

Accounting Records

Directors of private limited companies and PLCs must keep accounting records as section 221 of the Companies Act 1985 states: 'The accounting records shall be sufficient to show and explain the company transactions'. Under subsection A they should be able to disclose, with reasonable accuracy at any time, the financial position of the company, and under 3(a), accounting records must be kept of the daily receipts and payments of money. Under 3(b), a record of assets and liabilities must be recorded. Stocktaking records must also be recorded (section 4).

Again, these Companies Acts should in theory safeguard creditors, but in practice it does not as a high proportion of company failures are due to poor general administration (see Chapter 8).

It can now be seen that a private limited company's strengths have to be evaluated by checking their management's experience, the history of the company and financial stability. It is so easy to be misled by an impressive letter heading and order form that shows 'Ltd'. The vast majority of directors and managers are honest. The problem for all credit controllers is that about 85 per cent of all limited company failures may be caused by poor management. It has recently been stated that a further 15 per cent of company failures may be due to fraud (see Chapter 4).

UNDERSTANDING PUBLIC LIMITED COMPANIES (PLCs)

Before the Companies Act 1980, there was only one type of public limited company which, if it wished its shares to be offered to the public, had to go through a very thorough process via the London Stock Exchange to gain a listing. Since 1980 there have been further developments which have enabled smaller companies to raise funds by issuing shares and debentures to the public. From 22 December 1980 a public limited company, to be registered or re-registered, must have a minimum allotted capital of £50,000, of which one quarter must be paid up on each share. This is a Companies Act requirement.

Regrettably, there is still a loophole as it is possible to purchase an 'off the shelf' PLC. Therefore it is imperative to check if the PLC is:

- fully listed
- AIM – Alternative Investment Market
- OTC Market – Over The Counter.

As a senior partner of Coopers & Lybrand stated, when dealing with a PLC, it 'does not mean that they are a super credit risk!' (i.e. they will pay your account). The problem is that seeing the words 'Public Limited Company' on a letter heading or order tends to inspire confidence automatically. It is even more important nowadays to check the PLC status as the company may have had a relatively short history (see Chapter 4).

Basics of a PLC

A public limited company must have at least two directors and the company secretary must be qualified.

A Full Listing

As at 30 June 1997 there were 2695 PLCs, of which 533 were overseas domestic companies, which were traded on the Official List on the London Stock Exchange. These companies are major organisations which may have thousands of shareholders. Again, a warning: UK and overseas takeover battles are now more frequent and vicious. Therefore, constant monitoring of the press is necessary to keep up with developments. In the UK, fund managers of the large institutions are now playing an increasing role in the way major PLCs operate. Because many of the fund managers, who often represent insurance companies, are protecting their policy holders by trying to achieve maximum dividends, there can be dramatic changes of policy and profit when the City sentiment starts to move.

You may think that my previous comments have been negative, but it is my opinion that credit personnel have to be watchful 365 days of the year.

The good news, however, is that a full listed PLC has to publish far more financial information than the other types of companies which raise funds in the security market.

Raising Funds Through the London Stock Exchange

There has always been a need for expanding companies to raise finance through the Stock Exchange. In November 1980 the London Stock Exchange launched the USM (Unlisted Securities Market). Some of these companies had a checkered history and there were a number of failures. The USM Market was closed on 31 December 1996 and some of the companies transferred to AIM.

The Third Market was closed on 31 December 1990. There is still a small market for OTC (Over The Counter) shares which are sold by brokers.

The new AIM flotation which opened on 19 June 1995 offers a slightly less expensive way for young companies to raise funds.

There are no restrictions on the number of years a company has traded or market capitalisation. An AIM applicant must appoint and retain a nominated adviser and a nominated broker. It is believed that many entrepreneurs favour this type of flotation as it gives them a positive image. Since AIM companies flotations have been established there have been three insolvencies and a number of nominated advisors have resigned. As at July 1997 there were 286 AIM companies registered, of which 25 were operating overseas. The London Stock Exchange started a new structure in October 1997, and it is hoped that the electronic order book will reduce costs and stocks will be more keenly priced for companies listed on the FTSE 100 stocks.

When 'PLC' in a letter heading or order is noted, the very greatest care must be taken to distinguish it between a full listed PLC and an AIM or OTC.

Formation Cost

The formation costs for an AIM flotation can be anything between £250,000 and £500,000 for a smaller company and for a full listing can be far higher. Therefore, before the management and their advisers consider this course of action a considerable amount of research has to be carried out. It must be remembered that the Stock Exchange administration costs are rising, due to computerisation.

As a guide to some of the requirements that are necessary for a full listing, the Council of the London Stock Exchange state that the sponsoring member of the Exchange has to 'pay particular attention to the composition of the board of the applicant and whether the range of skills and experience necessary to the board is available'. The sponsors have to satisfy themselves that the directors can be expected to honour their obligations both in relation to shareholders and creditors. The expected market value of securities for which listing is sought must be at least £700,000 in the case of shares and £200,000 in the case of debt securities (debentures or loan stock etc.).

Three Years' Accounts

The company must have published or filed accounts covering the three years preceding the application for listing. Where there is an equity element the sponsoring member must state the nature of the company's business, its profit record before taxation for the past three years, and whether any profit is to be forecast for the current year or next. There are a vast number of other regulations which relate to the accountants' and auditors' reports.

PLCs, like all other companies, can and do become insolvent, but where an application for listing is made, the directors have to declare if they have ever been adjudged bankrupt or whether deeds of arrangement have been made with their creditors. They also have to declare whether there are any unsatisfied judgements against the directors, and whether any company has been put into liquidation (other than voluntary) or had a receiver appointed while acting as a director. Convictions of fraud or dishonesty, and when the court adjudged that fraud, misfeasance or other misconduct occurred, and finally, if the director has been refused membership of a professional body also have to be declared.

A public limited company has to file their accounts within six months of the end of the accounting reference date. Therefore, the information is a little less historic than in a private limited company. I have already mentioned that PLCs can get into financial difficulties and become insolvent.

The problem for credit granters is that, generally speaking, a PLC will spend far more on public relations and marketing of their total image than a private limited company will. This includes the annual report which can create the most attractive image it is possible to produce.

Chairman's Report

These reports can appear tremendously optimistic. Here are two examples:

> In view of the substantial increase in capital available to us, I would expect the future growth to be maintained at the same satisfactory level as hitherto.

> The Directors continue to have confidence in the future progress of the enlarged group.

Within a year, both the companies quoted above became insolvent with losses to creditors of millions of pounds. Incidentally, the annual reports were among the most beautifully presented I have ever seen.

OVER THE COUNTER (OTC) PLCs

This is another type of public company where shares can be sold through private dealers. This market commenced some years ago. An OTC flotation is not under the control of the London Stock Exchange. There are a number of market makers who now seem to be willing to market these shares. This does place OTCs in a difficult position. The OTC market was created when banks and other financial institutions were unable to increase their funding to small established family-owned companies. There are few accounting and reporting requirements. The very greatest of care should be taken when considering significant credit transactions.

LOCAL AUTHORITIES

A local authority will pay for supplies or services provided that the orders, acceptance, and all the formalities have been correctly carried out – but here is a warning! It is imperative that the accounts department of the business which is drawing up the 'invoice' to be submitted to the local authority knows exactly the correct method of applying for payment (see Chapter 8).

With council tax capping and more stringent controls by central government the morale of the staff in many finance departments can be low. Local authorities can take many months to pay accounts. Although there have been sensational reports of authorities running out of funds, it has not yet actually happened. The key point to remember is that local authorities, like other businesses, all have different characters. Credit controllers should credit rate their local authorities like any other customer. If you note from national or local newspapers that a particular authority is leasing out their town hall or lampposts, the outcome could be a shortage of funds at a particular time of the year.

Delayed Payments by Official Bodies

The Audit Commission announced in November 1996 that it would require local authorities to publish their payment record as a performance indicator in the next financial year.

NHS TRUSTS

The national Audit Office announced on 18 July 1997 that 95 of the 433 NHS Trusts were facing financial difficulties as at the end of 1995–6, of which 26 were serious. By the end of the third quarter of 1996–7 the number which had serious difficulties had risen to 47.

Under the NHS Residual Liabilities Act 1996, when a trust has financial difficulties, they have to merge with another trust. The credit granter must in future monitor their accounts with NHS trusts. If too many have difficulties, would it be possible for the Government to lend or give sufficient funding?

NEW TOWNS

A further indication of how careful a credit granter has to be when assessing a government-aided corporation is shown in the following example:

The *Financial Times* reported in September 1988, that the House of Commons Public Accounts Committee were very disturbed at the lack of financial discipline. This related to five new towns that were set up between 1947 and 1966. The towns – East Kilbride, Glenrothes, Cumbernauld, Livingston and Irvine – were run by development corporations. A sum of £852 million had been advanced and only £18 million had been repaid. It was reported that some £800 million may have to be written off.

PRIVATISED UTILITIES

The gas, electricity, rail and water companies and hospital trusts, for example, all have completely different payment systems. They are all responsible for payment of accounts providing that the work or services have been carried out in the correct manner. Again, payments may be delayed for months on end if the individual procedures are not followed.

MINISTRIES

Ministries, like local authorities, are responsible for paying for supplies and services, but again absolute care and accuracy has to be ensured to see that all the applications for payment are submitted in the way the ministry requires the applications to be recorded. Quite often an invoice will not be issued. Instead a certified payment certificate will be required.

THE COMPANIES ACT 1989

The Companies Act 1989 received its royal assent on 16 November 1989. The main provisions of the Act implement the 7th and 8th EC company law directives. The Act strengthens the law on consolidated accounts, and off balance sheet financing and removes the application of small- and medium-size groups and subsidiaries of EC parent companies to prepare group accounts in certain circumstances. It lays down the minimum requirements for the training of auditors and requirements of accounting bodies to apply for recognition.

New procedures for registered bodies and changes in the routine at Companies House plus the limitations to the capacity of a company and the authority of its board of directors are amended under the Companies Act 1985.

The majority of this Act's provisions are not yet in operation, but will be implemented within the next year or so.

NEW LEGISLATION AFFECTING CREDIT GRANTING

Small Company Audit Exemptions

The exemption for limited companies with a turnover of £90,000 was raised to £350,000 on 15 April 1997. Since this higher exemption came into force members of the Institute of Credit Management report that there has been a marked deterioration in the information provided.

VAT Bad Debt Relief

Changes to the VAT bad debt relief mean that suppliers will not be able to claim relief on live aged debts because if they do so they will have to write to their customers advising them that they have written off the debt. This new procedure will jeopardise any chances of recovering the debt in the future. The requirement to also notify every customer is so detailed, even for smaller debts, that the administration effort and cost will outweigh the benefit of reclaiming the VAT.

PLC's Reporting Requirements

Under Statutory Instrument 571, 4 March 1997, PLC's directors have to report in their annual accounts the percentage of days credit taken from suppliers. In 1996 under SI 189 the payment policy has to be mentioned.

POSSIBLE FUTURE LEGISLATION

Late Payment of Trade Debt

Late Payment of Trade Debt, Statutory Interest Legislation may be put through in the near future, although many interested parties do not feel that the new administration has thought through all the ramifications, including delays in the court system and the complexity of calculating the interest charges. It is understood that this legislation will go through although many organisations, including the Institute of Credit Management, are against these proposals.

In July 1997 Barbara Roche, the DTI Minister, published proposals on statutory interest which included the following points:

- Where no existing payment terms are defined, or no contract exists, the credit period should be 30 days from date of invoice.
- Businesses will not be able to contract out of the terms of the legislation.
- The proposed interest rate will be base rate plus 4 per cent. However, when the 'Late Payment of Commercial Debt (Interest) Bill' was published on 11 December 1997, it was announced that the interest would be base rate + 8 per cent – a huge increase on the original proposal.
- Small businesses will be able to claim interest on any commercial debt against large enterprises and the public sector (in the first stage). When the second reading took place in January 1998 it was envisaged that 'the right will be extended, after a period of two years, for use by small businesses against all enterprises of any size, including the public sector. Finally it is envisaged that the right will be extended again after a period of at least two years, to all enterprises, including the public sector, to use against all corresponding enterprises'.

Disclosure of Directors' and Secretaries' Home Addresses and Nationalities

A DTI Consultative Document was circulated in February 1997 and views from professional bodies including the Institute of Credit Management were submitted in May 1997. The basis of the consultation is that directors and secretaries are being pestered and security and privacy implications are involved. If this proposal goes through, it will be impossible to check the personal payment morality of directors for personal guarantees to be cross checked. If directors are constantly overseas it is not possible to address questions to them at creditors' meetings concerning the location of assets.

Data Protection Guidance on Debt Tracing and Collection

The Data Protection Registrar issued guidance notes on debt tracing and collection in 1997 for discussion in the industry. They refer to the 1944 Criminal Justice and Public Order Act when gathering information about debtors. The guide notes point out that 'personal data shall be processed fairly and lawfully'. It is understood that revised notes will be issued in the future.

SUMMARY

There is an enormous difference between the financial strength of a fully listed PLC and a private limited company with a share capital of £2. Do not be mesmerised by an impressive letter heading from any organisation.

- Have you the correct name of the business you intend to sell to?
- Do you understand the legal liability of the various types of business in paying their debts?
- Looking at ministries, local authorities and so on, do you know how their payment systems work?
- With new legislation coming in, how can you review your administration to counteract any additional problems that arise?
- Remember that privatised utilities may not have the same corporate strength as formerly.

4
The Unknown Customer

When an order comes in from an unknown customer it is often difficult or impossible to make an accurate credit decision based on a single fact. The order may arrive in the sales office simply by telephone or by post or fax on a letter heading which does not indicate their terms. Regrettably, the order could even be a fraudulent transaction (see Fraud).

The problem is that in some businesses the buzz of receiving a further order or an initial order means that all rational, commonsense considerations vanish. A set system of opening an account by using credit bureaux and other reference information encourages a disciplined approach. The madness of handing over goods or services to be supplied on credit without first checking or assessing the risk will then be reduced to a minimum.

Basically a credit bureau's strength lies in the following areas:

1. their knowledge in gathering consumer and commercial information which includes payment profiles and trade reference information;
2. their staff's ability and experience in accessing their clients' trade credit requirements;
3. the information passed to the bureau by their clients which builds up their report records.

Care has to be taken in choosing a bureau. Evaluating the way they collect data is important. For example, some bureaux telephone or write to the business that they have been asked to research and then report back their findings. The problem here is that the business will just give the information that suits them.

Credit bureaux can assist you, the credit granter, by supplying additional commercial and financial information which will enable your business to decide whether to:

1. increase the credit sales volume per month
2. leave the credit limit as it is
3. reduce the amount
4. monitor the account more carefully
5. obtain additional information
6. agree to a cash account with favourable terms, or a different form of sale.

A credit bureau will often specialise in a certain trade or segment of industry. This usually means that the majority of credit personnel in that trade will all use the same agency.

No agency can make a decision for you as to whether goods or services should be supplied. But agency information, plus the references and the other data which is gathered through the new business form, will help to reinforce your decision on which sales terms you offer. No one agency can supply all the information you may require. I have found that in the UK and overseas markets it is often far better to use two agencies to obtain information on a new customer. This is especially useful when the information is marginal or when the transaction is larger than you normally see. Fraudulent transactions do occur, businesses often say 'It could not happen to us.' But if a company is newly-formed and an order came in 'out of the blue' it could indicate fraud.

The following two interviews illustrate the need for vigilance.

FRAUD

When I interviewed Mr John Wood in 1989, the then Director of the Serious Fraud Office, he said: 'It's very easy to be wise after the event. Fraud is usually motivated by greed.' There will always be people who will try and get away with fraud because the sums involved are so vast. They invariably think they will succeed.

It is always possible that through 'white collar fraud' we, the suppliers, may be caught out. Precautions, however, can be taken, firstly by identifying who your actual customer is and verifying their track record (see Information Research).

John Wood told me that although fraudsters are typically motivated by greed, fraud is not necessarily limited to those who do not have much money. There are plenty of examples of fraudsters who are extremely wealthy and who still manipulate the system to become even more wealthy. He mentioned two distinctive types of fraud: crimes committed by the professional criminal and those committed by hard-pressed directors, who gradually drift into fraud. The former group normally carry out a 'long firm fraud'. They may go in at particular times of the year – for example before Christmas – over-order, get the goods, and not pay for them. They then sell the goods to the more dubious markets in the home market or abroad. These professional fraudsters may have started with petty theft or robbery and then graduated to fraud. Mr Wood thought that it was important to remember that, up till now, fraud has paid dividends, in the sense that one can get a lot of money quickly without taking the risks that are inherent in robbing a bank or a security van! Regrettably, Mr Wood pointed out, anyone convicted of committing a bank raid could easily be sentenced to a prison term of more than 10 years, whereas, in fraud cases, a term of three years and often less was quite possible.

City Fraud

As there has been so much publicity concerning the city financial frauds I asked Mr Wood how they begin.

There have always been instances of glossy advertisements, seemingly respectable, with a City of London address. The wording of the advertisement is often couched in highly impressive jargon, promising fantastic returns on money invested. Members of the public are persuaded by it, then send their cheques. Weeks later, the office suddenly closes and the directors vanish.

'Fraud is not generally a young man's crime, although there are examples of young men being involved in fraud'. In Mr Wood's experience, it was more likely to see a fraudster aged over 30 because experience is necessary to carry out such frauds.

I was interested to know how a limited company gradually became involved in fraud. Mr Wood pointed out that quite often there may be a small company trading perfectly properly. The company directors are anxious to further the business and make a reasonable living. There may be circumstances that change their business activity. The company starts losing money. Instead of getting professional advice, or going into voluntary liquidation, they fraudulently gain credit from a bank by submitting a false balance sheet to obtain a loan. They then order goods, realising that they cannot pay for them. The directors, who had no intention of being fraudulent when they started the business, led themselves into fraudulent conduct.

There are a number of cases that come to light when false documentation is used to obtain a loan. Banks, like other financial organisations, are often extremely reluctant to report these facts because it can draw attention to their own vulnerability. Therefore, a considerable amount of fraud is never reported and never receives notice in the financial or commercial world.

Mr Wood told me:

> We have found already that having accountants at our elbow has paid the most handsome dividends. They can identify very clearly those lines of investigation which you should not be pursuing. Although my department has only been operating for a few months, the concept of the team – that is, the police officer,

accountant and lawyer, with inputs of specialist advice from Counsel – is working out even better than we hoped.

LONG FIRM FRAUD – AN EXPERT'S OPINION

The following wording is a standard reply indicating fraud, when a trader asked a purchaser for references which appeared on the surface to be 'perfect'.

> We hope that this information is to your satisfaction. If we can be of any further assistance to you, please do not hesitate to contact us.
>
> (signed) Credit Manager

Talking to Laurie Harrop, who is acknowledged as an expert on long firm fraud, he confirmed that the above reference was one of the indications that a business could be suspicious. Mr Harrop, a former Associate Director of CCN Business Information Limited (now Experian), was previously a manager at the Manchester Guardian Society for 36 years and has unique experience on tracing fraudulent transactions. He has lectured at many detective training courses run by the Home Office and he is therefore able to advise of any changes in LF techniques.

He confirmed that from his agency's reports, less than one per cent of the enquiries they receive could relate to long firm fraud. This is surprising when one considers that this technique of purchasing large amounts of goods on credit without any intention of paying for them has been a practice in the UK for about 200 years. In the 1950s and 1960s the criminal fraternity diversified, adding hijackings and protection rackets to long firm fraud. Recently there may be some evidence that long firm fraud is tied up with drug trafficking. This money is then 'laundered' through business enterprises which are run in a fraudulent way.

I asked Laurie Harrop how these operations develop. He confirmed that although there are the backers and organisers along with 'front men' to run these businesses, most of the money required is received from the innocent creditors. An important point to remember is that the backers hardly ever appear on the premises. They may be shown as directors of a 'company' but they often resign three to four months before the failure. In this way they can deny any possible involvement in the fraud.

Timing

The success of these operations depends on timing and the quick dispersal of products. There are still places where consumer goods can be sold with few questions asked. Often it is only when the credit has actually been paid for the first or second order that they discover that the warehouse is empty. Creditors may be told that there was a burglary or a serious fire on the site. Quite often they discover that the office address is an accommodation address.

Pre-planned frauds often commence when a new business is set up with a lifespan of less than six months. The other method is for a group of fraudsters to take over an existing business. Credit is gained by building up the supplier's confidence. The initial sale may begin on a *pro forma* basis. The purchaser supplies false trade references (such as the example quoted above). The alternative method is to set up two or three companies in various locations and use these for fraudulent references.

SIGNALS FOR FRAUD

1. The bank reference may state 'a recently opened account' whereas the trade references state that they have dealt with the business over a period of years.
2. The letter from the company ordering the goods or the referee's letter may be beautifully printed. The directors all have 'professional qualifications'. However, when checked they are all fictitious. One vital piece of information is often omitted, and that is the company registration number. If the credit granter had cross-checked with their credit reference agency they would have realised that the 'limited company' did not exist.
3. Very often these letter headings look even more impressive as more than one telephone number is quoted. Fax and telex numbers are also printed and the business belongs to numerous trade associations. The actual trading address when traced is an accommodation address.
4. The trade references, when received, are drafted in the same way and produced on the same typewriter.
5. A representative is suspicious because a well-established business is under new ownership.
6. A substantial order is received from a new customer with no questions asked about price or quantity discount. The representative was surprised how easy it was to obtain the order.
7. A very large increase in the credit line is requested on an established credit account.
8. A large order is received for out-of-season goods.

Change in Ownership

Mr Harrop confirmed that when an established business is taken over it is often far more difficult to identify a potential fraud. A 'killing' can take place in an exceptionally short timespan. Because the business has an established banking history, a credit rating and a list of customers who have granted credit over a considerable period, the supplier has confidence. If it is a limited company, the new, fraudulent owners will delay filing the documents with the Registrar of Companies. In certain recent cases they delayed until the assets had vanished without any documents being filed at all.

When fraud is suspected, a major credit bureau should be contacted as normally a fraudster will place many orders over a wide area. Bureaux then receive a flood of enquiries which may indicate a possible fraud. Laurie Harrop pointed out that these commercial frauds receive very little publicity but in fact they cost businesses thousands of pounds each year. If suppliers would even telephone these perfect trade references to see if they were genuine, many write offs could be avoided. Total protection is not possible, but that little extra time spent on investigation could prevent a large loss.

Credit managers who are concerned about commercial fraud should contact CIFAS, the Credit Industry Fraud Avoidance System, 173/175 Cleveland Street, London W1P 5PE (Tel: 0171 383 0210).

CREDIT INFORMATION

Beware of the agency that simply produces a report by retyping the names and addresses of the directors and their shareholding from the annual return filed at Companies House. In the past they obtained a banker's opinion and if there was uncertainty they just stated that 'suitable assurances concerning payment should be obtained'. This type of report never helped the credit granter to make a decision. One must always enquire *when* the actual information was obtained. If the information is months or years old the report is virtually worthless.

If a large sum is being considered, it is advisable to purchase a report on the business from two separate bureaux. I often hear managers say that a single report costs £30 plus, and that they cannot afford to 'throw money around'. My reply is that if they are reviewing any transaction which is substantial in their terms, why is there not the profit margin to assess the risk? With constant changes in minimum base rates, funding a delayed payment can be extremely expensive (see Figure 1.2). I consider that 90 per cent of credit management is assessment. Therefore, if no reports are obtained, the total transaction proposed could be a total loss. For instance, if it is agreed that up to £50 be spent on sales valued £5000 and that £100 can be charged to your budget on a £10,000 order, it is then possible to negotiate with bureaux to arrange for volume orders.

How an Agency Works

There is no magic or secret method of gathering commercial or consumer information. Agencies do make direct approaches to a business without, of course, disclosing the name of their client who requires the information. They also gather a considerable amount of data by being in constant contact with the business and consumer world.

THE COMMERCIAL FIELD – LIMITED COMPANIES

With computerisation, every limited company, be it private or public, is noted on a database. Major bureaux purchase this information from Companies House, Crown Way, Cardiff CF4 3UZ (central enquiries tel: 01222 380801).

The name and registered office of the company and the full name and home addresses of the directors and secretary are recorded when a company is incorporated. Over 300 credit bureaux belong to two organisations in the UK which supply credit information on consumers and commercial traders, and also carry out debt recovery work.

The Credit Services Association has been formed by a merger between the Collection Agencies Association and the Association of Trade Protection and Debt Recovery Agents. The first body was formed some 17 years ago, and the latter was formed in 1902. The Credit Services Association has a strict code of practice. All membership applications are vetted thoroughly and are only accepted after at least two years' unblemished trading and that they are financially solvent. This has to be confirmed each year by the Council of the CSA. The Association is also a member of the Federation of European National Collection Associations. As at March 1997 there were 130 members. For further information contact: Credit Services Association, Ensign House, 56 Thorpe Road, Norwich NR1 1RY (tel: 0160 362 9105).

INFORMATION RESEARCH

The development of the credit reference agencies dates from the period of the industrial revolution. When transport and communication between towns started to improve, there was a great need for precise information when credit transactions were being considered with traders. Trading started to expand throughout the UK from 1800, but bad debts were frequent, due to lack of information.

It is believed that the first organised trade protection society was the Mutual Communication Society which was formed in 1801 at the British Coffee House, Cockspur Street, London W3. The rules of the Society included members' duty 'to communicate without delay the name and description of any person who may be unfit for trust . . . for the security of other members'. The rules also stated that 'no member shall give any improper or wrong information so as to manifest any malicious . . . intent'. This was the beginning of national credit reporting by independent, professional, commercial and consumer reporters.

MAJOR INFORMATION PROVIDERS

The following interviews with major credit and information bureaux in the UK illustrate how they are developing their services to help credit managers and controllers to assess their customers for risk and at the same time actually show how those same customers are paying their debts.

Equifax

In the previous edition of this book I reported that the oldest independent information bureau in the UK was the United Association for the Protection of Trade which was formed in 1842; subsequently they changed their name to Infolink. Infolink have now been absorbed by Equifax, who have also purchased Infocheck, another commercial trade information provider.

Equifax was established in the USA in the late 1890s in much the same way as UAPT. Their origins were in the retail and mail order markets to protect traders. They are now the largest providers of consumer information services in the USA and they also operate in Canada, Europe, the Far East, Latin America, Chile and Mexico.

I interviewed Simon Lees, Associate Director of Equifax, to see how they were developing their services for the consumer and commercial credit granter. Apart from being the largest supplier of volume commercial reports in the UK, they also have a significant market in supplying commercial lending reports to finance houses which has been their traditional market in the past. There is an increasing need to know what is happening in the local area, therefore banks are beginning to use Equifax's trade reports and their marketing data to increase their own sales promotions.

The change since 1989 is that this Group focuses on supporting the credit decision when there is less information available, for example limited companies who are not required to file full accounts. This is why they are producing rating systems with expanded commercial group structures. Another example is the way they are collecting payment data as against trading information, such as payment data on outstanding loans or leasing agreements which gives a pointer to the way a business or individual pays its debts. This type of information is, however, only available to certain closed user groups such as finance houses, banks, insurance companies, and so on.

Commercial and Consumer Data

To give an indication of this Group's database, if a director's full name is known, a full report on his or her company can be obtained, or if the same director is noted on their consumer database that individual can be searched so that their personal payment morality can be assessed if the application is for a personal loan.

There are 44 million consumers and 1.4 million limited companies entered on their current database of which 900,000 may be trading as at March, 1997. Interestingly only 400,000 of those limited companies are searched once a year and 50,000 of those are searched twice a year. This may be the reason why trade credit granters receive a shock when they are not paid, or their customer simply ceases trading or fails, said Simon Lees.

In the UK the number of commercial business names, unincorporated businesses, sole traders and partnerships number about 3 million. There are about another 900,000 sole operators that work from home. The total number of businesses on their database numbers 3.8 million, however, other information organisations think this figure may be even higher. Simon Lees emphasised that when his company reviewed business start-ups in 1996, 420,000 were launched, and 400,000 ceased trading.

Speed

Automated systems are in demand as Equifax have customers who require credit decisions within seconds. For example, it may be a leasing company who needs a quote by a business introducer, and they are ringing three potential leasing companies, and if it takes 20 minutes to turn the quote around, the business is lost!

A sales person visiting a prospect does have to know, if they make the investment in time, effort and research, that when the business is signed it is not going to be rejected by the credit department when they review the application. Therefore there is a need to rate the business before a visit.

Marketing

Equifax confirm that there is a need to look at the whole country in terms of the market place. They have the means to plot this market against geographic areas and branch networks, and by this method it can be seen where the prospects are located. Once this is carried out personal data can be overlayed so that the business can be assessed for positive and negative information.

Conclusion

This Group is still developing sources of information for credit granters based on their knowledge – of consumer, industrial and commercial databases. The services that they provide are likely to be particularly useful to the leasing, banking, building society, insurance and financing industries, or consumer sales, where speed is essential, and where the 'Closed User Group' contributes.

For further information contact Equifax Europe Credit Services, Capital House, Chapel Street, London, NW1 5DS (tel: 0171 298 3000).

Experian, Formerly the CCN Group

In an interview with David Coates, Managing Director of Experian's Business Information Division, Henry Davison, Manager Consumer Division, and Tim Morris, Sales Director, it was emphasised that only 20 per cent of the business community use credit reports. Many businesses in the UK do not recognise that they are running a risk. They are not prepared to pay for a credit report, or they believe that they know everything about their customers. Regrettably, many companies have to incur a few bad debts before they begin to realise how damaging lost profits can be to their business.

In reviewing the changes that have affected UK trade over the last seven years it is clear that there has been a dramatic growth of small businesses through the Thatcher years of privatisation, and through the downsizing of major corporations who employ small companies to carry out work that was previously done in-house. This trend has impacted on Experian as they now have to provide more information on those small businesses, many of which are unincorporated. This means that credit controllers are demanding far more information, and this group are responding by providing consumer information, on which it has a huge data bank.

From their research it can be seen that there is a fundamental relationship on how an individual pays their bills as a consumer, and as a proprietor or partner of a business. Essentially they are assessing the same individual who has unlimited liability in their personal and corporate life, however, an entire business will rest on his or her skills. For these reasons their research department is collecting thousands of current payment performance patterns through their review of a large number of sales ledgers which come from a spread of many sectors in industry and commerce.

What They Can Report

A credit granter looking at a small business needs to know: Is it real? How do they pay their bills? When was the business established? Can you take some measure from its payment records on the size of trade that is being transacted? The number of employees, the size of the premises and a check on any CCJ's which might have been registered against the business will build up a meaningful picture. But this has to be checked against other small businesses, as the person running the business may be running other enterprises under a number of different names. Linking the man or woman to the business is critical.

Another Trend

Sales ledgers are now changing, for example where there were 200/300 live accounts, there might now be 600 smaller accounts. Assessment can be handled through their consumer database, payment performance and credit scoring. Credit Control staff cannot gain this type of information from Companies House, therefore Experian is providing information from many sources. Large businesses are also changing because to win business they have to pull together as a team, so the credit policy is now inevitably determined by sales and marketing. The finance department may say that if you push for larger business the implication from a credit perspective is that there will be a percentage of higher risks. This is why a considerable amount of credit is now 'pre-screened' so that provided the account hits a certain score it is passed. The credit controllers' time is then focused on those big, tough exposures, and they will then take out of the main system anything that does not meet certain criteria.

The credit controller can now look at 2000 accounts and monitor them in a different way – either profitable/unprofitable, or risky. Importantly, all this type of information can be fed into the marketing system so that sales, marketing, finance and credit are now working together to create a revenue cycle.

Help for Small Businesses

Many small businesses do not have credit controllers nowadays so technology and scoring is being developed. For this reason Experian is being increasingly asked to design Credit Application Schemes. These are not the standard name, address and two trade references; now the proprietor's name and address, home address, and the same information on directors is required. Where there are also changes in a limited company there is another service called 'Constant Review', where a tick will appear on the on-line screen service.

Conclusion

This company has developed its services to incorporate what it thinks credit personnel will need in the coming years to assess risks and profits. To quote

Henry Davison 'there is a vast difference in interpreting a business that is 14 days late on 90 day terms, and a business that is paying 14 days late on 14 day terms.' See Figure 4.1, which illustrates delayed payment of J.H. Dewhurst, the high street butchers chain. This sector works on seven day terms.

Further information of their group's services can be obtained from: Experian, Talbot House, Talbot Street, Nottingham, NG1 5HF (tel: 0115 941 0888).

Dun & Bradstreet

The history of Dun & Bradstreet and its development actually began when, in New York in 1841, Lewis Tappan realised that he could no longer extend credit to country debtors without adequate independent credit information. In the panic of 1836 his firm, Arthur Tappan and Co., had suffered losses, but other businesses began to ask the Tappan brothers for credit information. This was the birth of Dun & Bradstreet.

Lewis Tappan formed the Mercantile Agency to improve credit reporting, using local people who could be trusted, often churchmen. Reports were then gradually compiled. As Sol Bergman stated in his book *Credit in Early America*, 'Subscribers came to the office to consult the reports'. In 1857, Tappan's agency was opened in London and Montreal, and in 1849 a rival agency called

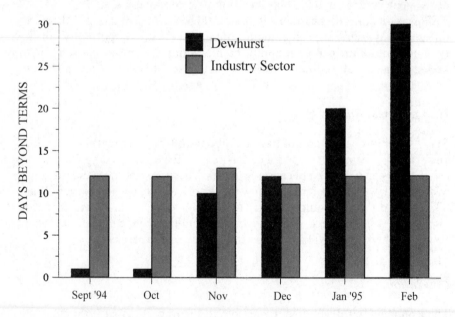

Figure 4.1 Payment performance

John M. Bradstreet was opened in Cincinnati. The two agencies merged in 1933 to form the R.G. Dun-Bradstreet Corporation.

Dun & Bradstreet can now supply, through their worldwide database of commercial information, reports on some 40 million businesses which are located in the 230 countries of the world (as at February, 1997).

In the past, many readers would have discovered these services by looking at the old style D&B Registers. These have now been superseded by the *CD-ROM D&B Credit Register* which for the UK covers 1.74 million businesses, including sole traders, partnerships and limited companies.

Their Reporting Service

Since reporting on this company in 1989 they have dramatically changed the way they deliver the data to businesses. Depending on the levels of information that a business requires to assess a new customer, or just as important, to monitor an existing customer, there are now seven types of key reports. These range from the Compact, for high volume transactions, to the D&B report, which highlights extra data to assess medium risks. Their Rating Report (see Figure 3.2 for example) gives credit granters warnings on potential failures; this database covers over 1 million UK trading businesses. There are also the Trade Reference, Executive, Financial Profile, Select, Industrial Norm, and the Company Document and Monitoring Reports. The Comprehensive Report is the most detailed, so I obtained one of these for an actual limited company which I was interested in monitoring. I received a thirteen-page report which immediately gave me a D&B rating report, analysed the condition of the company and stated the maximum credit that could be extended. Just as important was the fact that they were paying their suppliers 19 days beyond terms. There was also a payment score and a commentary on the payment performance. Details of Mortgages and Charges registered, and County Court Judgments including the amounts, courts, and plaint numbers were all listed up to five years.

The background of the directors, including home addresses, and the company names of their other directorships were all scheduled. The Balance Sheet and P&L Account was followed by two pages of analysis covering profitability, financial status, asset utility and employee ratios.

The in-depth analysis of payment habits was perhaps the most useful as D&B had collected 56 payment experiences which showed that invoices amounting to over £80,000 were being paid on average 19 days late. There was also a breakdown of these balances between £1000 and £50,000 which again showed how many balances were paid within terms and percentages beyond terms (D&B do in fact hold £11.6 bn. trade payment experiences per annum).

Publications

One of D&B's publications which I feel is essential for all credit personnel is their *Stubbs Gazette* which was first published in 1836. Each week in *Stubbs Gazette* there are listed County Court Judgments which appear to be of a commercial nature. Administration Orders, Bankruptcy Proceedings, Corporate & Voluntary Arrangements, and the critically important List of Creditors and amounts.

Conclusion

D&B are still developing new reports for credit granters, and their graphs transmitted through the software for Access for Windows are particularly good. In their data bank they do now have information on unincorporated businesses. They also have a special UK Call Centre at Newport where their 90 telephone researchers gather extra data on new businesses and update their current records throughout the world.

Further information can be obtained from Dun & Bradstreet Ltd., Holmers Farm Way, Booker, High Wycombe, Bucks, HP12 4UL (tel: 01494 422000).

ICC Information Group

Credit managers and controllers can often increase their sales and profits by looking intelligently at their sales ledger records. Regrettably, accounting staff do not always tie up the loose ends so that they have a total picture of a business. When ICC carried out a survey at the end of 1995 they noted that a quarter of British limited companies were making a loss. These were some of the major factors which were often overlooked when businesses agree to sell products or services to limited companies, without assessing the risks, said Annette Smart, ICC's Marketing Manager.

Adding Value

Since I reviewed this company in 1989 they have fundamentally changed the way they transmit the information on the 1.2 million live limited companies' records they hold, to their customers. ICC was formed in 1969 to analyse financial information. They are now the largest company in the Hoppenstedt Bonnier Information (HBI) Group. They still collect raw data which is analysed and added value is created, so that for example an enhanced credit scoring, credit limit and highest contract value sum can be studied by credit granters. This gives credit controllers the freedom to decide on what terms and how much

Identification **Anderson Haulage & Storage Ltd**

Address:	Shawlands, Northern Road, Chilton Industrial Estate
	Sudbury
	Suffolk CO10 6XQ
	UK
Telephone:	01787 - 881569
Registration Number:	2949011
D-U-N-S Number:	77-445-5067

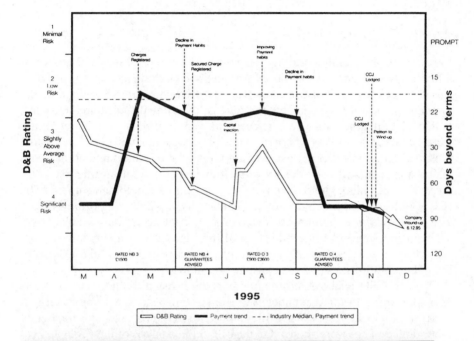

A PETITION FOR THE WINDING-UP OF THE ABOVE NAMED COMPANY WAS PRESENTED ON 25 .11.95. ON 06.12.95 A WINDING-UP ORDER WAS MADE.

Figure 4.2   Example of a D&B Rating and D&B Payment Score

credit to advance based on the strengths and weaknesses of a business. It must be remembered that mergers, acquisitions and disposals can often completely change the foundation of a business, therefore every scrap of information is vital, especially when businesses are planning a new sales and marketing scheme.

What They Provide

If a customer only requires a segment of information then the profile, over-view, financial, business or company director's reports can be accessed through a range of options. Their Juniper® service gives direct access to subscribers through Windows 3.1 and 95 on-line to the 1.2 million companies and to over 3 million live and dissolved companies in the UK. For anyone working from home the Internet Service Plum®, giving details on the 4.9 million directorships, shareholders and financial records, is a real advantage. (Incidentally, with this service the actual photographic images of the annual Accounts and Returns can be accessed.)

An Actual Company

In reviewing an actual operating company in the Juniper® service I looked at a full business report which was exceptionally well designed so that not only was it easy to read, but also the key factors were highlighted. For example the previous names of the company, the date of the annual return and accounts, and importantly the date when the accounts were lodged at Companies House were all noted, as well as whether or not there was an auditor's qualification, plus the banker's sort code, name and address, a credit limit and credit score which was reviewed over the previous four years, and an informative commentary which highlighted the strength of the ultimate holding company. The ICC Contract Value Figure of £250,000 was a vitally important figure, especially for those organisations who employ contractors on a regular basis. The contract limit gives an indication of the capability of a company to successfully manage a potentially large contract – particularly useful for Government, local authorities and the construction industry.

On page 1 all the above information plus the registered office, date of incorporation, and registered number was shown. On page 2 a complete list of directors, their addresses, when they joined or resigned, and the number of other directorships were shown. On pages 3–5 the analysis of the Profit & Loss and Balance Sheet was presented over a five-year period. On pages 6 and 7, 55 ratios were noted over the same period. However, the analysts have recently added 'sales to Audit Fees ratio'. This calculation plus the date when the accounts were lodged can often highlight an immense financial problem. On page 8, 22 growth rate calculations were shown over a four-year period.

On page 9 the company's figures were compared against 61 companies in a similar sector by checking performances in the lower, median, and upper quartiles. On page 10 was the Filing History – something which is sometimes forgotten, but is vitally important. This showed dates and changes of company name, dates of Memorandum of Satisfaction, Mortgage Documents dates, changes of the company's Registered Office and Alteration in the Memorandum or Articles of Association. Finally, on page twelve the unsatisfied CCJs were listed, the Judgment amount and date, and County Court and case numbers were all scheduled.

Other Reports

It is always more difficult to credit assess a newly incorporated company but ICC does have a Profile Report available on every limited company. Dissolved or name changes can also be searched through their data bank. If a subscriber does not have the correct name of a limited company then thirteen individual search criteria can be used to identify the business. Where an overview is required, a Trend Report is available which can cover up to 10 years data. An Interim Report is available on all public limited companies.

For high volume credit assessment the Credit Index on CD Rom again covers the 1.2 million live limited companies which give basic financial information, a credit limit and score figure, turnover, pre-tax profits, mortgages, winding-up petitions and CCJs. There are 20 search fields which include late filing of accounts, but they can also be used to search healthy companies via geographic locations for marketing purposes. This index is available through CD Rom and each month the CD is replaced with an updated version. This index is endorsed by Trade Indemnity, the Credit Insurers.

Bulk Data Supply

For any business wanting the entire database on a daily, weekly or monthly basis, their Damson® service can provide this information via magnetic tape/DAT, or Electronic Data Delivery (EDD) with overnight update by ISDN. For customers to gain the maximum benefit from this service ICC will provide on-site training courses which cover data analysis and risk management.

Internet

Anyone working from their office or home can access financial reports over the Internet. A choice of reports include a risk score, credit limit and CCJ data. The overview report covers risk related information, financial facts, and the key business ratios which are all available through their Plum Internet service.

The Help Desk

Having telephoned their help desk on a technical query about business ratios, I can confirm that their team are fully able to answer a complete range of queries covering balance sheet analysis and risk assessment.

Future Developments

During my research, I was told about ICC's future plans as at June 1997. They have signed an agreement with Companies House to produce a mortgage register which will be available at the latter end of 1997 and a shareholders register in the summer of 1998. In conjunction with Scorex Ltd they will be providing additional information not only on limited companies but also other types of businesses.

ICC Business Publications

ICC Business Publications Ltd also publishes many directories on limited companies which credit controllers and managers will find useful not only in assessing ongoing risk but also in reviewing prospects and competitors. 'Business Ratios' covers over 160 business sectors and to help benchmark the top companies, 26 key performance ratios are listed. The financial analyses of between 50 and 150 companies are included in each register.

'The Financial Survey' covers over 120 major sectors of business. In the reports the sales, profits, asset values and number of employees are given for over three years. The regional 'Sales Leads Directories' cover England, Scotland and Wales but exclude Northern Ireland. The value of these surveys is that checks can be made on an individual limited company before useless prospect calls are made.

For further information contact ICC Information Ltd, Field House, 72 Oldfield Road, Hampton, Middlesex TW12 2HQ (tel: 0181 783 1122).

ICC Site Search

Contaminated Land. The Department of the Environment have estimated that there may be up to 100,000 contaminated sites in the UK. Once land has been identified as being contaminated, the value can drop like a stone. ICC Site Search Ltd can report on industrial and residential property which may be contaminated.

For further information contact ICC Site Search, Nutmeg House, 3rd Floor, 60 Gainsford Street, London SE1 2NY (tel: 0171 357 6757).

Worldwide Reporting

Mr Derrick Kemp has been running Global Enterprises, an international credit reporting agency, for a number of years. He has been involved with the best correspondents throughout the world for 48 years and has a good reputation.

Further information from Derrick A. Kemp, Global Enterprises, 189 Gipsy Road, Welling, Kent, DA16 1HX (tel: 0181 301 3345).

Graydon UK Ltd

The company was established in 1940 in the UK. From 1987 it became part of the Graydon Group with headquarters in Amsterdam, Netherlands. The company is ultimately owned by NCM of the Netherlands, Hermes of Germany and Coface of France. Graydon UK's main product is Creditline, an on-line credit information service. They have a large database of incorporated and unincorporated businesses. Where companies are focusing on marketing operations, their Prospect pre-vetting system which is available on-line is designed to identify bad credit risks before time and money is wasted on salespersons' visits.

Graydon forms part of an online network of European information agencies called Eurogate.

Their services are now also available on the Internet.

Further information from Graydon UK Ltd, Hyde House, Edgware Road, Colindale, London NW9 6LW (tel: 0181 975 1050).

Qui Credit Assessment Ltd

In 1983 David Plevin decided to launch a model screening system which would give businesses speedy, clear and concise reports. He had worked previously for a major credit agency where a high proportion of the reports were constructed with the use of a computerised database.

Qui's current range of information services is still designed to meet routine and special requirements on limited companies, partnerships and sole traders. Their Status report incorporates a credit score which Qui has developed to analyse accounts and other company information. They also produce 'Quick Reports', 'Credit Check' and a 'Monitoring Service'. Their Bespoke Reports are recommended when the matter is important or complex. The fee is usually £20 to £300, depending on clients' requirements, the amount under consideration, the complexity of the case and the data sources used. Unless the client has specified a different budget figure when ordering, permission is sought to undertake any further work that might be necessary if initial investigations show that the final report is likely to cost over £50. It is helpful if, when placing instructions, the client specifies the information required and gives the reason for the request, to help the analyst to tailor the report to the needs of the particular case.

Further information from Mr David Plevin, Qui Credit Assessment Ltd, Saffron House, 15 Park Street, Croydon CR9 1TU (tel: 0181 686 7686).

Regency Consultants

Twenty-seven years ago Michael Scully formed Regency Consultants to provide clients with a more personal service in reporting. Mr Scully maintained that in 75 to 80 per cent of all commercial credit transactions 'neither party really knows who the other is'. Businesses believe that they know their customers and, fortunately, because the majority of people pay promptly, do survive in business. In Mr Scully's experience, the lack of commercial information on a business goes unnoticed. However, it is only when payments become slow that suddenly the commercial risk of non-payment assumes greater importance. He emphasised that the commercial world is never static. Its anomalies, errors, deceptions, constant changes of company names, directors, auditors and bankers mean that information has to be constantly updated to assess the commercial strength of a business.

Mr Scully has written a pamphlet, '*What's in a Name?*', for marketing and credit staff. In a simple and concise way he explains the reasons why it is so important to confirm the correct trading style and name.

Regency Consultants was one of the first agencies to recognise the growing Eastern and Asian markets, and they are founder members of the Malaysian registered TCM Group International with 40 offices throughout the world. A further development in July 1993 was that this agency became one of four in the UK to achieve the ISO9000 recognition and it is probably the first to obtain an Investors in People accolade. They have upgraded their computer systems many times and have a number of long-standing, experienced staff who totally understand what credit controllers require when assessing risks or even collecting a so-called simple 'overdue account'.

Regency Consultants are on E-mail and have their own WWW site. They market 'Creditcheck' for Business Information Technology Systems Ltd. This is a desktop system which enables total sales ledgers to be monitored against weekly updates of default information as well as the vetting of new customers.

Further information from Regency Consultants, The Grange, 1 Hoole Road, Chester, CH2 3NQ (tel: 01244 319912).

BUSINESS INTELLIGENCE

Readers will notice from the preceding selection of credit and financial information bureaux that there are a multitude of organisations which will help them to make a commercial assessment. I have so far excluded Balance Sheet analysis, which will be covered in Chapter 5. Meanwhile, there are other information sources which should be used in conjunction with bureau reports. This can be called your business intelligence section which is an ongoing update of day-to-day commercial news.

COMPANIES HOUSE

Since the Joint Stock Companies Act of 1844, companies were required to be registered, which enabled them to be sued and to sue in their own names. It was not until the Limited Liability Act of 1855 that limited liability was extended to members of a company. The Joint Stock Companies Act of 1856 consolidated the earlier Acts.

Under the Companies Act 1985 as amended by the Companies Act 1989, public limited companies, private companies limited by shares, companies limited by guarantee and unlimited companies, if they have a registered office in England and Wales, have to be registered at Companies House in Cardiff. Scottish companies are registered in Edinburgh. There is also a search room in Glasgow. Other offices where searches can be carried out are:

Cardiff	tel: 01222 388588	Leeds	tel: 0113 233 8338
London	tel: 0171 253 9393	Edinburgh	tel: 0131 225 5774
Manchester	tel: 0161 2367500	Glasgow	tel: 0141 248 3315
Birmingham	tel: 0121 233 9047		

There is a separate registry in Belfast for companies formed in Northern Ireland: Registry of Companies, IDB House, 64, Chichester Street, Belfast, BT1 4JX (tel: 01232 234488).

The main duties of Companies House are the incorporation, re-registration and striking off of companies and the registration of documents required to be delivered under companies' insolvency and related legislation. Companies House is also required to provide the above information to the public and enforce all the statutory requirements. From 3 October 1988, the then Companies Registration Office became the first executive agency of the DTI. On 1 October, 1991, they adopted a trading fund status. To give an indication of the size of their operation, at the end of March 1997, in England and Wales and Scotland there were 1,090,883 limited companies registered and to give a further indication on how many of these companies may be trading, 889,305 of those companies submitted an annual return. Companies who delay filing their annual returns and accounts do receive a series of fairly stringent letters, one of which points out that the directors or their agents will be personally liable for any legal obligations.

New Developments

Because not every company that is registered has a sophisticated accounting system, changes are only introduced at a speed that is reasonable to meet customer demand. For example, electronic filing of accounts can only be introduced when a significant proportion of their customers can relay the data. Intelligent Character Recognition is being developed so that when a company submits a document or accounts, instead of having to key in information, details will be scanned.

New Services

The Companies House monitor service is an ideal way for credit controllers to pre-order copies of specified documents the moment they are filed by the company that they required to be monitored on a continuing basis. Under this service, copies of documents can be despatched by fax or (for customers with a fax modem) directly to a PC. Alternatively the delivery of the document image files can be produced on a 4mm DAT tape, which is available to customers monitoring 3000 companies or more.

This service covers the whole range of documents which are filed. Therefore if a Mortgage or Charge has been added, or an increase or decrease in Nominal Capital, or any Voluntary Arrangements or other liquidation notices filed, these can be automatically 'pulled up'. This is an extremely useful service, as a sudden additional Charge can completely change the financial structure of a company and quite often indicates that a bank or finance house actually controls the company.

Companies House has awarded a contract to ICC (Inter Company Comparisons) to create a shareholders and share capital database. This service should be available in mid-1998.

Fast Track Name Change Registration

At the time when I visited Companies House at Cardiff in May 1997, they were operating a same day change of name and re-registration service. At the time of writing the fee for this service is only £100 including VAT and I understand that if a customer arrived at their office at Cardiff before 3.00pm with the correctly filled in documents (provided that the proposed company name is not 'sensitive'), the customer can take away the 'new' company name before 5.00pm. This is also an illustration and a warning to readers to be vigilant when a limited company constantly changes its name.

Conclusion

The strategy of Companies House is gradually to move away from their reliance on microfiche to reproduce documents. By the year 2000 they expect that a considerable volume of inward and outward information will be transmitted electronically.

OTHER INTELLIGENCE SOURCES

It is often difficult to make a credit decision based on an agency report or a set of accounts in isolation. The following sources will help in making a commercial assessment.

Newspapers

Most serious national dailies have a City page, but one financial newspaper which must be read by 9.30am each day is the *Financial Times*. It is unbeatable for every type of trading, company and world information. I despair when I hear that the FT is handed around the office two or three days after publication. The *Financial Times* is non-political and does not follow any party cause.

Cutting Services

If you brief a cutting service carefully and accurately on the type of information you require and the number of publications that you wish to be scanned, the business intelligence reports that can be assembled are truly amazing.

Romeike & Curtice Ltd employ over 140 readers who, using key words, scan and read about 4000 weekly and national publications and over 2000 trade, technical and consumer newspapers and magazines.

Further information from Romeike & Curtice, Hale House, 290–296 Green Lane, London, N13 5TP (tel: 0181 882 0155).

Local Newspapers

Local newspapers, if they publish a regular local business column or page, often report small facts which, if assembled, will give you the credit granter an immense advantage for reviewing the progress of a competitor, supplier or customer.

I have found that it has been worthwhile to take out a subscription for a particular local paper as my principal customer was located in that area. You may think that I am going to extraordinary lengths to gain information. I do not think so. I am just protecting the receivables, 'the debtors'. At the same time I am watching for those small reports which could indicate an expanding market and hopefully increased profitable sales. On the other hand, any reports of takeovers, changes of management or change of name could signal a warning. When this occurs the subject account should be placed on 'special watch'.

Specialised Magazines, Trade Associations, Journals etc.

In every trade and service industry there are specialised publications. Regrettably, in my experience, companies are mercenary about taking out subscriptions. For the credit or sales ledger department to function efficiently, the information must be scanned for positive and negative business news as soon as the magazine is received, because by the time the publication hits your desk the news can easily be four weeks old.

All the major clearing banks issue monthly economic reviews and these often highlight a specific trade or industry. Their writers are highly skilled and their economic forecasts are used by many other organisations in predicting growth and weaknesses both in the UK and overseas.

Many major UK chambers of commerce produce magazines and fact sheets which are only available to their members. The advantage for the credit granter is that the information which has been published is circulated to a relatively limited number of members, therefore it places the reader well ahead of the field.

TRADE REFERENCES

It is human nature for a prospective customer, when requested to supply a trade reference, to give names of the suppliers that they pay promptly. In other words, certain suppliers are 'kept sweet'. But I have also received replies which are so strongly worded that on this evidence alone credit would be refused.

The trade reference letter should be exceptionally well produced, as it is an advertisement for your business. The basic information which is being sought is the present transaction value and whether payments are to terms. Always allow plenty of space for the referee to make comments. Answers to four to six questions will usually give enough information for an outline decision to be considered (see below).

The first question to consider is who the referees are, and what their reputation and strength is in the trade. It is not unknown for a company to give an associate company as a reference. You may think that I am being ultra suspicious, but when companies are desperate for goods or services, their friends, associates or anyone who can give the business a 'good' reference will be contacted first. If you have any doubt on the reference, especially if the replies are vague, do telephone the referee. Begin, of course, by thanking the referee for their information. Your reason for telephoning is that you wish to clarify a few points. Do make it a commercial discussion. Thousands of pounds can be saved by making a five minute telephone call.

Comments which might arouse doubts are:

- 'Known some time' – find out how long they have traded altogether.
- 'Payments made to our terms' – ask the question, 'what *are* their terms?' There is a vast difference between 21 days after month end and 60 day terms.

There are two other problems for credit granters to consider. Often a customer will give the name of a competitor as a reference. The referee may wish to keep the account, so by carefully drafting their reply they may stop you from opening the account. On the other hand, if the account with the competitor is in arrears, the competitor may give a more favourable picture so that their risk is reduced. Again, this may not seem ethical but it can happen. For this reason, if you have a trade association in your business where informal discussions with colleagues take place, do develop these contacts. The odd word or comment concerning the prospective company will often underwrite or perhaps give quite a different picture from the commercial impression you have received by reviewing the information in referees' replies.

When considering payment terms, other sources of independent information are Dun & Bradstreet's and Experian's payment reviews (see earlier in this chapter).

BANKERS' OPINIONS

Bankers' opinions, which are sometimes known as status reports, are still in my opinion one of the best pieces of information on current financial trends which are available. The report alone cannot give the credit granter all the information on which to make an assessment, but it is part of the jigsaw which, when read together with other facts, will create a complete credit picture.

Since 28 March 1994 new rules relating to status enquiries were issued by the British Bankers' Association which required the express consent of the customers concerned before a 'status enquiry' could be forwarded to their bank. The credit granter no longer has to send the application to their own bank to be forwarded to the customer's but now sends the consent form directly to the customer's bank.

The cost of these reports, depending on which clearer issues the opinion, starts at £7.50. Some clearers charge more for personal opinions which might, for example, relate to taking up references for a letting agreement. Each clearer charges a different amount, some still requiring a single payment to be made for each request. Banks will not accept a faxed consent form and they will not normally allow repeat enquiries at a future date without a further signed authority from the credit granter's customer.

Since these new rules came into place many companies have stopped using status enquiries. However, recent research I have carried out shows that some credit managers are again using them, especially when there are unusual circumstances or large financial exposures. Individually, all clearers have their own consent forms (Figure 4.3 is an example of a form that a credit granter can use).

Be warned – all clearers seem to interpret the rules on obtaining status enquiries in their own ways, even between branches of the same bank.

When asking for a banker's opinion it is essential to request information on whether the bank or banks are holding any charges or debentures. If a bank is aware that charges are registered they are obliged to advise you, the enquirer. This information is vital as, if all a company's assets are secured to the bank for an overdraft or loan facility, all the assets are not controlled by the business – in fact, the bank controls the assets of the business. When requesting an opinion for 'are they good for £2500', the business is really asking the bank to confirm if a sum of £2500 is regularly cleared through the account.

If you, the credit granter, really wish to know whether your total credit line is secure, then you must either ask other credit agencies or trade suppliers for

---

To   The Manager
        . . . . .Bank PLC,
        . . . .

Dear Sir,

        I/We. . . . .
        Bank Account Number . . . .

        hereby give our consent to you providing a Bankers Reference to

For and on behalf of. . . . .
                        Company, Club, Society, etc.

Signature . . . .

Position . . . . .Date . . . .

Figure 4.3 Application for a banker's reference

this specific information. My definition of a credit line is the maximum credit which will be extended. This figure is the amount that is being transacted, plus the next month's sales, and any further credit transactions which will be charged up to the date when the initial cheque is received. It is dangerous to ask for an unrealistic figure in the opinion – one which is too high or too low will not reflect the actual credit transaction you wish to consider. Often I hear of companies multiplying the actual transaction they are considering by three and then asking the bank for their opinion based on the higher sum. This, in my view, can lead to totally wrong assessments.

The questions that always run through my mind when considering a credit application are:

- Can they pay the initial transaction?
- Will they pay?
- And what can I do if they do not pay?

Interpreting an Opinion

Bankers' opinions are written in a type of code. A banker will, of course, never undervalue the reputation of his client. The opinion will be based on the way debits and credits are transacted through the account. If cheques are never dishonoured or overdraft facilities exceeded the reference may be favourable for the sum that is regularly cleared. But regrettably there are areas of doubt:

1. There may be far more than one account
2. The accounts may be with different clearers
3. The bank may have far less knowledge concerning the background and current situation of their client's business than you do
4. With computerisation the bankers are more remote from their customers.

Tables 4.1–4.3 illustrate the type of replies that can be received from the strongest/favourable to the weakest/'do not touch' variety.

Please remember that the opening words of an opinion on a limited company, 'Respectably constituted private limited company' simply mean that the bank has seen a Certificate of Incorporation issued by the Registrar of Companies.

Table 4.2 highlights replies showing that the figure requested is above what is acceptable for a credit line. However, a smaller figure may be acceptable.

The final example in Table 4.2 is one in particular where 'bank' terminology, if read at face value, would appear satisfactory. From my experience this reference is a serious warning.

Table 4.1 Bankers' opinions – favourable

Reply	Interpretation
'Undoubted'	This is the highest reference and is not used very frequently.
'. . . which is good for your figure of . . .'	This sum is cleared regularly through the account.
'. . . which is considered good for your figure of . . .'	This again is a good reference, but not quite so strong.
'. . . which should prove good for your figure of . . .'	There is a slight doubt here, so further investigation should be carried out.
'. . . which is considered good for normal business engagements, including . . .'	Again, less strong, so further investigation should be carried out. In this and the next reference, a lower credit line may be the answer.
'. . . trustworthy for your figure . . .'	
'. . . should prove good for your figure . . .'	
'. . . should prove trustworthy for your figure . . .'	This sum is cleared regularly, but not such a good reference as 'good for your figure'.
'Respectably constituted company considered trustworthy in the way of business.'	

Table 4.2 Bankers' opinions – cautionary

Reply	Interpretation
'. . . Your figure is larger than normally seen but should prove good . . .'	
'. . . your figure is preferred in a series . . .'	
'. . . new customer to this bank but should prove good for your figures . . .'	There is also some doubt here.
'. . . the directors (or proprietors) would not enter into any commitments that they could not see their way to fulfil . . .'	Serious warning

Table 4.3 illustrates replies when clients may have even more serious problems.

Most head offices of the major clearing banks have special departments that monitor their clients who have borrowed funds and have commercial trading

Table 4.3 Bankers' opinions – unfavourable

Reply	Interpretation
'. . . resources fully committed . . .'	Funds constantly moving, very seldom a credit balance. Cheques may be dishonoured.
'. . . capital fully employed . . .'	Funds not always available to clear cheques. Cheques may be dishonoured.
'. . . cannot speak for your figure . . .'	Bank unwilling to give positive reference for the amount of the enquiry. Cash, not a cheque, may be the best way of transacting business.

difficulties. The banks, even if they have a fixed and floating charge on the assets of the company, obviously prefer to try and keep businesses operating if they can. These special accounts may be reviewed twice daily at the 9.30am and 3.30pm clearings. Banks can and do, however, place administrative receivers into companies with remarkable speed where they hold a charge or debenture. Normally their reasons for carrying out this action are because they can see no likelihood of their interest or principal being paid. Usually when this happens there is little chance that the trade creditors will be paid any percentage of their trade debts. The Rolls Royce liquidation was unique, as were the circumstances which led to the collapse.

Because of the constant monitoring by banks when their clients have cash flow problems and the care they take in drafting bankers' opinions, readers should read with the utmost care any opinion which has a change from previous wording. Bankers do have an added conflict, as if they misinterpret the information on their clients many of their customers could easily lose money. Therefore they have an added responsibility.

You will observe that all banks place a disclaimer clause on their opinion that it is given without responsibility on behalf of the bank or their officials. However, I would repeat that bankers do have a responsibility to be accurate but they can often only judge the strength and weakness of their clients' accounts from the debits and credits that regularly are transacted through the account. In carrying out interviews with many businesses who regularly receive opinions it is surprising how differently they interpret them. Bankers' opinion information must be reviewed with all the other pieces of information which fit into the jigsaw for assessing customers.

In an interview in 1989, Mr Bob Smith, a manager with National Westminster Bank PLC, on secondment to Croydon Business Venture, confirmed that with computerisation it was his bank's normal practice for their managers to review and monitor their 'out of order' customer accounts well before banking hours began. From 8.15am the daily refer list of customers would be checked against a clearing list. It is this type of intensive checking that enables the managers to control their clients' accounts and build up a picture of commercial and consumer activities.

SPECIALISED TRADE GROUPS

I can confirm that as a member of a specialised export sector group that credit managers and controllers who attend regular trade meetings do try to support their customers and at the same time protect their company's interest. I mention this fact because the general impression of protection agencies is one of 'put them on stop' and start proceedings. Starting from the new business stage, members, by interchanging trading experiences, can give a far more detailed picture of an account than by just asking for a trade reference. Slow paying accounts can be reviewed, but it is when suppliers in a particular trade are experiencing real payment difficulties that the joint knowledge of the trade can be beneficial. Basically it is in everyone's interest that a business survives. If suppliers can work together, quite often an insolvency can be avoided. If the financial position looks grim, the suppliers can reduce their own exposure by reviewing their own credit limits. Sometimes it is inevitable that proceedings or insolvency action has to be taken. The great advantage of using this type of agency is that the previous experiences of other traders, when collecting from the same customer when in arrears, can be obtained. A final benefit of becoming a member of these specialist trade groups is that not only can new government legislation be discussed, but also changes in legal procedures. It is these procedures that often make assessment and collections more difficult.

PERSONAL VISITS

There is no better way of obtaining an immediate picture of a business than by making a personal visit. Many credit staff that I speak to seem to say that they never had the time to visit prospective or existing customers. A personal visit will support or refute any other facts which are already to hand (see Chapter 2).

When visiting a business for the first time, an immediate impression is obtained. The condition of the premises, the attitude of the staff, the amount of activity or inactivity in the building, the condition of the company vehicles, can all be an indication of the state of the company.

Let me give you an example of a company that I visited some years ago. There were many people in the reception area waiting to be seen by the company's personnel, and the two receptionists were frantically trying to 'tannoy' various managers. There did not seem to be anyone available in the accounts department. This information I gained from talking to a man in a dark blue mackintosh: he was from the Gas Board and he was not going to move until the company secretary handed him a cheque. The atmosphere in the reception area was singularly unpleasant. The rubber plant and other greenery had not been watered and were dying. The front mat was threadbare. The switchboard office was untidy. To an outsider a different picture was projected, as the chief executive liked to run an expensive limousine. On leaving the premises with a cheque for £40,000 I had three immediate thoughts: 1) The company was in difficulty as it was not paying even the essential bills. 2) Their costs must be high if they are running expensive cars. 3) My cheque was going to be specially cleared! Somehow the company continued to trade until it was placed in voluntary liquidation years later.

Here are two more examples of visits. During visit one I immediately agreed to give credit because the company's sales office was so well-organised. Their staff were enthusiastic, cheerful and keen. On another visit to a different company the warehouse was so disorganised that I decided that our product could easily be damaged before it was sold.

Other Key Facts

Other information which it is quite possible to obtain are general facts about the business. Staff members of a company may actually mention that there have been management changes; that a new order had just been obtained; that layoffs, part-time working or redundancies were taking place. On the positive side, news of expansions can be good news. Always accept if asked, or ask if you may view the operation of the company that is to be supplied. Again, it is human nature for personnel to be interested in their company's administration. In meeting more people it will enable you to assess the whole operation in a more objective way. Often it is at this point that the management accounts will be offered for inspection. The other absolute advantage of a personal visit is that in the initial stages of a new account a far better relationship is established between the buyer and seller.

Sometimes the buyer can create a totally false picture if you fail to view the premises. Mr Bernard Chambers, retired insolvency partner of Booth White & Co, illustrated the problem on assessing the strengths and weaknesses of limited companies when he said: 'a limited company can easily trade for more than six years but actually be technically insolvent for the entire period. They just live off the credit of their suppliers'.

SUMMARY

A credit bureau with a large database of information, or a specialist agency which only investigates a certain trade sector, is an essential tool in assessing risks. Time spent in assessing customers will reduce bad debts, and a payment performance schedule from an agency will show how a customer actually pays their debts.

- Do you use a credit bureau to help you make a credit decision?
- If the order is too large, could the business wanting you to trade be fraudulent?
- Have you obtained a current payment performance schedule from a credit bureau?
- Have you considered using more than one information provider to obtain maximum information?
- Have you studied the trade references to see what they say and what they omit?

5
Making the Assessment

It is the credit department's responsibility to promote profitable sales – but how much credit do you grant? The following guidelines can be used as a framework.

In the previous chapter I mentioned some of the sources of information which can assist you, the credit granter, to make a decision. Now you will have to decide on what is an acceptable risk. It must be remembered that in these times of intense competition, marginal accounts are important to any business in maintaining their targeted sales. Sales very seldom remain stable and it is not often that a company has a unique product.

The credit controller's job is to put all the pieces of the information jigsaw puzzle together, which includes balance sheet analysis, so that he or she can decide on what terms goods or services can be supplied. Even if, at the end of the day, a credit decision is not considered to be advisable, never forget to offer an inducement for a cash transaction.

In every industry, trade or specialist service sector there is a bank of knowledge which has to be tapped to help the credit granter in finally making a decision on how much to grant. Sometimes it will be the 'grapevine', a trade association, or specialist magazines which will provide the information which will indicate a reasonable line of credit.

The structure in assessing the risk has to cover:

- the new account application
- the review of the existing accounts
- re-assessment of rejected credit applications.

When reviewing an account application, the size of the order and the excitement and pressure in gaining a possible new credit account should not induce anyone to make a rushed decision. Consider what the usual or normal order values in your trade, depending on your business, would be. A routine list of questions can then be constructed so that a business's strengths and weak-nesses is then available in a coded form. The code, once developed, can be used either on a manual or computerised accounting system.

QUESTIONS FOR ASSESSMENT

1. What is the age of the business? This will give an indication of its history – but remember that the name may have been changed in the past. This is an instance where one or more specialist bureaux can help you build up an accurate picture.
2. What is the experience and knowledge of the management? Have there been any changes of personnel recently? Are there any new appointments, resignations, management buyouts or take over bids? (see Chapter 4, Intel-ligence Information). If a sales force is employed they should be able to give some up-to-date facts, e.g. condition of building, activity, etc.
3. If the order comes in 'out of the blue' the question must be asked, 'Why did they wish to buy from this company?' (see Chapter 4, Fraudulent Trading). What is the type of legal structure you are supplying?
4. I have already mentioned the importance of checking the legal status of the business. Regrettably, a beautifully produced order or letter heading may disguise a paper-thin business.
5. What is the value of the initial order or enquiry? In some companies an initial limit is granted which opens the door to the customer. This will help to cement the relationship while full credit enquires are made.

In considering a credit limit it is vital to visualise the type of company or business you are investing in. An initial order of, say, £200 or £1000 may safely be despatched provided that your business or trade has actual trading knowl-edge of the buyer. Credit limits can and should be reviewed continuously so that realistic assessments of a customer's potential can be planned.

Here are examples of how a coding system can be used to develop a monitoring system:

New account	A
New business recently established	B
Business with good paying record	C
Limited company (no accounts filed)	D
Local authority, slow payer	E
Local authority, prompt payer	F
Expanding company	G
Adverse information (County Court Judgments, reports of slow payment)	H

A credit limit should not be set in tablets of stone, but it should be used as a workable guide to assessing the sum that the customer can support.

BALANCE SHEET ANALYSIS

The analysis of accounts is a further aid to assess private and public limited companies' strengths and weaknesses. The actual analysis is part of the jigsaw of information which, if fitted together, will give the credit granter enough information to make an objective decision in the following:

1. whether to supply on credit
2. the amount of credit that can be reasonably supplied
3. whether to supply on different terms.

There are five fundamental points to remember when reviewing accounts. One is that a set of accounts represents a 'day in the life' of a company. The figures that could be produced on the day after the accounts are published might show an entirely different picture.

Secondly, qualified accountants spend many years in training. One of their skills is to show a set of accounts in the best possible light. This may be considered by some to be creative accounting.

Thirdly, because of government legislation under the Companies Act 1985, Section 248 (1) and (2), small and medium-sized private limited companies are allowed to submit modified accounts to Companies House. This creates an extra problem when analysing accounts (see below). Small companies are exempt from publishing a directors' report and profit and loss accounts which, of course, include the all-important turnover figures where:

- turnover is less than £2.8 million
- balance sheet totals less than £1.4 million
- average number of employees is less than 50.

Medium companies are exempt from submitting the turnover figure where:

- turnover is less than £11.2 million
- balance sheet total is less than £5.6 million
- average number of employees is less than 250.

Obviously your analysis will be far more precise if you can persuade a company which has filed modified accounts to give you the actual turnover and profit and loss figures. I have not found it difficult to convince a business to provide this information. I have always emphasised that it is my company's policy to give maximum support to businesses by offering credit terms. I then highlight the fact that disclosure of these most confidential figures would also help their business in the future. It is important in a telephone call, letter, or in conversation, to indicate that this information is strictly confidential and will not be passed on to a third party.

Finally, under annual government budgets, changes in legislation can create benefits and penalties through taxation and grants for companies which change each year.

I have expressed the above points first as, although I am a firm believer in reviewing accounts, I would emphasise that a considerable amount of outside detective work has to be carried out in conjunction with analysis to ascertain the creditworthiness of a limited company. As partnerships and sole traders are not required to file accounts, provided that you arrange a meeting to discuss credit terms, normally the proprietor or partners will be more than willing to supply trading details (see Chapters 2 and 4).

Before looking at any set of accounts I try to visualise the type of business and the characteristics of the management. I would then consider what was a small, reasonable or large order, which might depend on the time of year or seasonal trends which would normally affect a particular trade, industry or sector in commerce. This gives me a picture of an order value which is reviewed with the accounts and compared with other suppliers' information. At the same time, I would review the economic conditions that were affecting trade generally.

But before looking at any accounts it is worthwhile considering that all companies have different accounting policies and that no two companies appear to present their accounts in the same way. Sometimes the method of calculating depreciation will have a marked effect on profits. This is why comparing companies in the same segment of trade can be so difficult. I am now in the right frame of mind to quietly review the accounts step by step and it is only at this stage that I would do so.

The Date of the Accounts

The first question I would ask is, what is the date of the accounts? Under the Companies Act 1985, Sections 238 and 241, all private and public limited companies must file their accounts with Companies House. Private limited companies must file their accounts within 10 months of the end of the accounting reference period. If a company does not notify the registrar within six months of its incorporation, the accounting reference date will be 31 March. You can now see that even if a company has filed their accounts within six months of the accounting reference date that the information on which you, the credit grantor, are basing your assessment, is already dated.

Allowing for the fact that many medium and small companies are filing modified accounts, which may not disclose the turnover or the profit and loss figures, the principal reason for analysing accounts is to check the general trend of the company. By comparing the figures from year to year it can be seen if a company's activities are progressing, declining or perhaps remaining stationary. It really is like viewing a company from a distance to see how the management and directors are performing.

Hours and hours can be spent on analysis, but normally there is limited time and your objective is to assess whether you can safely grant credit up to a certain figure. On the other hand, a three-minute scan of the accounts will mean that many trends will be overlooked. Therefore, it does pay to be thorough. My way of analysing accounts is to automatically break a company's figures into five distinct areas: asset strength, liquidity, profitability, capital structure and employment trends. First, though, I ask the question: are the accounts qualified?

Qualification of Accounts

Under the Companies Act 1985, Section 236 (1) and (2) auditors are required to state whether, in their opinion, the company's accounts have been properly prepared in accordance with the Act and whether a true and fair view is given in the balance sheet and profit and loss account. Also, under Section 237(1), auditors have a duty to confirm whether proper accounting records have been kept by the company, including branch records, and whether the balance sheet and profit and loss account are in agreement with the accounting records and returns.

There are various degrees of qualifications of accounts. A qualification should signal to credit personnel that they should be especially careful when considering any credit transactions. There is one type of qualification which is frequently used by a small company, whereby one or two directors make all the decisions and actually control many aspects of the company, such as:

> in common with many businesses of similar size and organisation, the company's system of control is dependent upon the close involvement of the Directors. Where independent confirmation of the completeness of the accounting records was therefore not available we have accepted assurances from the Directors that all the company's transactions have been reflected in the records.

Other qualifications have even more serious implications. For instance, the auditors may mention in their qualification that they have based their examination of the accounts on the continued availability of finance from the company's bankers or their group holding company.

There are three other points that have to be considered when reviewing the auditors' certificate on a set of accounts. The name of the auditors and their reputation will have a definite positive or negative effect on the way other businesses will react to that company. The date of the auditors' certificate, be it qualified or unqualified, should be checked against the date of the accounts year end. For example, when the accounts of a small company had been qualified, their accounting year end was 31 December 1985, whereas the chartered accountants' report was dated March 1987. The considerable gap between these dates suggests that the chartered accountant had difficulty in assembling all the financial data to carry out an audit and issue the certificate. I noted from the accounts that the turnover is lower than the preceding year but the cost of sales, administration costs and interest payable are higher. The company is also carrying forward an adverse balance (loss) in its profit and loss account. To conclude, the liabilities greatly exceed the assets!

Since 1993 when the Auditing Practice Board issued their SAS 600 'Auditors' Report on Financial Statements' there has been a new emphasis on disclosure. To obtain an unqualified opinion adequate disclosure of all information must be given. Inadequate disclosure is one of the reasons why a qualified opinion is often limited to a fundamental uncertainty. The 'subject to' comment has been banned.

When a fundamental uncertainty is issued the auditors should include 'an explanatory paragraph when setting out the basis of that opinion describing the matter giving rise to the fundamental uncertainty and its possible effects on the financial statement'. To quote Leon Hopkins, the editor of *Audit Report*, 'Auditors are not always good at making disclosures.'

In November 1994 the Audit Practice Board issued SAS 130 which required auditors to give more details when 'a going concern' qualification is issued by auditors.

Under Section 237 of the Companies Act the auditors' duties and powers are set out. Under Subsection four, if the auditors fail to obtain all the information and explanations which, to the best of their knowledge and belief, are necessary for the purpose of the audit, they shall state that fact in their report. A further requirement of the Act, under subsection six, is that 'it is the auditors' duty to consider whether the information given in the directors' report for the financial year for which the accounts are prepared, is consistent with those accounts; and if they are of opinion that it is not, they shall state that fact in their report'.

Readers who are interested in the reports of audits should obtain a copy of *Audit Report* (published monthly). *Audit Report* is published by Butterworth Customer Services, Butterworths, 35 Chancery Lane, London WC24 1EL (tel: 0171 400 2500).

In *Audit Report* a series of audit reports are critically reviewed and scored for nine factors including 'timeliness', i.e. the period elapsing between the date of the report and the company's year end. I highly recommend these reports as they exemplify the best practices and omissions of audit reports and evaluate them!

In theory it may appear that there are enough weapons in the Companies Act to safeguard the interests of shareholders and suppliers. I believe that, in practice, there is a grey area. Firstly, there must be a fear in auditors' minds that if they are too stringent they might not get the audit in future years and consequently their qualifications may be less severe. Secondly, directors, realising that auditors will arrive once a year, have months to disguise certain transactions. I am not saying, by this, that I distrust all sets of accounts and the statements from chairmen or managing directors. However, I am aware of the many hours of discussion that often take place before an auditor will pass a set of accounts, therefore I am wary and vigilant when reviewing accounts and directors' reports.

Professional Indemnity

Because of the risk of claims against auditors it appears that the qualification that states 'In common with many other businesses of smaller size' etc., may now be used more frequently by auditors. Recently there have also been some extremely expensive actions against accountants for professional indemnity when they omitted to spot a flaw in the accounts. Proceedings have been taken by companies which have purchased other businesses only to find that the stated current asset value was not true. For example, in Bowring's *Accountants' Professional Indemnity Quarterly* Spring, 1988 edition, they reported that a subsidiary of a major clearing bank had appointed another firm of accountants to conduct an enquiry into a frozen food wholesaler, as they wished to purchase some shares. A year later, when the audit was carried out, it was discovered that the stock had been overvalued by over £1 million. After the discovery, a receiver was appointed, liquidation then followed and the entire investment of the bank was lost. The bank then claimed against the reporting auditor and the company's auditors for alleged negligence. The claim was settled out of court on a 50/50 basis, split between the two accounting firms, less a 25 per cent discount.

Bowring's Accountants' Professional Indemnity Quarterly was published up to 1996. Bowrings are now planning a similar style newsletter which will be published early in 1998.

Chairman's and Directors' Reports

When reading a directors' report I try to read between the lines. First of all I consider what has been said, and what has been omitted. Here is an example. In the previous section I mentioned that a private limited company's accounts were dated 31 December 1985 whereas the auditors' report was dated March 1987. In the directors' report they considered that the trading results were satisfactory, but on closer examination of the accounts (apart from the auditors' qualification) they show an increased overdraft and reductions in fixed and current assets. The creditors could not be paid even if all the fixed and current assets were sold. These figures alone indicate that a credit transaction could be risky. But at this point I have only looked at the accounting. I have not reviewed any other information. I do not know, for instance, why the debtors figure is so low in relation to the creditors. If all the transactions were carried out on a cash basis, a cash-in-hand or in bank figure should have appeared in the accounts. It did not.

It is human nature for directors to be optimistic when they report on their company's trading and future developments. Many directors work exceptionally long hours and often sacrifice everything for their business. This should be borne in mind when reading a comment in a chairman's report such as, 'The electronics industry is experiencing a difficult period which is not yet over. I believe your group is well-equipped with products capable of holding their own in this competitive business'. This report goes on to say, 'We are planning for continued profitable growth this year, and are building a strong senior management team to achieve it.' The chairman's statement is far longer but it does give indications that there could be difficulties in the years ahead.

Here is another example of how a few extra words in a directors' report can signal that a business should be monitored. In a directors' report on a timber importing company, a dividend had been paid to shareholders, the retained profits had been reduced by £500,000, but it was stated that a cost-cutting exercise was being pursued. My immediate feeling on reading this note alone would be to monitor the company, but not refuse credit, and I would reconsider the credit line. I would, however, place a special signal in the sales ledger so that any changes in trading and payment could be reported. At the same time I would discuss the company's activities with the sales personnel and make a note to visit the company.

THE ACTUAL ANALYSIS

By this stage I have noted the date of the accounts and the auditors' certificate date. I have also checked whether there is a gap between these dates. I have ascertained whether the auditors' certificate has been qualified and I have reviewed the chairman's or directors' report.

I will now home in on a few fundamental features which help me to put a company's strengths and weaknesses into perspective by scanning the sections of the profit and loss account and balance sheet. For example, even if the turnover and profits are not stated, I will look at the debtors and then deduct creditors, overdraft (if any) and long-term liabilities. The answer to this fairly simple calculation will tell me, at the time of the accounting date, whether the company could have paid their debts. If the turnover is known, a quick calculation, by dividing the sales by 12, will give a monthly average sales figure. The monthly sales figures will enable me to decide on a realistic credit figure that I might extend to the company.

I am now ready to start analysing a set of accounts by noting the individual figures and then reviewing the trend. The latter can only take place, of course, if the company has traded for more than a year.

How Healthy is the Company?

Here is an example of a company, HCP Ltd, who have not filed modified accounts. The turnover, profit and loss, and directors' reports are therefore available for review. These are the questions I consider initially:

1. Is the turnover going up or down, and are greater or smaller profits being made?
2. Are the profits and losses reasonable considering the trade?
3. Are all the costs being controlled?

This company was formed many years ago, so I can check the accounts over a greater period. Turning to the profit and loss account, I look at two figures from the 1986 accounts, and refer to the corresponding figures for 1985 (Table 5.1).

Profit to Sales

I will divide the profit figure into the turnover to give a profit:sales ratio, e.g.

$$\frac{124,335}{3,194,729} = 1:26$$

In other words, it takes 26 units of sales to produce one unit of profit. In percentage terms, a profit of 3.9 per cent has been made on each pound of

Table 5.1 Turnover and profits, HCP Ltd, 1985/6

	1986	1985
Turnover	3,194,729	3,346,703
Profit before tax (but after interest receivable and payable has been deducted)	124,335	150,794

goods sold. For a comparison, Inter-Company Comparisons general report shows that their pre-tax marginal figure for manufacturers or sales and packaging shows an average return of 4.9 per cent for 1986, against the subject company's figure of 3.9 per cent.

A further question now arises. Why were profits in 1985 higher? This will be considered further when the costs are analysed. In Table 5.2 the sales/profit figure for the previous years is reviewed and a definite pattern emerges.

It can already be seen that the company have climbed out of a trading loss in 1983 to achieve profits in the subsequent years, although their profit margin on sales was reduced in 1986.

Still concentrating on the profit and loss account, I ask myself whether there is any indication of how the loss in 1983 was turned into profit in the subsequent years? Yes: by reading the notes to the accounts there was a large cost-cutting exercise in 1984. Staff were reduced and sales increased. Later in this section I will illustrate how helpful it is to use the number of people employed to measure productivity to sales and profits.

The notes to the accounts for 1984 indicate that the increase in sales in 1984 was partly due to a surge of export sales from £512,603 to £777,673; an increase of 51.7 per cent. The home sales increased from £1,918,215 to £2,382,579, an increase of 24 per cent.

When reviewing any profit and loss account it is critical to check the gross and net profits percentage changes. What is the actual gross profit margin and how does it compare to the segment of trade which is being examined? In Table 5.3, cost of sales items have been deducted to produce the net profit figure (see below). If the change in stocks, raw materials and other operating items are deducted from the turnover figure a gross profit percentage can be calculated.

As the gross profit margins for the year are virtually static, it can now be seen that the reduction in the net profit figure was due to two or three major factors, for although there was a reduction in 1986 in the raw materials consumed and staff costs, depreciation has increased.

Turning back to the profit and loss account for 1986 and reading the notes, the total turnover has decreased by £151,974 or 4.7 per cent. The notes show that the export sales increased by £7938, but home sales decreased by £160,912. The other figures in the profit and loss account indicate how the

Table 5.2   Sales/profit pattern

Date	Sales	Profit/Loss	Ratio	Percentage
1986	3,194,729	124,335	1:26	3.9
1985	3,346,703	150,794	1:22	4.5
1984	3,160,252	147,061	1:21	4.7
1983	2,430,818	(267,422) LOSS	(1:91–)	–11.0

Table 5.3 Net profit figures

	Note	1986 £	1985 £
TURNOVER	2 & 3	3,194,729	3,346,703
Change in stocks of finished goods and work in progress		18,605	(13,223)
Raw materials and consumables		(1,074,450)	(1,118,725)
Other operating charges		(606,439)	(600,731)
Staff costs	4	(1,298,527)	(1,382,283)
Depreciation		(104,102)	(76,459)
NET OPERATING PROFIT	5	129,816	155,282
Interest receivable		1,319	2,312
Interest payable	7	(6,800)	(6,800)
PROFIT ON ORDINARY ACTIVITIES BEFORE TAXATION		124,335	150,794
Taxation	8	–	–
PROFIT ON ORDINARY ACTIVITIES AFTER TAXATION		124,335	150,794
Retained profit at 1 January		1,127,507	1,051,713
Dividends		–	(75,000)
RETAINED PROFITS AT 31 DECEMBER		1,251,842	1,127,507

company was economising. There was a reduction in the raw materials consumed, and a saving of £83,756 on staff costs. In the accounts for 1985, a dividend of £75,000 was paid to shareholders, whereas no dividend was paid in 1986. The non-payment of a dividend may concern you, but dividends to the holding company have not been paid in every year of trading.

Certain questions may be answered when the balance sheet is analysed, but there is one figure still to be examined: the retained profits figure.

Retained Profits

The retained profits for the year end 1986 were £1,251,842, an increase of £134,345. The earlier figures were as follows:

1986	1985	1984	1983
£1,251,842	£1,127,507	£1,051,713	£1,204,652

Bear in mind that £75,000 and £300,000 in dividends were paid in 1985 and 1984 respectively, and that in earlier years no dividend had been paid. It would appear by just looking at the profit and loss accounts that the directors are carefully watching the management of the company, because since 1984 there have been no major peaks or troughs in sales or profits. I have not yet reviewed depreciation or taxation. A further check can be made on the operating ability of this company by comparing it with other companies in the same segment (Chapter 4, ICC Information Group).

In reviewing these sets of accounts I have just one ratio – sales to profit – but I have had the advantage of being able to review four years' figures. The work of analysing the balance sheet now begins, so that the profits to assets, capital strength and liquidity can be reviewed.

Fixed Assets

In the accounts being reviewed, the fixed assets are divided into tangible and investment assets. The fixed assets are valued at £850,337 but here it is important to study the notes to the accounts as they are broken down into the following areas:

- Freehold land and buildings
- Short leasehold land and buildings
- Plant and equipment.

The notes are sufficiently clear to show depreciation, additional purchases and disposals. Again, by reviewing the previous year's accounts it can be seen that over the last five years plant and equipment have been replaced, disposals have occurred and depreciation has been allowed. In this illustration there is an indication that the buildings and plant may be worth more than the value noted in the accounts, but it always has to be considered that market values can alter dramatically with changes in economic or political strategy. A personal visit to the premises is often the only way to evaluate the real value.

In reviewing fixed assets the question that I would like to be answered is: how are these assets being used to generate sales and profits? Buildings have to be maintained, and if it is leasehold property on a short lease a renovation clause may be in operation. Plant and machinery will gradually wear out. Apart from replacing and servicing parts of the equipment, reserves are required for updating and purchasing plant which will increase productivity. The amount that is depreciated each year should be set against the known value of these types of assets in the trade or service industry that is being reviewed.

Solvency Margin

Now let us review the trade and creditors figures and the amounts owed to group companies so that the total current debts can be examined.

	1986	1985
Trade and other creditors	290,468	290,145
Amounts owed to group companies	214,246	146,013
	504,714	436,158

Before reading the notes, if the debtors and amounts due from group companies are placed immediately below, a solvency margin appears.

Debtors	523,924	484,473
Amounts owed by group companies	25,587	10,537
	549,511	495,010

In ratio terms:

$$\frac{549,511}{504,714} = 1{:}1.08 \qquad \frac{495,010}{436,158} = 1{:}1.13$$

In comparing these ratios alone it can be seen that although the liquidity ratios have been reduced, at the accounting year end the company *on paper* had more than enough debtors to pay all their current creditors.

Turning to the notes on creditors, a far more detailed picture emerges.

	1986	1985
Trade creditors	99,489	109,834
Other creditors	71,815	59,353
Social Security	5,563	11,660
Accruals and deferred income	113,601	109,298
	290,468	290,145

The actual trade creditor figure has been reduced by a greater percentage than the reduction of turnover. There is no pointer to show why the other creditor figure increased by £12,462. In reviewing the trade creditors it is useful to carry out a calculation to see how quickly creditors are paid and then check to see how quickly debtors payments are received (see calculation in Debtors section, page 85).

To calculate the trade creditor collection period in days or percentage of sales:

	1986		*1985*
Creditors	290,468	Creditors	290,145
Sales	——————— × 365	Sales	——————— × 365
	3,194,729		3,346,073
	= 33 days		= 31 days
	or 9.1 per cent		or 8.7 per cent

Turning to the trade debtors figures it can be seen that the debtors are paying the company in 60 days on average in 1986 against 53 days in 1985. The reserves in the company appear to be cushioning this situation.

FURTHER KEY RATIOS

Liquidity

Once the current net assets and liabilities are analysed, it is possible to carry out a vast number of calculations which will help a credit controller or manager to decide whether credit can be safely extended. In the previous section, to ascertain whether there was a solvency level, debtors were compared to creditors at a particular date. A more refined ratio is the acid test – or quick ratio – to test short term liquidity. In this example the inter-company balances have been included as I always steer towards the safety factor.

	1986	*1985*
Current assets – stock	1,350,529 – 664,026	1,240,045 – 645,421
Liabilities	504,714	511,158
	= 1:1.36	= 1:1.63

The 1985 liability figure included a proposed dividend of £75,000.

This ratio shows that there were ample resources to clear short-term debts. A ratio of 1:1 is a favourable sign. In examining this company the ratio is even better. Many companies have a solvency ratio which is below 1:1, but are still able to pay accounts to terms by operating a carefully disciplined management system. When reviewing these ratios for pure cash flow purposes, the peculiarities of the particular industry or trade should also be examined. The total debtors outstanding in this example are £523,924 as at 31 December 1986, but at that date the debtors had not been converted to cash. From the calculation in the Debtors section (page 85), it can be seen that the average time it takes to collect debts is 60 days. Therefore, a question I always ask myself when considering whether I can extend credit is: what cash may be available to actually pay the debts? I ask this question because I invariably have one thought running through my mind when just looking at historic trade figures. That is, the 'what happens if' theory:

- What would happen if the associate companies require immediate payment?
- What would happen if the VAT, Inland Revenue, National Insurance or Utilities all demand payment?
- How quickly could the stock or raw materials be turned into finished goods?
- What is the estimated length of time it would take from manufacture of a product to the payment of the invoice?
- What would happen if the Bank or Finance House required repayment?

From the example, only estimations can be made to indicate cash flow generation time. Stock is turned over on average every 76 days (see below). A credit free period of about one month would normally be included when the customer is invoiced. It is also known that collection of accounts takes on average 60 days (see page 85). Putting all these facts together, even if the pure manufacturing time was just 30 days it would take at least four months before the payment for that production would be made. As a reminder, turning back to how the creditors were paid, the average number of days the company took to pay their accounts was 33 days.

Another way of estimating a company's daily cash flow is to divide the total turnover, less inter-company balances, by the number of working days in the year. I would emphasise that, for this estimation to be of any use, it must reflect the segment of the trade that is being considered. All trade and service industries have different trade cycles. In discussing these points I am estimating by 'blind reckoning' and a little common sense as to which funds might be available to pay a particular credit transaction.

Stock

A too high stock figure is a massive burden on any business. Not only is the stock taking up warehouse space, but the extra cost of heating, lighting, security and insurance can greatly reduce the profit margins. The Japanese method of 'just in time' (JIT) minimum stockholding has enabled the motor industry to become more profitable. With varying international interest charges a company which can buy in the required stocks at a moment's notice should achieve a far higher profit margin. Turning to our example, in the notes to the accounts the breakdown was set out as shown in Table 5.4.

Looking at these figures, the increase of £39,144 in raw materials has been countered by a reduction of £16,524 in the work in progress.

Now that the stock figure is known it is possible to calculate how many times the stock is turned over on annual sales. This ratio is a key indication of stock liquidity. A high ratio will show a quicker movement of stock which should in turn produce greater profits. One way of calculating the stock turnover figure is to take the cost of sales if available or if not the sales turnover figure and divide it by the average stock. The average stock is the opening plus closing stock divided by two:

	1986		1985	
Sales turnover	3,194,729	4.84 times	3,346,703	6.49 times
Average stock	659,724	= a year	515,304	= a year
		or 75 days stock		or 56 days stock

Table 5.4 Stock turnover

	1986	1985
Raw materials	473,579	434,435
Work in progress	187,380	203,904
Finished goods	3,067	7,082
Total	664,026	645,421

The above figures do not take into account any seasonal trends. In this example, although the stock level was higher and the stock turned over just under five times a year, this did not directly affect profits as savings were made in other areas, for example wages and salaries. The reduction in stock circulation and the decline in sales in 1986 has effectively helped to reduce the profit margin in sales by 0.6 per cent. If the profits on sales are reviewed over a two-year period a further picture emerges:

	1986	1985
Profit on sales	£124,335 1:26 or 3.9 per cent	£150,794 1:22 or 4.5 per cent
Stock as a percentage of sales	20.6 per cent	15.4 per cent

There are of course many other factors in the accounts of any company's figures which will dramatically change the all-important gross profit margins and final net profit figure before tax. Even allowing for the fact that I have deliberately omitted to interview the management, as I wished to show the limitations of just reviewing a set of accounts, by highlighting sales, profits and stocks, a picture is now emerging.

Debtors

How long does it take to collect those outstanding invoices? It is also worthwhile to consider that in any debtors figure there could be items that may have to be written off. The ratio of debtors to sales is a key ratio on which to judge the average time it takes a company to collect its debts. The longer the period or the higher the ratio the greater the indication that there are poor credit control methods, overtrading to produce low profitable sales, or intense competition between suppliers. In using this ratio I would recommend that a comparison with the same trade or service industry is carried out when considering whether to supply a large order on credit terms.

Debtors' calculation

1986

$$\frac{\text{Debtors} \quad 523{,}924}{\text{Sales} \quad 3{,}194{,}729} \times 365 \text{ days} = 60 \text{ days}$$

1985

$$\frac{\text{Debtors} \quad 484{,}473}{\text{Sales} \quad 3{,}346{,}703} \times 365 \text{ days} = 53 \text{ days}$$

It can be seen that it has taken seven days longer, on average, to collect the outstanding sales in 1986. Table 5.5 summarises the notes to the accounts in which the debtors are analysed.

Even with lower turnover in 1986 than 1985 the debtors may have been more difficult to collect. The large increase in prepayment and accrued income would have assisted the company's cash flow as it represents 12 per cent of total debtors. The company may have also had to increase its credit terms when there was pressure to obtain further orders.

A further factor now emerges which could directly affect cash flow. Turning back to the previous year's sales there was a reduction of £151,974. This is why the examination of creditors is so important. Normally speaking, if the

Table 5.5   Summary of debtors

	1986	1985
Trade debtors	458,852	441,263
Other debtors	2,325	5,266
Prepayments and accrued income	62,747	37,944

collection period gets longer, so will the payment of trade creditors. The only other ways for a company to get out of this syndrome are to:

1. increase sales which may increase costs
2. borrow funds which will increase costs
3. increase speed of collection of debts which will reduce costs
4. slow down the payment of creditors which will increase cash flow.

In this set of accounts the amount owed by group companies is shown separately as follows:

	1986	1985
Amount owed by group companies	25,587	10,537

To make any real sense of the figures when looking at any intertrading between associate companies, all the purchases and sales figures have to be reconciled from all the associated companies.

For the purposes of this review I have deliberately not contacted any credit bureaux for additional information, as I wished to illustrate the way in which trading trends could be extracted from a set of accounts. But in looking at the large increase in intercompany sales, this may be an indication of why profit margins have been reduced.

	1986	1985
Bank balances	£136,992	£99,614

There is, of course, another factor which may explain why the company has increased its bank balance. In the year 1986 the base rate fluctuated between 10.5 per cent and 11.5 per cent. If profit margins were stretched it might have been more attractive to keep unused funds on deposit to increase the cash balances.

Turning to the earlier years the bank balances were as follows:

1983	£38,858
1984	£52,554

Once the ratio for determining how creditors are being paid is matched against average debtor collections, the entire relationship between the need for cash flow, sales generation and payment of creditors can be plotted.

The next section to be reviewed is the current liabilities. Once these figures are analysed the net working capital ratios can be calculated.

Creditors

How quickly are the creditors being paid and what is the relationship between debtors and creditors? The answers to these first questions would help me to gauge – if I was a new supplier – what the average number of days would be that the company might take to pay (see Solvency Margin, page 81). This is vitally important as I wish to know at a definite date whether a company could pay its creditors from the cash flow generated from its debtors. In scanning the debtor figure, I have no knowledge at this point of whether all the debts are collectable. It should also be remembered that in this example there is no overdraft outstanding. If there is an overdraft figure noted in a set of accounts, this must be added to creditors when evaluating whether a business can pay its short-term debts. Short-term debts are defined as payments which have to be paid within one year.

Depreciation

It is not possible in analysing a set of accounts to isolate one figure. Therefore, when looking at the depreciation figure in the profit and loss account, the relationship to the fixed assets and notes to the accounts must be studied. The depreciation figure for the four years is as follows:

1986	1985	1984	1983
104,102	76,459	77,941	84,003

I have already referred to depreciation (see Fixed Assets, page 80), but for the moment, if sales and profit are measured as a ratio to depreciation it is another way of evaluating the way in which the net value of plant and machinery is generating sales and profits.

Taxation

In this particular company, as losses were made in previous years, no provision has been made for corporation tax. This relief was available under Section 258 of the Income and Corporation Taxes Act 1970. In the notes to the accounts, the group's current corporation tax liability has been provided in the accounts of a fellow subsidiary company.

Corporation Tax

There are changes in corporation tax and other tax adjustments in nearly every budget. If, in this example, HCP Ltd was not part of a group and had not previously been making losses, their corporation tax rate for the financial year 1988 would be 35 per cent. In the Finance Act 1988, the corporation tax for small companies, which applies where profits are £100,000 or less, was reduced from 27 per cent to 25 per cent.

Working Capital

How much capital is there in the company and how is it being used to generate sales, profits and dividends? Once the current assets and current liabilities are totalled it is possible to calculate the working capital. This is the difference between the current assets and liabilities. This calculation excludes the fixed assets. Measuring working capital against profit and turnover will show how effective the management of a company is in controlling all the segments of their business. As the working capital is the 'core' of the business, any significant changes should be examined with great care. Vast increases in sales, for instance, can create massive bottlenecks for production or distribution. Costs can easily rise ahead of profits. When sales are declining the costs may not be reduced at the same rate as sales.

One of the problems of sales management is that they obviously have to be optimists. They always feel that they will succeed in hitting their targets. Measuring the trends over a three-year period can often highlight a problem. In particular, when looking at the profit figure, it is essential to see how the accountant has constructed the profit and loss account. No two sets of accounts are drafted in the same way and although all the major accounting bodies do follow agreed practices, it is remarkable to see how the treatment of certain costs will change the profit figure.

The term 'working capital' should not be confused with the term 'capital employed'. Working capital refers to short-term funding, e.g. current assets less current liabilities. Capital employed is total assets, including fixed assets, less current liabilities. This figure is equal to the ordinary and preference share capital, all reserves and the profit and loss account balances. I have deliberately not used the term 'net worth' as although the phrase refers to shareholder funds less any intangible assets, there do seem to be a confusing number of definitions.

If the working capital is now measured against profit, turnover, stock and liabilities, a financial picture begins to emerge. The profit to working capital is a key ratio which basically plots how that 'core capital' is generating profits. Table 5.6 shows that in this example, depreciation charges have been deducted from the profit figure. The profit figure excludes interest receivable and payable, and taxation.

By reviewing the three years' figures it can be seen that in 1984 it took 4.3 units of working capital to produce one unit of profit, whereas in 1986, 6.5 units of working capital were used to produce one unit of profit.

Table 5.6 Ratio of profit to working capital

	1986		1985		1984	
Profit	129,816	1:6.5	155,282	1:4.6	151,091	1:4.3
Working capital	845,815		728,887		664,157	

Overtrading

Moving to the turnover figures, the ratio of working capital to turnover can indicate whether there is an improvement in sales with relation to the working capital. A rise in the ratio would normally be seen as a positive sign. If there is a massive increase in sales and the working capital core is not increasing at about the same rate, overtrading can take place. Overtrading can be signalled in a number of ways – an increase in the borrowing of funds, a slowing down in the payment of creditors and a large increase in stock and creditors.

If overtrading is taking place, the statements made by the company's management may get more and more optimistic. When considering a transaction where overtrading may be taking place, credit staff can request a payment profile from Dun & Bradstreet. This will at least list a series of recent payment experiences which will serve as a guide to how much and how long it took the business to pay (see Chapter 4).

Table 5.7 shows that in this example there is no indication of overtrading.

In a different form, 26 per cent of working capital is required to generate sales in 1986, whereas in 1985 only 22 per cent of capital was used.

Stock to net current assets is a useful guide to how much of the working capital is held in raw materials and finished goods. It should be remembered that high stock levels do not necessarily create sales and cash flow. When looking at the total current assets, the most liquid items should be reviewed to highlight from where the immediate cash flow can be generated. In this example, the stock levels are turning over 4.81 times in 1986 against 5.18 times in 1985.

Table 5.8 shows that if the working capital is measured against stock it will indicate if minimum stocks are being held to operate the business. High stock levels increase warehouse costs, insurance and interest charges.

Table 5.7 Ratio of working capital to turnover

	1986		1985	
Turnover	3,194,729	1:3.7	3,346,703	1:4.6
Working capital	845,815		728,887	

Table 5.8 Working capital against stock

	1986		1985	
Working capital	845,815	1:1.2	728,887	1:1.1
Stock	664,026		645,421	

It can now be seen that although the actual stock levels have increased fractionally, the movement of stock has slowed down. The net current assets picture has changed because of the following movement in 1986:

- Current assets increases   £
  - Stocks   18,605
  - Debtors   39,451
  - Amounts owed by group companies   15,050
  - Bank balance   37,378
  -    110,484

- Current liabilities increases
  - Trade and other credits   323
  - Amount owed to group companies   68,233
  -    68,556

Capital Employed

The net increase in the capital employed was 41,928 before allowing for the fact that a dividend of £75,000 was not paid in 1986. This increased the capital employed to £115,928 on the 1985 figure.

Table 5.9 Capital employed

	1986	1985	1984
Called up share capital	15,550	15,550	15,550
Other reserves	506,042	406,042	406,042
Profit and loss account	1,251,842	1,127,507	1,051,713
	1,673,434	1,549,099	1,473,305
Capital employed	$\frac{1,673,434 \times 100}{} = 7.42\%$	$\frac{1,549,099 \times 100}{} = 9.73\%$	$\frac{1,473,305 \times 100}{} = 9.98\%$
Profit before tax and interest	124,335	150,744	147,061

Return on Capital Employed (ROCE)

This ratio is a key to the entire performance of a business. In Table 5.8 profits are measured against all the resources of the business. Table 5.9 illustrates figures from more than two years to show the trend.

In this instance it can be seen that there has been a general reduction in profitability.

Another way of measuring the same trend is to use the sales/total asset ratio to check how a business is utilising its assets. Sales to current assets and fixed assets can also be used as a further measurement. The key to using these ratios is to see how the proportion of fixed and current assets are used to generate sales and profits.

	1986		1985	
Sales	3,194,729	1:1.4 or	3,346,703	1:1.5 or
Total assets	2,258,148	70 per cent	2,140,257	64 per cent

In a ratio form, it disguises the trend, as in 1986 sales are down and total assets are higher. But if a percentage of total assets to sales is calculated, this gives a clearer picture showing that greater assets are generating less sales.

Employment Ratios

Another strength which is often forgotten is the asset value of the employees. How much productivity and profit are generated by the employees? When looking at any set of figures the significance of the numbers of people employed and the wage cost can often be overlooked. In this example there has been a gradual reduction in the number of workers employed. Has this increased productivity and profits per head?

	1986	1985	1984
Number of employees	195	214	237

The first calculation relates sales to employees to determine the productivity.

	1986		1985		1984	
Turnover	3,194,729		3,346,703		3,160,252	
	—————	= £16,383*	—————	= £15,638*	—————	= £13,334*
Employees	195		214		237	

* per employee

Secondly let us look at the profits generated before tax and interest:

	1986		*1985*		*1984*	
Profit	129,816		155,282		151,091	
	——————— = £665		——————— = £725		——————— = £637	
Employees	195		214		237	

It can be seen that there has been a considerable improvement in the value of sales generated per employee. In 1986, the profit per employee had declined. I believe these trends illustrate the real advantage in taking extra financial measurements.

The Average Wages to Employees

	1986		*1985*		*1984*	
Wages	1,129,508		1,197,712		1,170,234	
	——————— = £5,792		——————— = £5,596		——————— = £4,937	
Employees	195		214		237	

Although there have been increases in wages year by year, if the profit and turnover per employee is set against the above figure, as in Table 5.10, a different picture emerges. Profits are lower, but productivity is up.

Table 5.10   Profit and turnover per employee v. wages

	1986	1985	1984
Average wages	5,792	5,596	4,937
Turnover per employee	16,383	15,638	13,334
Profit per employee	665	725	637
Number of workers	195	214	237

In Table 5.11 percentage profit increase is set against the increase in average wages.

Table 5.11   Profit v. wage increase (%)

	1986	1985	1984
Percentage profit	3.9	4.5	4.6
Percentage wage increase	3.5	13.3	10.7

In using the above figures it can now be seen that the average wage increases are ahead of profit increase. Have any other savings been made to compensate for higher wages? The other operating charges in the profit and loss account are as follows:

1986	1985	1984
606,439	600,731	534,120

However, looking at the notes:

	1986	1985	1984
Director's remuneration	75,650	95,912	93,471
Number of directors	4	5	6

Conclusion: in only looking at the administration costs there has been a slight increase in other operating charges. Against this the number of directors employed is less and there is a slight reduction in average remuneration.

Here are a few further suggested ratios which will help to plot trends in the efficient use of the capital in the business. Measuring the capital employed to each worker will show the way in which the two assets of the business, capital and employees, are working to create sales and profits. The higher the ratio the greater the use of the capital employed.

	1986	1985	1984
Capital employed	1,673,434	1,549,099	1,473,305
Employees	195	214	237
	= £8,581	= £7,238	= £6,216

In this instance there is a considerable improvement. Does the company hold on to too many employees and is the wage bill reasonable, or average, for the trade that the business is in? Part of the answer to this question could be checked by using the SIC code.

The Standard Industrial Classification is a list which describes types of business activities. Once the precise code number is identified, it is then possible to compare the numbers employed and wage costs with other businesses of the same type. Intercompany Comparisons Ltd is a company which specialises in this field.

It is always difficult to compare average wages per employee, as regional costs of living allowances and national and local union agreements can distort wage costs.

GEARING

Earlier in this book, I highlighted the need to distinguish between the issued share capital – which may be just two pounds – and authorised share capital. This is fundamentally important in judging what proportion of the personal funds the directors and other shareholders are willing to invest in their company against outside borrowing.

If the share capital in a company is minimal, the business relies on bank overdraft facilities, short- and medium-term loans and directors' loans to support it. These types of loans will normally be secured by a charge against the assets of the business. Consequently when looking at a number of loans in a set of accounts, I always find out who holds the security by checking the Register of Charges, held by Companies House. The basic question I am asking is – who actually controls the company when loans are secured on the assets?

The term 'gearing' is the ratio used to describe the relationship between risk capital – which is the share capital subscribed – and loan capital. A high geared company relies on outside funding. If the gearing is very high, this can be a danger signal. On the other hand, if the gearing is exceptionally low, the question may have to be asked – is the capital of the company being used in the best possible way? This is especially true when interest rates are high. It must be considered that a company will normally only pay a dividend if a profit is made. However, if they are highly geared the interest charges still have to be paid.

In the following example, the company does not rely on outside borrowing to support its operation.

- There is a share capital of £15,550
- Other reserves are £406,042
- Balance on the profit and loss £1,251,842.

The only long-term borrowing is the £80,000, 8.5 per cent mortgage loan repayment which is due in 1992. Although there is an £80,000 term mortgage loan repayable in 1990, there are no other loans or overdraft facilities. The company's called-up share capital may be only £15,500 but their other reserves and retained profits totalling £1,657,884 show that there is a more than adequate cover for this loan. There are a wide variety of gearing ratios and many different definitions. There are two versions:

$$\frac{\text{Fixed interest loans} + \text{Preferential share capital}}{\text{Shareholders funds}} \times 100$$

$$\frac{\text{Fixed interest loans} + \text{Preferential share capital}}{\text{Ordinary share capital}} \times 100$$

In this instance, using just one ratio and not relating it to all the other information would give a totally misleading picture.

Outside funding can make a dramatic difference to the structure of a business, so I will show below an example from an entirely different company.

	£	£		£
			Share capital	100
			Profit and loss account	8,123
Fixed assets		21,663		
Current assets	118,929			
less current liabilities	131,969			
net current liabilities	(13,040)			
If the deficit on current assets/ liabilities is deducted from fixed assets and allowing for a £400 deferred expenditure	13,040 400			
		13,440		
Net assets		8,223		8,223

Turning to current liabilities

	£
Trade creditors } Corporation tax } Social security }	84,036
Hire purchase	7,839
Other creditors	8,073
Bank overdraft and bank loan account	10,650
Directors' loan account	16,371
Dividend proposed	5,000
	131,969

In this instance the £10,650 bank facility is charged against a debenture. This is a fixed and floating charge on all property and assets, present and future, including book and any other debts. This means that the bank has a preferential claim on the assets of the company if it went into liquidation or called in a receiver.

The directors' loan account has not been secured against the assets of the company. Quite often there is a clause in the bank's debenture which excludes further charges being raised without the bank's consent. To gain the overdraft facility, the directors may have also had to give personal guarantees on their personal assets. In reviewing these figures I would always ask the same question: if in fact the directors wish to withdraw some of the loan capital from the business, would the business still be viable? Is there enough cash flow in the business? The total turnover is £450,000. The cost of sales and other administration is £441,000.

It can be seen in this example from a different company that as there are minimal reserves the bank facility and directors' loans actually support the entire structure of the company as at 31 August 1986. By August 1987 the picture has changed, as the sales are up by nearly £100,000. There is a net current asset figure of £7,500 whereas in 1986 there was a deficit of £13,000. There has been an increase in profits and no dividend is being paid. It appears that the reserves are being ploughed back into the business.

I think that this small amount of scanning shows up three grey areas:

1. one set of accounts will not give a financial picture;
2. the activities of a company can change dramatically within one year;
3. without information on the character of the directors, their trading experience and knowledge of the business, an accurate assessment is difficult, but it can be seen that liquidity is restricted. Further enquiries would also have to be made for example in the trade and through other sources (see Chapter 4).

Source and Application of Funds Statement

This is a relatively new statement which is added to sets of accounts where the turnover is more than £25,000. This statement can assist credit granters as it highlights the financial changes that took place in the preceding year. The balance sheet and profit and loss accounts will just state a figure, whereas the source and application statement shows how profits have been used and the movement of fixed and current assets and liabilities.

THE CHANGING PICTURE

Since reviewing these accounts of HCP Ltd, a further set of figures has arrived for the year ending December 1987. I also understand that there has been a change in the company's structure. The directors' report shows that the company had merged with a fellow subsidiary. Within one year how has the picture changed?

The net operating profit has increased by £223,762, an increase of 367 per cent from the previous year. The sales increased by £241,376. A fourth set of accounts means that the analysis has to be re-examined and the trends redefined. For example, staff numbers have been reduced by a further 20 people, saving the business £143,539 in wages costs on the previous year. I think this addendum illustrates how an increase in sales and a reduction in staff can dramatically alter the picture.

THE CREDIT LINE

The purpose of looking at a set of accounts is to decide how much credit can safely be granted to a customer. Would I grant credit to the subject company? The answer is yes. The maximum credit that can safely be granted at any one time can be calculated by using at least three cross bearings.

- Financial measurements
- Cash flow
- The company's historic trading.

Financial Measurements

Here are three financial measurements which are often used in calculating credit lines:

1. Ten per cent of net current assets:
   net current assets in 1987, £1,149,397.   10 per cent = £114,939
2. Twenty per cent of working capital:
   working capital in 1987 £1,836,103.   20 per cent = £367,220
3. Ten per cent of trade creditors £578,386.   10 per cent = £57,838

These may seem large credit lines but all measurements are linked to a customer's basic financial strength and historic trading. If credit granters are anxious about extending such large sums of credit, the lower maximum credit figure could be authorised.

Cash Flow

Another way of testing the life blood of a company is by just calculating possible cash flow from annual sales. In this example, taking 211 working days per year and dividing them into sales turnover of £3,436,105, the cash flow per day is £16,284. Ten days' cash flow indicates a possible credit line of £162,840.

Historic Trading

This entire exercise has been based on reviewing financial information on a company which has been established since 1932. In practice, if I was actually to open an account, I would carry out all the credit formalities of taking out references and obtaining a credit report (see Chapter 1, Assessment). My reason for being prudent is that although I have confidence in this company, changes have taken place since December 1987. In fact, there was a name change to Beldam Packing & Rubber Company Ltd, and then on 1 May 1988 the company transferred their activities to Beldam Crossley Ltd. The turnover for 1988 has increased to £10,163,912 and pre-tax profits were £422,286. The picture has therefore changed again, so an entirely new analysis needs to be carried out to assess a suitable credit line.

DOMESTIC CREDIT INSURANCE

The insurance of debts, in my opinion, is a service that enables business personnel to have one less worry. They will be paid a high proportion of the debt if the business they supply becomes insolvent or if it is proved that there has been a protracted default. There are only two provisos. The insurer will look most carefully at the total sales ledger before agreeing to underwrite a policy, so that the basket of risks is balanced. They will also inspect the entire sales ledger and credit control administration to make sure that the assessment and collection procedures are maintained.

Credit insurance is definitely not bad debt insurance. Companies who are accepted by insurers normally have a high standard of credit administration. Their bad debt record will have been reviewed for at least three years. If a claim is presented – provided that a company who have taken out credit insurance have not breached any of the conditions – the insured would be paid within 30 days of confirmation of debt. See Chapter 11, Credit Insurance.

SUMMARY

In assessing a business for a credit transaction the experience and reputation of its management are vital factors. A large proportion of limited companies are not required to file full accounts, therefore assessment is becoming more difficult. Sole traders and partnerships are not required to file their accounts publicly therefore any financial information should be carefully considered, as sometimes it is far more difficult to cross-check.

- What is an acceptable risk, and have you got confidence in the transaction?
- If a sole trader or partnership wants to trade with you, what do you know about them?
- Looking at the balance sheet of a company:
  - are the accounts qualified?
  - have they any liquid assets to pay your account?
  - are there any registered charges?
  - what is the trend of the business and its sector?
- If you do not have enough confidence in a business to extend credit, can you offer a discount for a cash transaction to avoid losing the sale?

6
The Administration of the Sales Ledger/Credit Control Department

INTRODUCTION

Since I reviewed the sales ledger accounting process in 1989, there have been a number of developments which will also affect how the accounts are collected. Although credit control never seems to receive the funding that marketing and research and development receive, the new credit management computer systems can be linked to word processing, spread sheets and fax and E-mail programmes. It is no longer a book keeping exercise (see Chapters 6 and 7). Throughout the UK and the western world staff numbers are being reduced, but there is more pressure on the credit staff to assess, reconcile and collect at a faster rate. With mergers and demergers, reorganisations and re-engineering some businesses will find they have many more small accounts to control whereas others will have few accounts but with huge balances. The 20/80 Pareto ratios are changing. However, in spite of all the new technology and computerisation, credit controllers and managers are still complaining that:

1. they cannot find invoices
2. hours and hours are spent in reconciling accounts
3. they were not consulted when a new accounting system was proposed.

Although the following notes on reviewing the administration of a sales ledger were written in 1989, the principles are still the same. However, I have added to the section on choosing the right computer for your business.

The organisation and management of the sales ledger is the core around which the entire credit control system operates. The purpose of the department is to keep accurate records so that not only can the invoices, credit notes and cash receipts be identified, but all the routines can be fitted into a precise workable system. Figure 6.1 illustrates the way in which the many individual activities in credit granting and collection are linked together.

There are three principal areas of work:

- Assessment
- Processing of documents
- Collections.

The sales ledger, debtors or receivables, is one of the most valuable current assets in any business. The speedy and accurate document flow will increase cash flow. The debtors in a business can represent up to 40 per cent of the current assets.

Depending on whether readers work in large, medium or small companies, all the basics of the sales ledger may be carried out by one person or many. It does not matter whether the system operated is computer driven or still manually run. Many larger companies have separate sections which deal with invoicing, cash posting and reconciliation, collection, assessment and reappraisal of accounts. Whatever the size of your business the following routines will normally have to be carried out to protect the sales ledger:

- New account applications
- Name, address, and account coding
- Order vetting
- Invoicing
- Statement processing
- Cash listing
- Reconciliation
- Applications for payment
- Reassessment
- Customer account review
- Statistics

If the records are well organised the sales ledger will highlight customer purchasing and payment trends. These statistics will help the sales department to plot any changes in market conditions. The advantages of monitoring the accounts as a routine exercise are that the signals from the sales ledger are sometimes the first signals of genuine expansion, overtrading or financial difficulties.

A vast amount of management information can be obtained if pre-planning is carried out. The sales ledger must not be considered a back room occupation. It is the core that generates the cash flow.

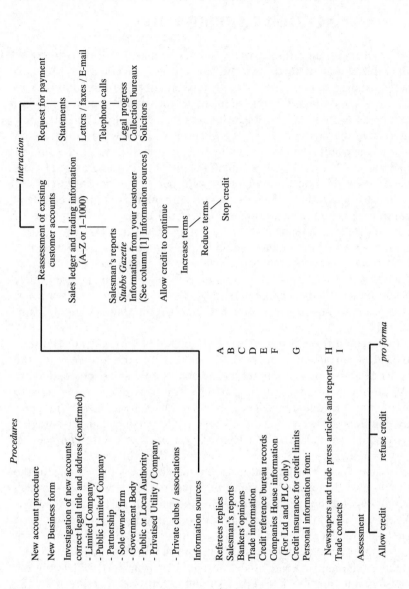

Figure 6.1 The administration of a credit control/sales ledger department

ACCOUNT APPLICATIONS

In Chapter 3 I mentioned that it was essential to make sure that the exact name and address was verified from the new business form details. Mistakes in the name, trading style or address can cause an enormous amount of extra despatch work if goods are being supplied to an incorrect delivery point. There can be an even greater problem if services are required, and the operator cannot find the new customer. If a section of the new business form is used to confirm where the invoice and statement should be sent, hours of work can be saved. It sounds simple, but many invoices, statements and letters either never reach their destination, or are returned by the post office.

Once the credit account has been sanctioned by the person in the company who is authorised to take the responsibility, the account can be opened. If there is no set routine, anyone could be opening accounts. This is not practical, it is dangerous, and the practice could lead to the business losing a fortune by not sanctioning accounts correctly. The way to ensure that accounts are being opened only by authorised personnel, is to have a formal credit policy which is set out in a credit manual agreed by, for example the senior partner, proprietor or managing director (see Chapter 7, Credit Manual, under Training of Staff).

Once the account is opened, the customer should be formally advised. The letter should be attractive and eye-catching. It is an advertisement for the business. The credit limit, trading terms and conditions can be included in the letter. A clause can be added stating that the company reserves the right to claim interest on overdue debts. The rate should be shown and provided the customer confirms the terms this will give the credit personnel an advantage if future payments are delayed. The Reservation of Title clause can also be added if it is relevant to your business or trade (see Chapter 1). It is good practice to keep a copy of this letter on the new business file. Copies of the letter should also be sent to the representative and sales and order branch offices. It all depends on the individual selling organisation. The whole idea is not to keep your customer waiting for goods or services.

If, when granting credit, your business can use credit limits or a code system, this information can be placed on record. Then the sales and order departments, regional or head office, despatch or transport, will know the maximum amount they are allowed to supply before they need to refer the account to the sales ledger/credit department.

THE INDEX OF CUSTOMERS

The entire accounts department can come to a halt if invoices are posted to an incorrect account. Again, it need not happen if enough digits are planned when the system is designed. Looking through a telephone directory, it is possible to ascertain that there are more names beginning with some letters than others, and these particular letters need far more space. Often a mistake can happen when the one person who knows the entire system is away and someone else tries to help out. A further safeguard, apart from the credit manual instruction, is always to have an extra authorised person who has been trained to allocate and input new account numbers.

If the company is using a manual or computerised accounting system, it is absolutely essential to have a cross reference system for account numbers and customer names. This safeguard can also save many hours of work, as when an incorrect name or account number is discovered there is an immediate, simple cross-check available. With some software packages it is not possible to add the customer's telephone number in the name and address file. If this can be carried out, the index can be used as a customer directory. The customer's telephone number can also be slotted into a variety of other working documents which makes collection far easier (see Chapter 8). Tables 6.1 and 6.2 show examples of customer indexing: Table 6.1 numerically by account number and Table 6.2 alphabetically by account number.

Overloaded Systems

I am still hearing of accounts departments where they have run out of account numbers due to the computer system's limited capacity. One way to overcome this problem is to cancel customers' accounts which have not been used for, perhaps, two or three or four years. These old account numbers are then reallocated to new customers. However, this crisis method can cause

Table 6.1 Example of customer indexing (numerical)

Account no.	Customer
261426	Experian
261526	Dun & Bradstreet
261626	Graydon
261726	Equifax

Table 6.2 Example of customer indexing (alphabetical)

Customer	Account no.
Dun & Bradstreet	261526
Equifax	261726
Experian	261426
Graydon	261626

enormous problems, especially if the 'old' customer wants to start trading again. The old customer, the accounts and the sales office staff could be using different account numbers. The only safeguard, if there is no other way to operate, is to keep a separate index of cancelled and reallocated account numbers. Any changes should be advised immediately to the sales, order, despatch and sales personnel.

Nil Balances

I have found that it is good commercial practice to advise an 'old customer' whose account has not been used for a considerable period that, since no trading has taken place, the accounts department is considering transferring their details to a non-active section. The effect on the old customer will be that they will either respond by purchasing or, if they reply to the contrary, the account can be closed. As a general rule, nil balances should be reviewed on a regular basis. Firstly, it is important that if an account has not been active, liaison is maintained with the sales personnel to find out why there has been a period of no sales to the customer. Secondly, if the particular account system issues nil balance statements at the end of the month or account period, there should be a method of stopping these going out. The postage alone is a total waste of money month by month.

Account Numbering

The account numbering and coding of invoices can get far more complicated when a head office only receives the statements. Quite often either an individual depot or shop will place an order and the goods or services will be delivered to that receiving point. Alternatively, the centralised purchasing office of the customer will issue an order which lists many individual dropping points to be carried out. It is essential, if either of these systems is used, to be able to identify the exact unit that received the service. If the units do not pass the delivery note or invoice a coding system can be designed to trace any delayed payments.

For example, the group statement number could be 16819000. The 9 denotes a group. Then up to 999 digits can be allocated to individual receiving points. In some systems the actual invoices have extra digits. These codes are highlighted on the statement, so that the location of the site can be traced, (see Clearing Queries, page 116, and Reconciliation, page 127).

When a special offer is being advertised and there is very little chance of the customer purchasing any other product or services, an account number for that offer can be set up. This saves the enormous amount of work involved in constantly opening and closing accounts. The only problem that has to be tackled is identifying the customer and matching the remittance. Provided that there are enough digits in the account number, special invoice numbers can be issued which are added to that particular special offer account number, for example:

Special offer 01400:   0001 Mr A A Brown
                        0002 Mrs A D Smith

The same system can be used for staff purchases where the debit and credit entries would always agree.

The only pitfall of this type of system is that these accounts must be constantly reconciled and they must not be left to gather dust. If this ever happens, I guarantee that write-offs will take place.

The Number of Computer Accounting Systems

In an interview with Maurice Hamlyn Associates, a business which evaluates computer software systems, they confirmed that in July 1997 there were 2028 software products which were available for sales ledgers and 312 packages for credit control. They emphasised that 35,000 packaged software applications marketed by 5400 UK and 2000 European suppliers, and these have to be broken down into some 280 specific areas such as engineering, farming, hotel administration and banking.

The Millennium Date Change

Maurice Hamlyn is particularly worried that not only will many computer systems not be convertible to the 2000 date change but that they will simply be discontinued by the manufacturers and suppliers.

EMU Compliant

The only companies I have come across which have already planned for monetary union accountancy conversions are the multinationals and companies with a turnover of £500 million plus who have their own computer staff.

Maurice Hamlyn Associates have produced a checklist highlighting the question, 'Can your computer system offer multi-currency, the ability to work to six significant figures?' They advise companies to obtain written confirmation from their suppliers that their computers will accept the year 2000 transactions and that it will accept EMU accounting and conversions. These problems cannot be put on the shelf.

Further information from Maurice Hamlyn Associates, Winchester House, Winchester Avenue, Chorley, Lancashire, PR7 4AQ (tel: 01257 262776).

I have discovered that many accounting packages are not listed in the major software and hardware reference books. The *KPMG Directory of Financial Software for Business* is useful in helping to understand what is on offer. One of their twice yearly *Softworld in Accountancy & Finance* Exhibitions is at Earl's Court, London, and their directory gives an overview of all the major suppliers products.

YOUR COMPUTER SYSTEM

In choosing a system it must be the right package for your particular business. I have heard time and time again of companies who have lost thousands of pounds because they have an unsuitable system. I interviewed Mike Willstrop, the Managing Director of Beaver Corporation. This company specialises in installing sales ledger and credit control accounting systems. Such systems can be tailored to suit special needs.

He confirmed that there are two principal questions which should be considered first:

1. What is the right package?
2. How ready is the company, with their present manual or computerised system, to convert to a more efficient programme?

How to establish the best system is then discussed with the management. The accounting system that is chosen will depend on whether the company is a single organisation or has a multi-branch or parent and subsidiary network.

The next question that he considers is what type of management reports are required. Basically, the size of the business usually dictates these requirements. The number of orders and invoices processed per month and the size of the customer base and stock held, if any, are reviewed. This ensures that growth can be planned beyond the immediate future. With the constant number of complaints I hear about computer systems, I wondered if it was really worthwhile. I asked whether there was any saving in time or staff numbers. The answer was immediate. Companies who put in the right system get far better information and seem to succeed in developing their business at a greater rate than those who rely on antiquated systems. Usually there are staff savings, as once the system is in operation the original accounts staff have more time to carry out other work – such as chasing overdue accounts. Turning to the entire accounting system, the normal planning process is for the sales ledger, then the nominal and purchase ledger to be computerised. If stock is carried it tends to be incorporated in the second phase.

In Mr Willstrop's experience it is far better to commence operating a new system at the beginning of a financial year end. It is vital to liaise with the company's auditors when the initial discussions take place. The involvement of the auditors and the company accountant creates a smooth-running planned process. Mike Willstrop stressed that where a project leader in the company is chosen to take responsibility for the project, an even greater success rate may be achieved. Further information from Beaver Corporation Ltd, 21 Whitefriars Street, London EC4Y 8JJ (tel. 0171 936 2828).

Accounting Systems

Many computerised systems dictate the size of the fields and the information that is available to users. The information generated and the appearance of the reports cannot be altered once the system is installed.

One of the accounting systems that the Beaver Corporation works with is called *dBFLEX*. After reviewing many systems, *dBFLEX* is highlighted because it is totally flexible. Mike Willstrop explained that as they are issued with a *source* code they can alter an accounting programme very easily. This also means that management reporting systems can be tailored to precisely meet individual departmental requirements. The other major benefit for managers and section leaders is that they may not know what their final requirements are. As the business develops, systems can be introduced without altering all the software. In fact, there are no restraints whatsoever; only time and money are necessary to produce an accounting system which will develop according to the needs of an individual system.

I then visited Dataflow (UK) Ltd who introduced *dBASE* to the UK in 1982. Talking to Mr D. Moghtader, Managing Director, he confirmed that their system was not a complicated one.

The first version of the accounting package was written with the sole objective that if extra management information was required by the user it could be provided easily. A number of versions and upgrades have been designed. There are now 1000 sites using *dBFLEX* software. In response to the vast number of problems I am constantly hearing from harassed sales ledger staff, I asked the following questions:

- How does he make sure that businesses have enough account numbers?
- How do they deal with unallocated cash?
- What systems do they have for highlighting queries?
- How do they tackle journal entries?

The Account Number

Mr Moghtader recommended that a six character alpha-numerical account number is used, for example 'COS 369'. He explained that by using the first three initials, of a customer's name there was already a built-in control to reduce misquoting of account numbers. The 999 numerical code gave ample space to allocate numbers.

Unallocated Cash or Invoices

This does not cause any problem at all. If an item of cash could not be matched against an invoice it could still be posted to the correct customer account number. On the customer account enquiry menu a note which either explains why the cash cannot be matched or which gives credit or debit numbers can be keyed in. These narratives act as an immediate reminder to the sales ledger staff. Unallocated cash just cannot be forgotten. There is a permanent record through the *Unallocated Cash Reports* which notes the account number, date of payment, cash or invoice, the transaction number and value.

Under the *dBFLEX* system everything has to balance and no entry can get lost. Although the sales ledger is an open item system after the payments have been matched every entry gets transferred to a different file so that there is a history of all postings. When a journal entry has to be made there are 26 digits that can be used for the notation.

AN END USER

Being a little cynical about all sales managers, I then visited Mrs Joan Gifford, the accounts supervisor of Lucis Press Ltd. Lucis Press Ltd publishes the books of esoteric philosophy written by the late Alice Bailey. It is associated with Lucis Trust Ltd, an international educational charity dedicated to the establishment of right human relations. Mrs Gifford chose the *dBFLEX* accounting system after spending nearly a year examining other computer systems.

I first asked how she approached the planning in order to decide which system best suited their needs. Mrs Gifford is very methodical. She has to be, as there is a staff of only 10 full time members. She first showed me her long-term aims. The profile set out four objectives:

1. to increase the availability of books, but ensure that costs were covered;
2. to minimise the time and effort of accounting and the keeping of other statistics;

3. to have information available to assist in the marketing of books;
4. to have a cost-effective system for transportation, storage and pricing of books.

This profile was produced some 18 months before the system was installed. Mrs Gifford listed the major work that all the various departments carried out. A departmental work profile was then produced which highlighted the interaction of publishing, printing, stocking, re-ordering and reprinting. It should be noted that as the printing is carried out in New York, a considerable amount of pre-planning had to be done. There was discussion between departments and their statistical, marketing and accounting requirements were then submitted to their auditor for his consideration. This work took 12 months to complete. Turning to the general ledger accounts, the final profile listed eight principal accounting areas. These descriptions show exactly what was required from the accounting system.

During this period at least three other accounting systems were reviewed. I asked why *dBFLEX* was chosen. The answer was that it was simple to use. Dataflow UK Ltd supply a sample programme so that a prospective user can get to know the system before making a final decision to purchase. Lucis Press Ltd purchased a *dBFLEX* system in January 1988, basically because they felt that other systems were too rigid.

Although there are only about 300 live accounts which are divided into shop outlets and individual purchasers with about 100 stock items, the system must be able to identify the book title and location immediately. On reviewing the system I was struck by the exceptional clarity in the way it identifies the customer account and book title. Because the alpha-numerical index system can be adapted, a four letter alpha plus two numerical digits can be used for account numbers. If a major book store has many branches requiring separate accounts, the alpha code can be shortened so that 999 locations can be identified.

Aspects of the Sales Ledger

As the previous system was a manual system the ledger cards had just been colour tagged to indicate debit or credit balances. Before changing to a computerised system the entire customer balances were checked over a three-year period so that credit limits could be allocated. The credit limits are noted on the aged debtor analysis which also acts as a chasing spreadsheet, as the customer's telephone number is printed against the customer's name. The system has the facility to specify that statements are never printed automatically and very small balances and credit balances can be omitted. The statements are printed in a clear heavy type. The following information is included to give precise payment instructions and speedy allocation of cash:

- Company bank; name and address
- Sort code
- Account number
- Precise reference number for previous cash postings
- Large print invoice reference number
- Large print aged analysis.

In publishing and many other trades there are various price bands. In this system there were ten price bands and there could be any number of facilities for trade discount. Turning to the problem of unallocated cash, there were at least ten options to use when posting cash. I was delighted to see that there was space in the system to actually print reasons why cash had not been allocated.

In this short summary it is not possible to review every item on an accounting system, but I will highlight three final fields. The stock control system was clear and concise and everyone knew the stock position. The audit trail statistics really showed how a transaction progressed through the system. There were 15 different sales analysis reports which gave a complete picture of the marketing of their books.

For a system that cost just over £2500 in 1989 to purchase I believe that Mrs Joan Gifford's statement that 'the more I find out about this system the happier I am with it' is an indication of how well it works for a small company which does not employ specialist computer staff.

A COMPUTER SYSTEM ON OPEN ITEM

Here is a picture of a multinational company with a turnover of £300 million plus. As there was a need for confidentiality, I cannot name the company, but I hope that the following review shows how a system can be developed. The open item system was first introduced in 1968 and was updated in 1978, 1984 and 1988. Their own programming staff have designed the system after extensive discussions with the credit manager. The manager, with many years' experience, detailed his requirements so that every tool to assist assessment and collection techniques was available to his team.

The Sales Ledger

'Cash that comes in today is keyed in today.' This is a rule that cannot be broken. Suspense accounts for unallocated cash do not exist. As soon as the cheques are received, they are input by the cashiers direct to the credit of the sales ledger account, the balance of which is immediately updated. At the same time, this produces a record which acts as the paying in slip for banking the remittances. Once the sales ledger staff receive the remittance advices, they allocate the value of the payment in the computer system by matching each paid invoice. If there are any differences arising from short payments or customer debit notes they can allocate up to six codings to indicate, for instance, price query, technical problem, delivery dispute, etc. A cash payment selected for allocation must balance back to zero. The system will not allow the clerk to proceed if a difference remains outstanding. Debit notes issued by the customer are posted to the sales ledger account at the time of cash allocation, under the reference number of the debit note.

As an aid to matching cash to invoices, each invoice on the screen is given an alpha symbol, A to M. When matching cash the clerks need only to key in the letter to allocate the payment instead of punching long invoice digit numbers, which saves a considerable amount of time and greatly reduces the possibility of mistakes. In this particular business, there is a large volume of debit notes. To control this problem, printouts are produced to show each outstanding debit note and the length of time taken to clear each item. Individual queries are highlighted so that the exact reason for the deduction can be followed up.

Account History

On first appearances the account history screen looked like any other system. However, there were subtle differences in the presentation of management information which made the ongoing assessment and monitoring of major accounts into a highly sophisticated practice.

It should be remembered that the original computerised system was installed in 1968. Computer specialists have been appointed to develop the entire system to the highest possible standard. Scanning the history file, I noted that the individual ledger clerk responsible for the account was shown both on the screen and on the customer statement. The account status was divided up into a series of ten codes. For example, a code denoted that all orders should be referred to the department before shipment of goods. Another code, 'supervision', was inserted so that especially difficult accounts were constantly monitored.

Turning to basic accounting data, the following information was all available on the same screen:

- the last cash allocation number
- date of the last payment
- value of the last payment

- total balance outstanding
- total due

and, vitally important,

- total not yet due.

Management Information and Communication

The accounts are allocated and controlled by the credit controllers working through operating divisions. Information from the sales division and credit controllers is constantly being interchanged. The credit manager, by having down-to-earth, up-to-date and readable facts can make an immediate decision. These decisions are not only based on statistical information, but also on solid contact between customer, sales department and credit staff.

This company uses a sophisticated financial analysis system which compares the financial performance against the individual averages, and also predicts the likelihood of company failure within a limited time scale unless suitable action is taken by the directors of that company (see Chapter 8 for further details).

THE INVOICE

What is Its Purpose?

An invoice should show clearly precise details of a sale so that there is no possibility that the transaction can be queried for lack of information. The invoice should be attractively designed as it is an advertisement for the business. A poorly designed invoice will get lost in any company. For instance, by adding payment terms in heavier type the invoice becomes the first collection letter. By including a block which states:

'for any accounts or despatch queries please telephone or fax . . . or . . .',

this small detail can greatly reduce queries and speed up collections. If, in your company, it is more appropriate to contact the sales or order office, a system must be developed so that those queries are passed to the sales ledger department on a daily basis (see Clearing Queries, page 116).

Speed is of the essence in invoicing. Converting the sale into an invoice at the earliest possible moment should always be the objective. Quite often I hear of companies which bunch or batch invoices because it is considered to be 'convenient' by the sales or computer operations department. This method can seriously damage a company's cash flow. A meeting with the sales order, invoice and manual or computer departments to explain the results of delayed invoicing will normally produce an improvement in invoice flow. There is only one warning: personnel get used to carrying out a routine in the same way, so it is necessary to monitor invoice flow in the same way as cash flow.

There are further advantages in early despatch of an invoice. The customer cannot use the excuse that the invoice was late, and missed the cut-off date for the bought ledger to post onto the account. It also forestalls a further complaint that the delivery note, or copy of the delivery advice, has not arrived or been lost; because, due to late invoicing the proof of delivery has not been matched with the invoice. These are standard excuses which can be reduced by operating precise invoicing instructions.

Delivery Notes

When a delivery or despatch note has a different number from the invoice it is essential to have the number printed on the invoice. This procedure alone can cut down enormously the amount of time wasted in trying to trace a delivery or the supply of a service. In the sales ledger department, a further time saving device is to design a simple delivery note/invoice customer schedule which shows corresponding numbers. In some businesses the order set includes a delivery note, despatch note and invoice which have the same pre-printed number. If each sales document is printed in a different colour it becomes far easier for the customer and your sales ledger staff to trace a transaction.

In many companies' invoicing systems, the actual processing of the invoice is delayed until the latter part of the month. Sometimes it is due to the time taken in finalising the previous month end figures. If a start was made in just invoicing high value invoices first, the cash flow increase would be dramatic (see Chapter 8). I have often heard of problems in computerised systems when invoicing is not given priority. Many companies still post invoices by second class post. This may not be a saving, especially at the end of the month, as it gives the customer another golden excuse for further delaying their payment. Sales departments are always under intense pressure to achieve sales targets and therefore the late sales invoice will help them, but it can create extra problems when trying to convince the customer that the account is due for payment.

Debit Notes

Many companies, when they disagree with an invoice immediately issue the supplier with a debit note. This note is the difference in value between what they believe they received and the original invoice value. If, in your industry, this is standard practice you must have a debit note symbol in the body of the statement and a clear system of posting debit notes detailed in the administration manual. But, more importantly, there must be an organised system to clear debit notes. Without this there can be pure chaos, as not only do the customers' debit note numbers have to be cross-checked with the invoice number, but if a credit note is issued, all documents must be cross-referenced. Without this check the sales ledger staff will continuously have a monumental task (see Clearing Queries, below).

It should also be remembered that some companies make a habit of issuing debit notes. Unless the whole operation is very tightly controlled the entire sales ledger staff stop normal work and the cash flow slowly disappears! (See Reconciliation, page 127.)

Credit Notes

A credit note should be as well designed as an invoice. The problem for the sales ledger/credit control department is two-fold. Firstly, if there is little information on the credit note to show why it has been issued, or if the actual invoice and/or delivery number of the original transaction is not stated, then the sales ledger clerks will have a difficult or nearly impossible task in matching the credits to the invoices. There are still computer systems where this simple cross-reference has not been considered. One way to reduce this problem (if it exists) is to create a credit note record schedule which actually records reasons why a credit was issued. As in the invoice process, if a schedule of credit note numbers issued is listed against original invoice numbers, the reconciliation is far speedier. The other problem which arises when credit notes cannot be found or are not issued, is that customers will use this as an excuse for not paying their account (see Clearing Queries, below).

A graphic example of this technique occurred when I tried to collect a cheque for £11,500 from a company which was actually owed a credit note for £9. I tried to persuade them to deduct the £9 from their cheque but they would not do so. One person in my company thought that it was not important enough to issue small credit notes – but he never delayed in issuing credit notes again! The delayed cheque took 12 days to arrive and, as at that time the interest rate for borrowing was 11.75 per cent, the cost to us was over £44. Another way of looking at this is to consider that if the cheque for £11,500 had arrived on time, this sum could have been placed on a deposit account at 10.25 per cent. A profit of £38 could have been made, which was four times the amount of the delayed credit note!

CLEARING QUERIES

Queries are one of those unattractive jobs that few people like to tackle but if they are left the problem develops into a monster. It is impossible for there to be no queries in any business. If there are queries, it is vitally important that there is a defined system for clearing them. A query register is one way of controlling them. The sales ledger or credit control department must be able to identify which outstanding invoices are uncollectable because of queries.

In every company there are different types of queries. I list below a series of problems which will hit a sales ledger department with regularity.

1. Goods not delivered
2. Goods incomplete
3. Goods returned
4. Service not carried out correctly
5. The price is (a) incorrect, (b) no discount given, or (c) special offer, no reduced price
6. Duplicate invoice required
7. Copy invoice required
8. Proof of delivery
9. Goods unsatisfactory
10. Awaiting technician to install
11. Incorrect address.

The system of clearing queries should be described in the administration manual, but if you can design a query register to chase the progress of outstanding problems, not only will you know how much is uncollectable but you will be able to highlight which system is not working correctly.

Table 6.3 shows an example of a query register which can be adapted for a company's individual needs. Totalling the number or value of individual types of queries at the end of a week or month end is the first stage in reducing a non-profitable activity. Repeat business can be lost for ever if constant mistakes are made in servicing customer's orders.

THE ORGANISATION OF THE SALES LEDGER

Order Vetting

So far I have concentrated on the importance of the invoice and I have not yet mentioned the order vetting and monitoring of the accounts through the sales ledger. By using credit limits, it is quite possible to vet every order before an invoice is posted. The only problem for the credit controller is that cash, invoice and credit posting must be up to date so that an accurate decision can be made.

At this point I am going to stick my neck out by saying that if you have a manual system it may be easier to make a decision on whether to supply the

Table 6.3 Design for a query register

Query No.	Date	Customer	A/c No.	Value of invoice	Type of query	Action follow up

customer or consider what action should be taken. Notice that I do not recommend just placing a stop on an account. If the computer system is down, what written records are available to refer to? My recommendation is that it is far, far better to keep a refer list of customers with overdue accounts (see Table 6.4). This list should be constantly updated so that the order or sales office can advise the sales ledger or credit control clerks when a customer telephones or sends an order in.

Many credit controllers seem to delight in the fact that they have so many customers on stop. This, in my view, is suicidal as the object is to keep the account open by negotiation and liaison. Stopping an account may give your customer the opportunity to place their business with a competitor. As a result, a further sale is lost and the payment is still outstanding. Depending on company policy, there is a great difference between an account being overdue and putting a stop on the account, which is far more serious. When a decision has been made to put a stop on a customer a whole series of reviews should already have been considered (see Chapter 8, Collection Techniques). It is my belief that when a further order arrives from a customer whose payments are overdue, it is a wonderful opportunity to collect the balance before supplying more goods or services.

One simple technique is to telephone the purchasing manager to say that you would be delighted to supply, thanks for their order, but could he/she

Table 6.4 Overdue list for sales force

THE FOLLOWING ACCOUNTS ARE OVERDUE. Can you help us collect?

Account no.	Customer name and address	Amount	Month	Your comments please

help to speed your cheque. At this point I aim to liaise, communicate and keep the good will. A further method is to telephone the customer's bought ledger department confirming that you have received the order and, at the same time, confirm when the payment was sent, or will be sent. Before any of these techniques are used the customer record card or computer records should be studied (see Chapter 8).

When compiling a refer list of customers who have either just overreached their credit limit or their payment time limit, it is also worthwhile sending a list to the individual salesmen and women. You can design the list so that your sales force can return the second copy with their comments. This system engenders good will, as the representative knows how much is outstanding. If a further order is held, the sales force could lose commission or bonuses in that month, therefore it is in their interest to assist the accounts and sales department to help to collect a cheque. I do not believe that the salesforce should be employed as permanent collectors, but quite often working as a partnership means that the cheque will arrive and a further order is released.

These are some actual comments that I have received from sales personnel by using this system.

1. 'Don't put a stop on them, the previous order has been returned.'
2. 'I am going in there next week and I will collect the cheque.'
3. 'The customer is a pain in the neck – do what you like!'
4. 'Whatever you do, do not stop that order. It took me six months to open the account and we are trying to get the business from our competitor . . . Ltd.'

Comment (4) is the most difficult one to deal with, as, firstly, the character of the representative must be studied to see whether the comment is 'hot air' or fact – in other words, do I have confidence in the salesman? Secondly, being cynical, it is possible that this customer wishes to buy from us because their previous supplier – our competitor – refuses to deal with them because of non-payment of the account.

Stopped Accounts

When you have done everything possible to collect and the payment has still not arrived, a decision to stop the account must be taken. The sales office, the order vetting clerks, despatch, transport and the salesforce must be advised to stop any additional orders being processed. Every door must be closed, including the despatch of sample orders! The stop list should be printed in a different colour and again the sales force should be given the opportunity to assist in trying to keep the account open, rather than close it (see Britvic interview, page 19).

Communication

One of the reasons why the sales ledger department can sometimes get a bad name is that they forget to advise all the operating departments when an account has been paid. The order department and the salesforce should be the first to be told. Even if personnel are miles apart they must be advised. It is common courtesy to let them know, especially if they have helped you to keep a customer and not lose one. By using the telephone and fax, sales and marketing personnel can be speedily advised that the account is open again. The only time that a different approach may be required is when it is known from the record card that their previous cheque has been dishonoured. This is a device that unscrupulous customers sometimes use to gain supplies when they are desperate (see Cash Sheets, page 125).

FILING

Whether your business uses a computerised or manual system of accounting, it is essential that the printout or second copies of all these documents are filed neatly in good quality files. These, as the old Sale of Goods Act states, should be 'fit for the purpose'. It is not cost effective to use lever arch files where the pins are disjointed so that these most valuable records are torn or lost. The correct computer files for storing records must be used. Admittedly, these types of stationery are expensive, but it is far cheaper in the long run to invest in quality filing than to write off invoices due to lack of proof that goods or services have been supplied. Nowadays computer records must be properly backed up and secure.

New Methods

Microfiching of documents is now becoming obsolete and imaging or DIP (document imaging systems) are replacing microfiches, because software and hard disk space is far cheaper.

Storing

It saddens me to hear of companies who write off large sums because their past records have been badly stored. Either the records cannot be found, or labelling is so poor that nothing can easily be identified. The VAT authorities require that all records be kept for six years. It is sometimes necessary to trace an entire transaction or analyse previous years' customer accounts. A well-ordered and planned area which is dry, warm and well-lit for storing accounting records is a real investment.

STATEMENTS AND THEIR DESIGN

A statement of account, like the invoice, must be well designed and attractive to look at, so that its impact on the customer is immediate. These are your objectives in the design and construction of a statement:

1. it should be a record of all uncleared or unpaid transactions;
2. it should be designed in a clear and concise way so that your customer can, without difficulty, check their bought ledger transactions, your invoice, and make a speedy payment;
3. the design should incorporate a marking off system so that when the payment is received the sales ledger clerks have far less work in matching the remittance to the invoice, etc.;
4. it should act as a first class reminder letter.

The Design

Many statements of account produced by computer do not look attractive. They are poorly designed so they do not receive attention. There is no customer contact. The way to overcome this drabness is to print the statement in more than one colour and plan with the printer and computer personnel all the features that are to be included. Management may say that it is too expensive to print in more than one colour, but remember that the statement is a reminder to your customer to pay. It is, in fact, the second reminder, as the invoice acts as the first notice.

The proof of an attractive statement is that within five days of despatch the cheques start to flow in. If you can achieve this response, enormous savings in time and staff resources are made. There is no need to chase for payment by telephone, and you do not have to send any reminder letters.

A Checklist for Features

- Is the customer's account number clear and distinct? Many computerised account systems use poorly designed numerals which can be difficult to identify.
- Are your company's name and address, telephone number and fax numbers clearly printed? If the accounting address where cheques are received is different, is there a large printed box to show the address clearly?
- If your accounting system is geared to paying by traders' credits are your banker's name, address, sort code and account number clearly shown?
- Are your payment terms printed on the statement in bold print?
- Is there room for a monthly analysis? Depending on the trade it may be better not to use the words 'overdue account analysis', as perhaps the customer may consider that the credit granter accepts delayed payments.
- Are the accounting details clear enough to be easily read, and is there sufficient space for marking off items? Even with computerised systems, statements do have to be reconciled.
- Can you design the statement so that the following notice appears?
  To ensure that your payment is credited correctly, please enclose the detachable slip with your remittance indicating which items you are paying.
- Most businesses get queries from customers. To save time, can you print the name and telephone extension numbers of a contact who is able to answer queries?
- The whole essence of the system is to make it easy for the supplier and customer to communicate. You may remember that this query liaison point can also be printed on the delivery note and invoice. In some companies it is necessary to highlight an account query point as the order, despatch and accounts offices can be many miles apart.
- Are you starring any invoice which is on query? This simple device can save much embarrassment.
- If you export:
  - Do you have sufficient space for a larger customer name and address section? This can be a problem for the programmers if the system is only designed for 21 digits per line!
  - Is there space for the: documentary credit number
    Bill of Exchange number
    acceptance payment date?
  - Do you have a separate ledger for overseas accounts? With monetary union on the horizon will you have a facility for dual calculations?
  - Are the statement details printed in the overseas country's language?
- Is there room to place a sticker which states 'overdue'? Does the statement actually show that the account is overdue and is the balance now due clearly highlighted?

- To assist reconciliation from the customers' and suppliers' accounts sections, are the previous month's transactions marked to show how the payments have been reconciled to the invoices and credit notes? Depending on the accounting system, this suggestion can save both parties hours of work, especially when there are different cut-off dates for invoice and cheque posting.
- Does the statement show the last date when payments, invoices and credit notes are posted to the account?
- If your business has many 'one-off' transactions, have you considered combining the statement with the invoice? This can save a vast amount of paperwork.
- If your company offers discounts for prompt payment, are the terms printed on the statement? Quite often your customer's bought ledger section may not have been advised; therefore the discount notice acts as a reminder.
- If your payment terms are the 20th of the month following the month in which goods are delivered, can you despatch the statements well before the end of the month?
- Is the VAT payable clearly itemised? Does the statement also show the VAT rate or zero rated items? Is your VAT registration number printed on the statement? This is a requirement when selling to the EC.

STATEMENT PROCESSING – THE MONTH END

Whether the system is manual or computerised, no statements can be produced until all the invoices, credit notes and remittances have been posted. This sounds simplistic, but if a business is trying to hit a sales target there will be a tendency to put through every possible invoice on the last day of the month. Meanwhile, the sales ledger staff are desperately trying to agree all the month-end totals for sales ledger control accounts.

Earlier in this chapter, I mentioned that delays in invoice batching obviously delay statement processing. My reason for highlighting this point again, is that unless there is continuous document control throughout the working month, bottlenecks will occur. One way to overcome the problem is to have a set time each day or week for batching cash, invoices and credit notes. This is not difficult to carry out provided that there is a set procedure for invoice vetting, cash listing and allocation and reconciliation.

RECEIVING PAYMENT – THE DAILY ROUTINE

Envelopes containing cheques, cash, trader's credits and other payments should be opened by a responsible, trained person who can check that there is a remittance advice and/or customer name. The remittance amount should be circled so that there is a corresponding check that the total cash received equals the remittance advice which will be posted to the sales ledger. Depending on the size of the business, the remittances can be sorted in product line or in segments of the A to Z ledger, (see page 127, Reconciliation). The listing of cash must be a daily operation to safeguard against any possibility of cheques getting lost or mislaid.

Examination of Cheques

When the cheques are first received – that is before the listing – they should be checked to make sure that:

1. the words and figures agree
2. they are dated
3. they have been signed.

It is sometimes possible that a bank will accept a discrepancy on a cheque provided that the customer agrees to the alteration of the cheque. But the main purpose of the examination is to stop the cheque being returned by the bank which in turn creates many extra debit and credit entries. In many accounting systems it is still difficult to identify a returned cheque. Regrettably, if a customer has severe financial problems, they may try to send a cheque which has not been signed or has such a small discrepancy that it is difficult to spot. This ploy can give the customer at least another two weeks' credit.

Another safeguard, when a new credit account customer pays their first month's account, is to keep a copy of the cheque and then place it in the customer's history file. This acts as a useful reference point if a future banker's opinion is required. It can also happen that a company changes their bankers, and the new banking details are often the first indication of financial or management changes that have occurred.

Dishonoured Cheques

When a cheque is dishonoured, the bank's actual wording on the cheque will give a further clue as to whether the cheque will eventually be cleared or totally dishonoured. An endorsement can be the first indication of the insolvency of the business. If the bank holds a charge on the assets of the limited company or individual, it already puts the customer with the dishonoured cheque in a weaker position. The creditor may then have to take speedy action to protect their interest. Bankers, having the immediate access for totally monitoring their client's account, have an enormous advantage when deciding whether to appoint a receiver.

You may think that the writer is the most suspicious person you have ever come across, but even the endorsement 'words and figures disagree' can be a ploy to gain at least seven days' extra time to pay. At the same time, the drawer of the cheque may try to order further goods or services by saying to you, the supplier, 'There is a cheque in the post.'

Once any cheque is returned dishonoured, I find that the best policy is to telephone the company secretary, director, chief accountant or proprietor and say 'If I re-present this cheque marked "Refer to Drawer", will you honour it?' In my experience, although the drawer of the cheque may try and say that it is the bank's fault, the business or individual who has drawn the cheque has the responsibility to see that there are adequate funds to clear any cheques drawn. If the signature on the cheque is legible, a telephone call to the person who signed the cheque can also be made. In commencing the conversation I have always mentioned that he or she has drawn a cheque which has not been honoured. Do allow plenty of time for the person at the other end of the telephone line to consider and answer the question of the endorsement. This is a situation where the best policy is to listen first. Do not get angry or lose your temper (see Chapter 8, Telephone Collection Techniques).

CASH SHEETS

You may have heard of a paperless office, but if there is one essential piece of paper it is the cash listing sheet. These sheets should be numbered and a separate register must be kept for security purposes. We do not live in an ideal world, and it is therefore always possible that due to postal or communication delays, power failures or computer faults, a payment has to be traced.

I have already mentioned the importance of identifying the account number. The cash sheet need only show the date, customer account number and name, and the amount (see Table 6.5).

Where there is to be more than one banking, the time the sheet was issued can be crucial in tracing an item.

Table 6.5 Cash sheet

Serial number	Total brought forward	Date Time
Account number	Customer name	Amount £
	Total carried forward, sub-total	

Because the initial sorting and identification of cheques is so vital, the following routines will help to reduce the problem of delay in the presentation of the payment into the bank, and the subsequent matching in the sales ledger.

UNIDENTIFIED PAYMENT

It is remarkable that a cheque can arrive without any remittance advice, tear-off statement or account number. For this reason, a rule should be made that a responsible person should supervise the opening of the cheques. The payments should be identified and coded as early as possible. Where a cheque arrives without identification, the envelope should be kept.

I have found that companies with large accounts sections often have a separate cashier department which first receives the cheques. These cashiers sometimes do not seem to realise how important it is for the sales ledger/ credit control staff to be advised of the payment the moment it arrives. Again, if this is the situation, it is vitally important to gain a good working relationship with the cashiers. Why not invite them to see how the credit control sales ledger system operates in the morning? It is also essential to visit their department as the interchange will normally give rise to a better operating system. Whatever system is used to list cheques and other remittances, there are two overriding tasks:

- to identify the customer and the account number
- to pay the cheques into the bank at the earliest opportunity.

The account identification can be achieved by using an up-to-date computer or manual index. If there are problems, it is normally possible to find a name by using the complete set of UK telephone directories and the *Yellow Pages*. If this proves impossible, then the following routine should be considered.

An Unidentifiable Cheque

It is possible that after an intensive search, the customer cannot be identified. All the available directories have been searched. If this problem occurs, I would photostat one copy of the cheque, enter the cheque in the suspense account and pay the cheque in on a separate paying-in slip. It is not a good policy simply to place the cheque in a drawer hoping that something will happen. The use of the cash suspense account should be kept to a minimum and the entries should be reviewed regularly to clear the outstanding items. My reason for keeping a photostat is that in the event that a sale cannot be matched to the cheque, a further photostat of the cheque with a covering letter can be sent to the manager of the bank requesting that he pass the letter to the drawer of the cheque.

If the sum is exceptionally large and the cheque is drawn on a limited company then a search at Companies House will at least identify the last known registered office.

Some readers may subscribe to the Dun & Bradstreet register on CD Rom. If they refer to this reference volume there is a list of companies in alphabetical order which is cross-referenced to five individual areas of the UK. *Who Owns Whom* is a further publication which lists parent and associate companies, and vice versa. Other advantages of this reference volume is that under the pink section there is the gazetteer which lists 20,000 place names. The blue section lists all bank sorting codes, which is useful when a trader's credit slip has to be identified. The yellow section lists all the authorised deposit taking institutions. I have used this in the past to gauge the strength of a bank that was not known to me.

RECONCILIATION

The reconciliation of the sales ledger accounts is a highly skilled job. Whether the system is computerised or manual no-one should be thrown into the task and just told to get on with it. Training must be given and a routine for posting should be set out in the accounts administration manual. I will refer to the various systems that can be used to help staff under Training in Chapter 7.

The one basic point I will make on reconciliation, is that personnel either enjoy it or dread it. I have found that women are often far more thorough and accurate than men when reconciling. If the work is carried out in a slipshod way it does not take many months for any ledger to become a complete jungle. Businesses who let this happen then have to spend considerable time and money in reallocating invoices and cash. Regrettably, the write-off can sometimes be enormous if care is not taken when planning a system.

DEPOSITING SURPLUS CASH

You may wonder why I am so anxious that all receipts should be paid into the bank at the earliest possible moment. Any cleared funds can be deposited through the overnight money market – minimum value £50,000. The minimum value quoted by NatWest Bank and the Midland Bank's Treasury Department was £250,000. As an example the Midland Bank quoted 6.5% for seven-day deposits for sterling in August 1997. There are other rates for different currencies and they also confirmed that for sums from £10,000 they could quote rates depending on the length of time and the sum deposited.

WORKING CONDITIONS

Before turning to the actual reconciliation of the sales ledger accounts there are two aspects of the job which are often forgotten. The first basic practical point is whether the physical conditions in the office are right for the task. The second point is whether the sales ledger person, group or team have had the right training. Do they also have the right personality, approach and attitude to carry out a demanding operation? Training is discussed in far more detail in Chapter 7.

The physical conditions in an office, if they are good, will create a happy working relationship. Staff absenteeism through sickness will drop and the personnel will not dread coming in to the accounts office each day. Here are a few questions that you may have to consider in your sales ledger credit control office planning:

1. Are the chairs adjustable and are they comfortable? Does the department have enough chairs for their staff?
2. Are the desks large enough to deal with the paperwork?
3. Is the lighting suitable, or does the fluorescent light reflect against the computer screens?
4. Is there enough space for the essential working papers and records so that they are to hand?
5. Is the heating adequate? I have had to work in offices where there were severe draughts, broken windows, or such intense heat that it made concentration difficult.
6. Is it too noisy? Where there is a considerable amount of machine noise there are types of screens that can partly reduce this hazard. Other types of screens can successfully reduce the amount of noise which is carried from a different section. These are particularly useful if used with fabric floor tiles, especially if people are using the office as a short cut!
7. Are the refer and stop lists easily within reach and can they be accessed by computer? Are there enough telephones – external and internal – and fax machines to deal with queries? Are there enough calculators?

The first six questions relate to comfort. The seventh question is concerned purely with making the operation easy to carry out. (For example, if the cash listing is carried out by the sales ledger staff and not the cashiers are the customers indices readily to hand?)

These all seem simple matters, but if the staff constantly have to 'make do' it will create extra problems. If the staff are constantly interrupted because of the lack of space or equipment, or the noise level is too high, then mistakes will appear, the atmosphere gets more tense and working relationships decline. Staff may then leave and this is an enormous loss to any business.

SUMMARY

The sales ledger can represent 30–40 per cent of the current assets of a business. It is vital that there is a comprehensive system for passing orders, raising invoices, chasing payments and reconciling receipts to invoices.

- Can you find an invoice and reconcile it to an incoming payment?
- Have you enough account numbers?
- Have you an accounting system, computerised or manual, which is just right for your business?
- Do you know why you are getting so many queries and can you reduce the problem?
- Can you improve the design of your invoices and statements?
- Could you find a remittance if it was allocated some months earlier?

7
Training for Credit Management

A credit person has to combine many skills to be able to tackle numerous complex situations. Credit control staff firstly have to have the ability to communicate with everyone. They must like people! But this is not enough, a knowledge of marketing and product policy, accounting, company law, economics, general principles of UK business law, plus mercantile law for exporters and importers is also necessary. It is a long list, but help is available (see Training).

BASIC SKILLS AND PERSONALITIES

I mentioned earlier that often sales ledger staff never chose to join that section, they were just told to report there. This is not the most helpful and effective way of choosing the right staff for the right job. It has been estimated that a large proportion of the country's workforce may be in jobs that do not suit their personalities. In the sales ledger/credit control field it is critical to choose the person with the right personality to do a certain type of work. Where the business is small, the accounts person might have to carry out every task including credit control. But here there is a difficulty. For example, the character of the person who posts cash and reconciles accounts should be meticulous and thorough. However, the person who is required to put all the reference material together for assessing a new account must not just be thorough but also have imagination and operate as a detective, accountant and salesperson.

Turning to the collection side of the work, the initial ability to communicate plus nearly every skill that I have previously mentioned are required to protect that investment. When collecting, the person also has to ascertain whether the customer should be helped. Company trading and marketing policy knowledge will then be required to decide on the best course of action.

It is impossible to make all these decisions without training. I have seen personnel shake with fear on being asked to carry out tasks where no training whatsoever has been given. This, in my opinion, must never happen. It takes time to understand the complete cycle from initial assessment and sales ledger procedures, to collection techniques. Both internal and external training will enable credit personnel to really enjoy their work.

TRAINING

Help is at hand. Do not be put off by my list of skills required. The best direct training that can be gained is by joining the Institute of Credit Management. This institute was formed in 1939 and it now has over 8500 members. They also run their own examination system. Over 45 colleges run courses in credit management in the UK alone. The present syllabus covers Credit Management 1, Business Law, Business Environment, and Accounting and Finance. In the final stages there are more advanced studies in 'Credit Management', Law of Credit Management, Legal Proceedings and Insolvency, Applied Accountancy, and Principles of Management and in part 3 there are case studies on Trade, Consumer and Export Credit.

A distance learning scheme for people who live too far away from colleges is available (see below). A correspondence course for part 1 of the examination is run by the Rapid Results College. They also run part 2 in Applied Accounts and Principles of Management.

The Distance Learning Scheme

This scheme is designed to provide a framework in the same way as if the student were attending one tuition session a week at a college. Each set of lecture notes uses only two or three text books which are constantly referred to in the notes. In 'Credit Management 1', for instance, the course has been prepared with the assumption that the student has never worked in a credit department before. Theory and practice are intertwined in the notes, as they are written by practising professional credit managers with years of experience.

The Preliminary Certificate

The Preliminary Certificate in Credit Management was first introduced in 1991 and was designed to provide employees with a sound knowledge of the basic skills of credit management. It is a one-year course and it involves attending a college for one evening a week.

Institute of Credit Management Examinations

Examinations are held in May and November in many centres in the UK and overseas. Students with four GCSE passes at grades A, B or C including Mathematics and English Language, can join. There are other qualifications which are recognised as equivalent, including a BTEC First Award and SCOTVEC Stage I. If a student has reached the age of 21 and has suitable employment experience but does not possess the educational qualifications, they may be allowed to register as a student.

If readers are considering these courses of examinations it is worthwhile remembering that BTEC and SCOTVEC higher level passes, and other examination passes with other professional bodies, may enable the Institute, at their discretion, to grant exemptions. As general standards are being raised year by year, it is becoming far more difficult for even mature people to be admitted by direct entry. The Education Committee is at present developing an NBQ/SVQ in Credit Management.

Where credit staff wish to be associated with the Institute but they do not have sufficient time to study, there is a new grade of Affiliateship. This is particularly useful for older people who may be starting a new career and wish to be kept informed of developments in the credit field. All grades of members receive the monthly journal, *Credit Management*. In my opinion it is the best publication in its field and is far superior in quality and content to the many other professional credit magazines. The only comparable one is *Business Credit* (see below for other professional credit associations).

Seminar Training

The Institution of Credit Management organises well over 50 seminars a year. Here are just a few examples of the range of titles and the subjects presented:

The Fundamentals of Credit Control. The development of the credit control clerk – The link between sales and credit – Assessing the risk – Letter writing skills.

Credit Control Workshop. A two-day course. The role of the credit department – The art of communication and a role-playing exercise – Telephone collection technique – Letter writing skills – Risk assessment – The balance sheet – Time management – Credit control and sales ledger.

Negotiation. The process of negotiating – Preparation and planning – Conduct of negotiation – Tactics for success.

Export documentation. An introduction to exporting – Documents of finance and payment terms – Shipping and other documentation.

The Branch Network

A further way of increasing professional skills and at the same time make contact with other specialists, is to join one of the 27 branches in the UK. Being a credit controller or manager often means that a decision may have to be made in isolation. Having a group of professionals who are quite willing to discuss problems and give informal advice is a unique source of help. Newcomers to the credit field need this extra support. From my commercial and industrial credit-granting experience I have found that certain unusual situations appear from time to time. The credit manager who has been around for, say, 25 years has often experienced those situations before.

Special Interest Groups

The Institute also runs the following Special Interest Groups:

● Building and allied trade group
● Petroleum group
● Secured lending group.

Future Developments

The Institute of Credit Management's Council agreed in March 1997 to introduce a Voluntary Continuing Professional Development programme for members. Because of technical and legislative changes, new techniques and economic and competitive pressures, it was considered that this CPD scheme was essential to update members knowledge and skills for the future.

Appointment Bureaux

Another advantage of joining the Institute is that they can advise employers on the specialists who are available in the entire credit field. Members are also helped to obtain superior positions so that their careers can progress far more rapidly. Credit assessment and collection work is a specialist area. Regrettably, the general high street staff bureaux often do not really understand the depth of work required. I therefore interviewed an official of the Institute's staff bureau to gain a picture of staff selection from the employer's and employee's side.

Many companies do not call a vacancy by its correct job title. This can create problems for the candidate unless the company who require staff provide a very full job description before an interview. A problem in many companies is that the position of credit controller actually entails the responsibilities of a credit manager. In the same way, the sales ledger supervisor's job in some businesses may be considered to be a credit controller's position.

I asked the reasons why credit staff seemed to want to move frequently. Often career advancement appears to be the answer. Sometimes promotion is blocked, and after five or six years in one position it is usually not possible to develop or make any further improvements in the systems. Relocation, redundancies and takeover bids often force credit staff to move. With the increasing use of information technology, less staff are required where new computer systems are installed. However, an increasing number of smaller companies are beginning to understand the significance of employing professionally-trained credit staff. This is particularly evident in the electronics field.

What are the initial questions an applicant will typically ask about a prospective company? It may seem simplistic, but the usual concerns are: the size of the company; how much is known about them; the number of live accounts; how many staff the candidate would be responsible for; salary; benefits and company car.

The age of the candidate is less critical than the all-important experience factor. Sometimes, where a company is looking for someone in their own field they are not so concerned whether a person has completed all the examinations. What really counts is their knowledge of the other competitors in their particular trade.

From the middle of 1995 there has been increasing evidence that the employment market has improved. Companies are asking for higher academic standards and often require evidence of ICM examination passes. Salary scales are gradually rising and where specialist knowledge, such as credit analysis or sector specialisation is required, salaries can be far higher.

Further information from The Institute of Credit Management, The Water Mill, Station Road, South Luffenham, Oakham, Leicestershire LE15 8NB (tel: 01780 721888).

The Chair in Credit Management

The Institute of Credit Management, in conjunction with a number of major company sponsors, had in 1993 established the world's first Chair of Credit at the University of Bradford's Management Centre.

Professor Nick Wilson was appointed to the Chair and immediately started to include credit management in their existing BSc in Business & Management degree. The Credit Management Research Group initiate a research programme into aspects of trade and consumer credit and the impact of development on information management and IT.

The research into credit and debt levels and ways of improving credit operations and bench marking are ongoing. The list of papers and publications and research activities is already too long to list here but is available from Bradford University. In late 1997 the Credit Management Research Group will publish the first totally independent quarterly *Credit Survey*.

The Annual Credit Management Forum in November gives delegates an insight into current and future credit management developments.

Further information from Professor Nick Wilson, The University of Bradford Management Centre, Emm Lane, Bradford BD9 4JL (tel: 01274 733466).

Training by Commercial Organisations

Dun & Bradstreet Ltd present a number of credit courses which cover assessment and collection techniques. They are currently running a series of four different one day seminars. There are also two-day courses in advanced credit management.

Further information from Dun & Bradstreet Ltd, Holmers Farm Way, Booker, High Wycombe, Bucks, HP12 4UL (tel: 01494 422000).

FEDERATION OF EUROPEAN CREDIT MANAGEMENT ASSOCIATIONS

The Institute of Credit Management is a founder member of the Federation of European Credit Management Associations. The following organisations belong to this body of professional credit managers:

Belgium	Association Belge de Credit
Denmark	Dansk Kreditchef Forening
Finland	Luottomiehet Kreditmannen ry
France	Association Francaise des Credit Managers
Ireland	Irish Institute of Credit Management
Israel	Israeli Institute of Credit Management
Italy	Associazione Credit Managers Italia
Netherlands	Nederlandse Vereniging voor Credit Management
Norway	Norsk Kredittforum
Spain	Association de Gerentes de Credito
Sweden	Svenska Kreditmannaforeningen

Contact is maintained with many individual credit managers in other European countries. Many UK credit managers are beginning to use this contact group especially when their companies expand or open branches in Europe.

Further information from The Institute of Credit Management (tel: 01780 721888).

FCIB – NACM

The National Association of Credit Management in the USA was formed in 1896. The Association has a membership of about 30,000. There are many affiliate branches which are members of the central body. The FCIB (Finance Credit and International Business) is their international arm operating in the USA and Europe. The value of joining this group is that some 120 to 150 credit managers from all over the world meet in different European cities three times a year and are also in contact with each other throughout the year.

NACM's monthly magazine *Business Credit* publishes many articles which highlight credit development in the USA, including research and current practices. Further information on fax 00 1 410 740 5574.

THE ADMINISTRATION MANUAL

The purpose of an administration manual is to serve as a working guide for staff, to help them follow the correct procedures. It can also assist new employees to understand the routine of their department. In all businesses routines can change, therefore the manual must be kept updated. If a loose-leaf system is adopted, immediate changes can be made.

Introduction

Depending on your type of business, an organisational chart showing the departmental structure, branches and the names of managers and their assistants will help the sales ledger/credit control staff to communicate. A list of all departments, names of staff with job titles and telephone extension numbers may seem a long and complicated task, but this list will greatly assist a new member of staff to understand your business.

Description of Operations

The procedure for carrying out every facet of the business can be included. For credit staff, the key areas will be firstly, how an account number is raised and authorised and secondly, how the invoice is posted. Examples of all the operating documents should be included. The routine between the sales order desk, despatch and sales ledger can be illustrated by using a flow chart.

Payment terms can be listed, and a copy of the company's conditions included for reference. Where different terms may be demanded, the name of the manager who is authorised to agree to a variation should be given.

If credit limits are used, the method of inputting onto the sales ledger records should be explained. Where a computerised system is used it may be appropriate to re-translate from the computer manual, so that one particular operation can be understood in its entirety. For example, where a credit limit is to be increased or reduced, the complete codes to input, the persons authorised to change limits and the documents required to carry out the procedure can be described and illustrated.

Posting Cash

No two businesses ever carry out this routine in the same way. Showing how the payments should be checked and account numbers coded when received, is especially useful when the usual staff are absent due to sickness or holidays. The actual reconciliation process can include an audit trail which basically shows how to find records. Copies of customer indices and serial numbers to show where an invoice was raised can be included.

Credit Notes

Whether a credit note request authorisation has to be issued or separately sanctioned by more than one person or department should be clearly stated. Quite often personnel are allowed to issue credit notes up to a certain level. If these levels are noted, it is far easier for the credit and sales staff to clear the queries. The entire routine of issuing a credit note will help create customer good will.

Stop, Refer, or Legal List

To stop the excuse 'I did not know they were on stop', the forms or routine used to place an account on hold should be displayed. Where necessary, the salesforce and/or regional offices, should be allocated code numbers and these should be available for immediate reference to advise that an account is on or off the stop or legal list.

Journal Entries

It is often a problem in accounts departments that when entries are being adjusted it is uncertain what the correct account number is. Frequently used accounts such as: discount allowed, loss or profit on rates of exchange, or damaged stock can be listed. The method of carrying out these entries, including a sample which shows the corresponding debit and credit entry, can assist the ledger staff in understanding the double entry book-keeping method.

Month End Balancing

The routine for balancing weekly or monthly posting of invoices, credit notes and cash, with deadlines for each task, will create a disciplined approach to operating the entire sales ledger. The manual may need to show priority tasks and, where a computer is used, a priority time for inputting data.

Future Planning

No manual can be written on tablets of stone. Accounting procedures in a fast-moving commercial world need to be constantly reviewed. The administration manual is a training aid, not a museum piece gathering dust (see below, Improving the System).

IMPROVING THE SYSTEM

With the constant pressure for greater profitability, the sales ledger/credit control section can increase a company's profits in several ways. It does not necessarily need to be a computer-generated miracle. More often quiet thought and careful monitoring of the department will contribute to improving a system.

Questions that could be considered:

- Can the invoices be sent out any earlier?
- Are there too many queries in proportion to the number of invoices issued?
- Are there too many accounts out for collection?
- Is there enough assessment?
- Are the accounts reviewed regularly?
- Can the cash flow be improved?

- Why are there so many unreconciled accounts, etc.?
- Which customers are in arrears?
- How is the time divided between assessment, reconciliation and collections?

This list could go on for ever, but the following schemes may help to improve the general efficiency of the section.

The result of a survey in which customers are divided into categories of arrears by account balance, type of customer and age of debt, will enable the credit controllers to re-plan their system. Once a survey of the sales ledger has been carried out, the reassessment, collection and follow-up procedures can be adjusted.

Under the Pareto principle, 20 per cent of the customers account for 80 per cent of the turnover, therefore it is possible, by applying this theory, to high-light not only cash flow but other operating problems. In the following example, 2042 accounts were reviewed to see why there was a reduction of cash flow. When a survey was carried out, the following picture began to emerge:

Number of accounts on ledger	Outstanding balance
2042	£2,908,866
387 accounts out for collection	= 18.95 per cent of ledger
1190 accounts had no queries	= 58.27 per cent of ledger
465 accounts had queries	= 22.78 per cent of ledger
2042 Total	100 per cent

Examination of these figures prompts various questions. Why are so many accounts in query and out for collection? Is there something fundamentally wrong with the system? If there are so many queries – why? Is enough time and cost spent on assessing customers? An enquiry and audit trail into queries could show where the real problem lay. For example, were documents being mis-posted or was it due to a delay in issuing credit notes?

Turning to cash flow, from those 1190 accounts clear of queries, how is the age analysis of debt broken down?

Account number		Amount owed	Percentage value
1190		£1,127,000	
480	3 months overdue	422,176	= 37
322	2 months overdue	302,125	= 27
88	1 month overdue	122,066	= 11
300	Paid to terms	280,633	25
1190		1,127,000	100

When the ledger was examined more closely it was discovered that there were unallocated cash balances of £220,000. These credit items related to hundreds of known and unknown debtors.

The first priority, in this example, is to reconcile the accounts and examine why the system has broken down. By just reviewing the age analysis a totally false picture was produced, as the unallocated cash was not included in the total of £1,127,000. If the accounts were correctly posted, many of the 465 queried balances and some of the collection accounts may not have been necessary.

Are the Collections Improving?

The Days Sales Outstanding (DSO) calculation in its many forms is a way of measuring the success or failure of the collection routine. Here is an example based on routine calendar days – not company sales periods (not a four- or five-week month).

Sales Ledger Balance at 31 March: £307,000

Sales in		
March:	155,000	
February:	114,000	
January:	151,000	

To calculate the DSO figure:

		Days
total debtors	307,000	
deduct March	155,000	31
	152,000	
deduct February	114,000	28
	38,000	
deduct January	38,000	7.8
	DSO = 66.8	

January sales are:

£151,000 ÷ 30 days

= £4,871

therefore

$$\frac{38,000}{4,871} = 7.8 \text{ days}$$

By plotting the DSO figure month by month, it is possible to prove that changes in collection procedures have had an adverse or positive effect.

Who is Succeeding?

In every sales ledger section there are different methods of carrying out the same basic tasks. Some companies prefer specialisation so that one individual is responsible for reconcilation, while another person approaches a group of customers for payment. Another method is for a senior and a more junior person to work together, the senior credit clerk tackling the difficult accounts. Whatever the system is used, records can be kept which will indicate where there may be a problem. If reconciliation is slowing down or payments are sluggish, it could be that one or more of the team has too much work. The reallocation of accounts may be necessary.

In Table 7.1 there are four credit clerks who reconcile and collect.

Table 7.1 Reconciliation and collection

Clerk	No. of live accounts	Number collected by month end	Percentage collected
A	403	391	97
B	92	86	93
C	109	77	70
D	590	499	84.5
	1194	1053	

Table 7.2 Time and resource survey

Activity	Hours spent
Coding	—
Posting	—
Reconciliation	—
Queries	—
Chasing *via* fax	—
Chasing *via* telephone	—
Chasing *via* letters	—
Meetings	—
Visits, etc.	—
Total per week/month	—

Clerk C has to deal with local authority accounts. The percentage on collections gives an indication that although there are only 77 accounts for C to supervise, help may be required.

The problem for many businesses is that the same accounting routine is carried out each month. If a time and resource survey is carried out (Table 7.2), planning a reorganisation can be a real success.

My only proviso in considering a new system is that the credit staff and other members of the company should have time to consider and discuss the plan before it is implemented.

SUMMARY

Credit control has often been considered a 'back room' task that anyone could carry out. If a large business needs professional training and a carefully planned administrative manual, how much more important is it for a small business where every order is essential for its survival?

- Have you sufficiently experienced staff to run your sales ledger?
- Has a member of your staff considered contacting the Institute of Credit Management for specialist training?
- Do you or your sales department know which customers are over their credit limits or on stop?
- Could you increase the credit limits for any of your customers?
- Reviewing the month end, are you doing well or might there be a cash flow crisis in the future?

8

Collecting the Outstanding Account

POLICY

Is there a policy and procedure for collecting outstanding debts?

In many businesses enormous conflicts occur between sales and accounts because the initial trading terms were never actually defined. The fear, in the view of the sales management, is that if pressure is placed on the customer, repeat business will be lost. But without a collection policy it is impossible to anticipate when cash receipts will be available. The payment terms can be varied to suit the profitability and competition in the market place.

It has been said many times before that a sale is not complete until payment for the transaction has been made. But there is a fundamental fact that is often forgotten. Until the payment is received, the business is self-financing the sale which normally produces a small profit. Dun & Bradstreet in their *Key Business Ratios* publication reported on 372,871 limited companies to produce average ratios for Great Britain Ltd. The average profit margin before tax for 1995 for all these companies was only 3.7 per cent. The average number of days taken to collect debts was 48.6 days, allowing for the fact that some payment terms may be less than 30 days.

I then reviewed their Industrial Quartiles (Table 8.1) where the following statistics show an even greater collection period.

It would appear from my research that in a large number of companies, because there is no collection policy, the customers actually dictate the payment terms.

There is a vast difference between following a planned collection routine which is part of a company's sales and profit policy and just trying to collect outstanding balances. Customers should be reminded before a payment is overdue. Once an increased cash flow is developed, these funds, if they are not

Table 8.1 Industrial quartiles

1995 Industrial Quartiles		
Upper	Medial	Lower
20.6 days	47.9 days	77.3 days

immediately required, can be placed on deposit. The interest received will quite often be far higher than the profit margin on the product or service provided (see Chapter 1). Once the collection can be seen to be cost effective, these profits can be ploughed back into the collection department to create even greater improvements. Planned collections do actually achieve the results and normally staff morale dramatically increases. The other great sales advantage is that by having a small number of delinquent accounts, the actual sales turnover is far higher. By placing hundreds of accounts on stop, you are just giving business to competitors! (see Chapter 6).

PROCEDURES

It is profitable to time-plan the actual method of collection each month. If customers receive the same requests on the same day for each collection period, they will normally never pay a day earlier. They will just respond to these routine requests. The collection plan should include the alternative use of a variety of letters, telephone calls, faxes and personal visits. For larger sums it should not be forgotten that a courier collection service can be most cost effective.

The Outline Plan

By reviewing the dates and methods of despatch of the invoices and statements for the preceding months or period it is then possible to plan an individual procedure which will create the maximum customer interest. For instance, if the aged debtor schedule is reviewed on the last accounting day for the period, a list can be produced showing which customers on the ledger have made no payment. From my experience, by noting the largest outstanding balances and the accounts with the most arrears first, a priority list automatically highlights the key customers. On many computerised systems, lists can be produced in which the highest balance outstanding, last date of payment, credit limit and last date of action are included.

Another method that can be used to plan the collection routine is to count the total live accounts and check to see how many customers actually paid their accounts in the preceding accounting month. The difference within the two will show the number of delinquent customers – that is, if they are on standard monthly terms. It is only by reviewing previous payment patterns that planning to improve the speed of collections can be made (see Chapter 7, Improving the System).

Here is an example of a live ledger of 1900 accounts where time planning has been used to increase cash flow:

- 327 accounts were on the refer list.
- 14 accounts were out for collection.
- 60 per cent of all accounts were in arrears as at the first of the month on payment terms.
- 60 accounts were in query on the first of the new month, 86 accounts were paid.
- By 11 o'clock the 30-day customers who owed more than £5000 were telephoned.
- A different person telephoned the 12 customers who were overdue on the 90-day terms.
- 726 letters were despatched by first class mail where the account was just overdue.
- 112 final notice letters were sent to customers who were more than a month in arrears.
- 126 accounts which required special attention would be telephoned, visited or faxed. This was part of the month end review of delinquent accounts.

FURTHER COLLECTION ROUTINES

Letters

Many businesses put those request letters aside because they are unattractive, dull and do not elicit the immediate interest of the customer. Although the speediest method of gaining contact with a business is by telephone, a faxed letter can often trigger off a payment if the message is clear and concise. A vast number of collection letters which are printed by computer are not eye-catching. Again, if the printing is in two colours and well designed, the result will be an increased cash flow. Companies are already developing E-mail systems for the future.

Many companies now only send one collection letter. Before deciding on the number of demands which are sent, the business must review its profit, cash flow and marketing policy. For instance, it may be cost effective to send letters to a particular type of customer where the actual order value is low and leave the credit control/sales ledger staff to telephone the high value, high risk accounts. Again, once this policy is agreed, the timed collection plan can be slotted in.

The Letter Style

It may take many months to perfect a letter which creates the right response, but I would emphasise that the rewards of spending a few hours in designing a well thought-out letter will create an immediate increase in cash flow. The only problem for credit granters is that an identical application for payment should not be made month after month. If letters are being despatched, a series of up to six letters can be designed which really convey the same message but look entirely different.

The paragraphs, layout and the number of words per line can be altered. All letters should be signed personally, preferably in black ink. A letter which has a rubber stamp endorsement does not command the same attention. If you can address the letter to your customer, quoting the name of the actual bought ledger clerk that passes your account, the response will be even better.

Types of Letter

The title of the letter will have a direct effect on the way your customer will initially react. Therefore if the following headings are printed in heavier type:

- Overdue Account
- Final Reminder
- Final Application
- Legal Notice

your customer expects that they are being advised to pay an overdue account by a definite date.

Your customer's bought ledger department is used to receiving hundreds of demand letters each month. It is therefore a priority to highlight three key facts:

- How much outstanding
- Which months
- When payment should be made.

The initial letter need not be long. There is no need to apologise in the letter for requesting payment. Here is an example of a short, first overdue letter:

Dear Mr Jones,

Overdue Account December 1997

Our records show that £2498.00 is now overdue for payment. We look forward to receiving your payment by _____ If you have any queries, please advise this office immediately.

Yours faithfully

The signature on the letter should be distinct and the telephone extension and fax numbers should be quoted.

The letter in Figure 8.1 was used in a company when payments were being withheld due to queries on products. However there was a desperate need for cash flow and therefore the 'overdue account' and 'cheque to the office' box were in extra heavy type.

Here are some illustrations of phrases in a letter which do not give a clear indication of when payment is required:

We are sorry to note that payment of your account is currently overdue as shown above. We would appreciate your remittance without delay, etc. . . .

In another letter, which quoted an aged debtor's analysis, there appeared to be a current item plus balances of up to two to three months old. The letter stated that the account was overdue and to avoid further action a payment should be made within nine days. My reaction on receiving these letters would be to await their next action. These requests give me an opportunity to extend credit.

Final Notices and Legal Action

These letters must be well-produced and whatever is stated in them should be carried out – otherwise it is just another threat. However, here are examples where it is unclear if the company will take action:

We would advise you that it may be necessary to place your account with our County Court if the debt remains unpaid after 14 days from the date of this letter.

If we do not receive your remittance to clear the balance within the next four days further action will be taken.

CREDIT CONTROL DEPARTMENT
Please Ring Extensions 22, 23, 26, 33, 101

our ref:

your ref:

date:

OVERDUE ACCOUNT

£

Dear Sirs,

We note from our records that the above account is overdue for payment.

We would remind you that our terms of sale are that your payment should be made on the last day of the month following the month of delivery.

Please forward your cheque to this office by [   ]

If you have paid this amount recently, please disregard this letter, otherwise please complete this form, and return it to this office as this will save us all further correspondence.

Yours faithfully,

Credit Controller

1. The account was paid on ....

2. Our cheque is enclosed

3. The date our cheque will be sent ....

4. Payment is withheld for the following reason ....

....

....

Figure 8.1 Example of an overdue account letter

Are they stopping supplies or taking legal action?

If it is possible to *type* the legal letter (Figure 8.2), I have found that the response is even better. In this example, the name of the solicitor or credit bureau can be stated. If you, the credit grantor, wish to take your own

The Financial Director   7 January 1997

Dear Sirs,

We regret to note that you have not responded to our letter of 2
January 1997 when we requested payment of the above overdue
account.

We must now give you notice that your account will be passed to
our agents who will commence collection procedures on the 14
January 1997 if payment is not received by this date.

Your payment in full by return will avoid this most distasteful action.

Yours faithfully

Legal Department

RECORDED DELIVERY

Figure 8.2   Typed legal letter

proceedings, then the letter can state when the action will be commenced and
at which court.

The key words 'distasteful action' will normally trigger a payment.
However, as it is an extremely strong letter, the accounting facts must be
correct.

When using these types of letter where a deadline is quoted it is essential to
hand the account over to the agent or solicitor immediately so that the mo-
mentum is maintained. If liaison is maintained with the third party they can
telephone or fax the debtor after the first post on the deadline day. This is a
particularly successful method when the supplier does not wish to reopen the
account and large sums are involved. Companies which carry out their own in-
house legal procedures can also arrange to start the process immediately the
deadline is reached.

When considering whether to stop supplies a marketing decision also has to
be made for the future. For this reason it is advisable to use more than one
type of final notice as you may wish to supply in future on a cash basis with
discount, or use some other more restrictive method.

Telephone Collection Techniques – Queries

In most commercial organisations, queries do take time to clear, so it is advisable to log all queries including telephoned queries onto a query register (see Chapter 6). When listening to your customer's complaint you, the seller, understand your customer's problem, you apologise and give your name. Your customer will then realise that you are taking personal responsibility for that query. The following up of queries is essential to cash collection. Once a customer realises that queries are not cleared, the chances of routine payments arriving weaken month by month.

EXCUSES

Some businesses seem to raise queries just to delay payment. By logging all telephone conversations it will soon become clear which are the genuine queries. One procedure which I have found has worked on copy invoices, is to actually arrange to send duplicates automatically to a named person in the bought ledger department. Another way is to suggest that these proofs of delivery are sent to the person's home address as your documentation never seems to get through their office accounting system. You, the caller, are not 'having a go' at the bought ledger person, you are just trying to get your job done in a professional manner. Of course, it does not stop there. If you are in a position to send copies of documents you can then negotiate, and say 'If I send these copies to you today, will you guarantee to pay me?' The answer you receive could be positive, but apart from a commitment to pay there must be a confirmation of when the actual cheque will be sent. A further query could then be raised, such as that the company secretary or accountant is away, and two signatures are required. It is then that you can gradually change your attitude. You must ask for the name or names of the persons who are the decision makers and who sign the cheques. At this point there is still no need to become angry. You are just persistent, polite, pleasant and cheerful. At the same time by listening to the customer and projecting a helpful attitude, 95 per cent of customers will normally be helpful in return.

I will now describe how these three rules can be used to construct a collection framework.

COLLECTION RECORDS

The customer record card or computerised record should be 'written up' when the customer's account is opened. The full name, address, account number, credit limit, telephone numbers and fax details, should all be clearly noted. If the customer's bought ledger or accounts address and telephone details are different, plenty of space should be allowed for this information. If necessary, there should be space for the buyer's name as well. The one name or names that must be highlighted are the bought ledger or accounts person who actually authorises or passes payment. You may think it is difficult to obtain the name but it is vitally important to do so for two reasons. By telephoning or writing to the right person you will save weeks of wasted time. Psychologically, people like to be addressed by their own name, as it is far more personal. The primary reason why enormous care should be taken in obtaining these initial details is that this record represents the core of the entire collection system.

CREDIT CONTROL DEPARTMENT   **CUSTOMER RECORD**

A/C NUMBER_____   TELEPHONE NUMBER_____

NAME_____   CONTACT_____

ADDRESS_____

Date	Tel	Letter	Agrd to Pay	CQ No.	Stop List Date	Trasfer to Legal Dept	Details
						£	

Figure 8.3   Collection record card

COLLECTION TECHNIQUES

The early bird catches the worm. Even if your invoice is correct and a statement has been despatched, the payment will not automatically arrive without a reminder. I have already mentioned in the sales ledger section (Chapter 6) that the invoice and statement can be designed so that they act as a request for payment. The planning of the collection routine is essential. It must never be a hit and miss activity. Often it is not known how a new customer will actually pay until the collection procedure commences. Customers will either pay through a set routine or by the seller's credit control department triggering off the response. Once this response is recorded, action can then be taken to reduce the time delay and increase the cash flow.

TELEPHONE CALLS

The Switchboard Operator

The communicator or ambassador for any business is the switchboard operator. I would recommend that this is the one name which should be added to the collection record. The switchboard operator knows the entire operation of the business you are selling to. Do treat the operator as a real person. One suggestion is to open up the discussion by saying that you realise how busy he or she is, but could they help you. By carefully listening to the operator it will often give you, the caller,' an immediate picture of the company you are trading with.

Once friendly contact is made with the operator they will often give you the name of the bought ledger person. However, if the operator is very skilled and has been trained to stop all bought ledger calls, a warning sign has already been signalled. Then a different approach will be required which I will outline below under 'The Blocking Response'.

The Approach

Before attempting to telephone, do have all the information on the account at your fingertips. It is also vitally important to be in the right frame of mind before making the telephone call. Do be calm and relaxed. Be confident and look forward to having a conversation with your customer. Having a conversation is not the same as talking to your customer. Allow your customer to talk to you. It is imperative for you to use silence positively, so that your customer can respond in a relaxed way. There is no need to rush the call. You are cheerful and enthusiastic and can therefore communicate. You enjoy your job. Never lose your temper or be abusive. Arguing will not help but through discussion and by asking questions you will start to reduce the tension in the other person. Changing the tone of your voice and showing interest will establish a far better framework. This is especially important when you have never spoken to the person before. Even if it has been a long day, you do not sound tired. In fact, you are enthusiastic. You not only like the job but you also support your company's product or service.

Telephone collection is a highly skilled job. No-one should be asked to telephone a customer unless they have been given training and have had an opportunity to listen to a person who knows the customer. If you are working in a company where there is no-one available to give advice, the following guidelines will help in planning the conversation.

Telephone Technique – Listening

It is human nature to feel aggrieved if your company has not been paid. But never show anger or annoyance in making your call. Your job is to listen to the customer so that their comments can be calmly noted on the record card or computer. Just saying, for instance, 'Good morning, Miss Jones, can you help me? My name is . . . from XYZ Ltd.' Then listen for the response. This is the crucial part of the conversation. It is so easy to just carry on by saying 'the amount outstanding is . . .', etc., but this will not allow your customer any time to respond. So do listen. Listening to their response will help you to plan out your negotiations.

In this part of the discussion you are trying to gauge the person's character and personality and also to get a feeling for your customer's business activity. You, the caller, are in fact intelligence gathering. The intelligence gathering will also allow the person at the other end of the line to get to know you as an individual. At this point you can ask whether the outstanding debt has been cleared for payment. The listening time is also necessary at this stage as you can then judge which response to give. In your mind the next question is: 'When is a cheque being sent?' If the customer tries to put you off by saying that the cheque will need two signatures, it is logical to confirm when the cheque will actually be sent. There is still no need to be aggressive, just be persistent.

Some companies have a definite policy of only paying after 60 or 90 days. It is your job to create a trigger mechanism so that an exception to their rules will be made. Most companies also have a manual system of payments apart from a computerised method. Payment may come through the system weekly or fortnightly. Other companies have a policy of only paying when threatened, or, more seriously, when proceedings are issued. For larger transactions a pre-check through a credit agency should warn potential suppliers – but it can still happen.

Always thank the bought ledger person by name and confirm the agreement which has just been made. By recording the comments on the record card or computer system, noting the person's name and the time called, if the payment does not arrive on the due date you can often achieve your objective by just quoting the customer's actual comments. The payment will arrive because the person at the other end will realise that you are a careful, methodical person.

The Next Stage

There are often warning signs that can be detected when a business is trying to head off requests for payment. The person is never available – they are 'at a meeting'. When these responses are obtained, do ask questions as to when that person will definitely be available. By obtaining the name of the person who is speaking to you, even if they are trying to block calls, you will create the impression that you are not going to give up. If the listener becomes aggressive and demands to know why their name is required the answer is simple – 'We, as a company, like to communicate with our customers.'

Objections

There is no such thing as a perfect world and sometimes customers have genuine reasons for not paying the account. The customer may state that the invoice has not been received or that the goods or services were not satisfactory. If this is the case, do listen to all that your customer has to say and make a formal note of the query. When listening to the query, do plan your response. For instance, just because the invoice for £42 is incorrect there is no need for the customer to withold a cheque for £520. An appropriate response is, 'Can I confirm with you that you will pass £478 on the account for payment?'

The Blocking Response

I have come across switchboard operators who have been skilfully trained in stopping all calls to the bought ledger or accounts section. They may say, 'he/she is out'; 'they are at a meeting'; they are 'away on sick leave'; or 'on holiday'. Before the operator puts you off, ask questions, change the operator's style or rhythm. For instance, ask when Mr or Mrs or Miss Jones will be in. If the answer you are given is that they are part-time, state when you will be telephoning. If it seems that you are getting nowhere, ask to speak to the accountant, purchasing manager, sales manager or company secretary. If all these people are unavailable, ask to speak to their secretaries or their assistants. Remember that while this conversation is taking place you, the supplier, are noting it down on your record card. By keeping the operator's attention you are also stopping them from carrying out their other normal duties. This, in itself, may sometimes force the operator to 'crack'.

If the situation seems critical and if it is a limited company, a search for the director's and company secretary's private address will enable you to telephone and gain contact. When dealing with consumers, sole traders or partnerships, by carrying out a search through Experian or the data banks of other major credit bureaux you may often be able to track down the home addresses of the proprietor or partners. Where a bureau has specialist knowledge of a particular trade, they often have a list of known defaulters.

When carrying out this technique you have to be absolutely certain of your ground. The person answering at the other end will often be angry, abusive and outraged. You explain that you have tried every method and time to contact their office. You quote from the record card or computer record the times when previous approaches have been made. These telephone calls should not be made late at night or very early in the morning as it is possible that you may breach Section 40 of the Administration of Justice Act 1970. In Section (1)A it states that a person commits an offence if, with the object of coercing the other person to pay money, claimed from the other as a debt due under a contract, he 'harasses the other with demands for payment which, in their frequency or manner or occasion of making any such demand, or the threat of publicity by which the demand is accompanied, are calculated to subject him or members of his family or household to alarm, distress or humiliation'. The other subsection of the Act refers more to written communications.

General Timing

With many businesses operating with part-time staff, it is often vital to telephone in the morning when people are available. Psychologically a person on a bought ledger will often be brighter and more alert in the morning, say between 9.15 and 11.30. It is therefore best to make these telephone calls to hit the peak attention time. In the afternoon, I have found that between 2.15 and 3.30 is about the best time to telephone. When dealing with small businesses it may be advisable to avoid Thursdays, as this is the day when wages are being prepared. Again a note on the customer record card will highlight when and whom to telephone.

SUMMARY

In many businesses collecting the debts is only carried out when the management suddenly realise that they have a cash flow problem.

- Have you a monthly plan to collect your debts?
- Can you improve your collection techniques?
- Do you change the layout and style of your collection letters?
- What does the customer record history show?
- Can you improve your telephone technique?

9

Thinking About
Taking Proceedings

It is human nature to be annoyed when a debt has not been paid. But first a policy decision has to be made on whether the supplier wishes to continue to trade with that customer. While considering this marketing point, a financial and economic analysis has to be made on whether that same customer has any assets which are unencumbered. Obtaining a pre-suing report is one way to judge whether your customer who is in default has any assets which are available for creditors if proceedings are to be considered. Remember that debt recovery and legal proceedings can cost considerable sums if proceedings prove abortive, or are defended. If the decision is made on marketing grounds that the customer should be helped, then a personal visit or meeting must be arranged.

The key to a successful outcome is to first make sure that all the management in your company, including sales and finance, agree on the new policy. If a customer needs help, extending the terms may not necessarily be the right course of action. They may actually need your expertise to help them collect their outstanding debts.

Before taking proceedings, are you absolutely sure that there is no dispute or query which will delay the action and create a defence? By rechecking the customer sales order and credit files, time will be saved and needless proceedings avoided if there is an unresolved problem. Speed is of the essence. Do not delay either making the decision or taking corrective action. There is no doubt that when a customer owes a company money, many other businesses are also owed. The first creditor who takes legal proceedings is very often the only creditor who is paid in full.

DIFFERENT TYPES OF PROCEEDINGS

Again, it is tempting to rush off and try to take proceedings which may be lengthy, expensive and result in total failure. These questions therefore have to be asked:

1. Has the debtor any assets on which to execute?
2. Which will be the most cost effective and speedy way to collect the debt?
3. Are you going to use a debt recovery agency or a solicitor to collect the debts?

Every customer is different, and no two collection cases are alike. By reading the customer history file and reviewing the customer records, their payment history will emerge.

I have mentioned in this chapter that timing is essential; there is only one further rule. If you state that you will take a course of action in a telephone call, letter or fax, this course of action should be taken. For example, if the name of your debt recovery agency or solicitor is mentioned in your final letter which quotes an action date, do keep to the follow-up dates (see Chapter 8, Collections). If you the creditor do not wish to take a course of action, then your initial collection letters must be re-drafted or the method of negotiation on the telephone altered.

There are numerous types of action which collection agencies and solicitors can take but you, the credit granter, should be in complete control at every stage. Vast sums – which are *your* profits – can be completely thrown away when pre-suing research is not carried out.

COUNTY COURT OR HIGH COURT?

County Courts in England and Wales

An action for a debt for any sum can be commenced in any County Court. In June 1997 there were just under 250 County Courts in England and Wales. (It should also be remembered that when a debt of £25,000 or below is commenced in the High Court, and it is defended, it is most likely to be transferred to the County Court for a hearing.)

A Default Summons issued through the County Court can take many weeks to be processed, and their files can get mislaid! As at June 1997 the minimum fee for issuing was £10 and the maximum fee £500. However, if a Default Summons is issued through the Summons Production Centre in Northampton the minimum fee is still £10 but the maximum fee is reduced to £75 (see the Pritchard Joyce & Hinds interview on page 169 for details). Where a debt is in excess of £1000, a creditor may obtain a certificate from the County Court to allow them to issue a High Court Warrant (see Nathan & Company interview, page 170).

Disputes

It is vitally important to make sure before an action is commenced that there are definitely no disputes or queries concerning the delivery of goods or the supply of services. In a defended action a date for a full trial hearing can be months ahead. Another aspect which creditors should consider is that the Defence and Counterclaim particulars that appear on the County Court Summons seem to be a debtor's charter for delaying, reducing, or disputing payment.

It is confirmed from many sources that the County Court Bailiffs who try to execute on the debtor's goods, or try to obtain a full or part payment, are less successful than the High Court Sheriffs Officers in executing the debts, as the Sheriffs are paid by results.

Statutory Interest

In the County Court, statutory interest may be claimed on any sum, under Section 69 of the County Courts Act 1984 at 8 per cent per annum (as at June 1997) from the invoice date or dates to the date of the issue of the Summons. Further interest under the same Act can be claimed from the date of issue until the date of Judgment or sooner. In the High Court interest accrues until the debt is paid (see New Legislation, page 34).

Policy of the Lord Chancellor's Department

Over the last ten years it has been the policy of the Lord Chancellor's Department to route as many default judgment debts as possible through the County Courts. There is also a trend to close smaller County Courts and concentrate the work in fewer but larger county courts.

At the time of writing it is not known how much of Lord Woolf's report 'On Access to Justice' will be implemented by the new Labour administration. However, there are now indications that the cost of putting in new reforms to speed up litigation could be hugely expensive.

High Court

Taking proceedings in the High Court is far faster than the County Court. The one great advantage of debt recovery in the High Court or the District Registries is that it is still possible to issue a writ within a day. The only drawback is that legal expenses and fees could be higher. However, on amounts between

£600 and £2000 costs are in fact lower. The minimum amount that a Writ can be issued for is £600, which attracts a fee of £120 plus £1.25 costs, and the maximum fee is £500 for debts in excess of £100,000. This attracts solicitors' costs of £89.25 (as at June 1997).

A Range of Options

Once it has been agreed that legal action needs to be taken, the threat of any of the following actions may result in your customer paying the overdue amount before any of these procedures are commenced in the County or High Courts.

- Attachment of Earnings Order
- Charging Order
- Garnishee
- Oral Examination
- Warrant of Execution
- Statutory Demand (where the debt is over £750)
- Liquidation or Bankruptcy Proceedings.

Attachment of Earnings Application

If an individual is employed, it is possible to apply to the Court for an attachment of earnings application, once a Judgment has been obtained. These actions take time as the debtor and his firm have to provide the Court with details of earnings. There is also a minimum protected earnings relief, therefore only a small sum may be available to clear a debt. If a debtor leaves his or her employment, payments will cease, and it may be expensive to continue the action. In the 1990s many employment contracts are exceedingly short and it should also be noted that Attachment of Earnings Applications cannot be issued against self-employed, bankrupt or unemployed persons.

Charging Orders

After a Judgment has been obtained, a Land Registry search can be carried out to ascertain if certain property belongs to a debtor. Where a limited company is involved, and where they may also own property, government stocks, stocks registered in England and/or Wales or unit trust or trust funds, it is advisable to first examine at Companies House the Company Charges and Mortgages Register. This action is vital as often the bank, banks, factors or finance houses will already have a fixed and/or floating charge on a company's assets.

Garnishee Proceedings

In England and Wales when it is believed that the debtor has monies owed by a third party (the Garnishee), then after obtaining a Judgment, a Creditor can then Garnishee the third party. The debtor may have funds in a bank, building society or post office savings account which can be attached. For a successful action there must be sufficient monies in an account, or which are due to be paid by a third party. Once the Garnishee proceedings have been issued and served the third party must 'freeze' any monies that they hold until a Hearing takes place, when an Order will be made by the Court for the monies, if any, to be paid over.

Oral Examination

If no payment has been made by the debtor after a Summons has been issued and Judgment gained, it can be a shock for the debtor to learn that an application can be made to the Court for an Oral Examination where, questioned under oath, an individual is asked about their present means and circumstances.

If a Limited Company has been sued, then a Director or the Company Secretary named on the application will have to attend, or if a firm has been sued a Partner will be requested to attend. Although the court fees have increased over the years for this type of action and some Courts might like to dispense with the hearings, there is one great advantage. If the debtor is served with the application but fails to attend the hearing, a Committal Order for Contempt of Court may be ordered. This could also mean that if after service of a Notice of Adjourned Heading the person fails to attend Court again, he/she could be committed to prison.

Warrant of Execution

In the County Court once Judgment has been gained a variety of enforcement actions can be taken. In most cases a Warrant of Execution will have been issued. This is an instruction to the Bailiff to levy on any seizable effects that the debtor may possess. The problem for creditors is that if the Bailiff cannot arrange a payment, trying to sell second-hand goods through a local auction room is time consuming and often the final payment after expenses is exceedingly low.

In the High Court after Judgment is obtained a Writ of Fi-Fa (Warrant of Execution) is issued. This is sent to the Sheriff's Officers to deal with (see interview with Nathan & Co., page 170).

Statutory Demand

Where a debt or Judgment exceeds £750, a Statutory Demand can be issued and served. If the debtor is a Limited Company the demand has to be sent to the Registered Office. The demand informs the debtor that they have 21 days from the date of service to act, failing which Winding Up Proceedings can be issued. If the debtor is an individual or firm, the form states that Bankruptcy proceedings may be issued. This is a strong threat, however, it appears that the Courts are not in favour of using this procedure just to obtain payment of one debt.

In this chapter I have interviewed a debt recovery agency, Intrum Justitia; two solicitors, Pritchard Joyce & Hinds and Nolan Macleod of Glasgow; sheriff's officers, Nathan & Company; and two insolvency practitioners, Malcolm Cork, of Moore Stephens, and Steve Hill of Coopers and Lybrand, to illustrate how debts occur and how they are collected.

A MAJOR COLLECTION AGENCY

To give readers an overview on professional debt recovery I visited several of the offices of Intrum Justitia to show their attitude and philosophy when collecting commercial and consumer debts. I spent many hours interviewing Gerard P Barron, MD (Commercial Division), David B. E. Thomas, Client Service Director, and Mary Colorado, Debt Surveillance Supervisor.

Undercapitalised Businesses

Too many businesses are undercapitalised, especially those with less than five years' trading history, who have therefore not had time to create a capital base. There is a big danger: overtrading has to be funded somehow. If there is a good solid capital base with reasonable margins, that is fine. The issue at the moment is that if a company obtains too much credit, it can fall apart through lack of credit policy. The business then cannot pay and the cycle starts all over again.

Credit Policy

It all relates to credit policy. A good company can grow properly, maintain margins and still retain turnover and profits. Cash flow management is the key. Too many businesses live from hand to mouth, using, for example, the sales this month to pay the salaries for the end of the month. As more customers resist payment because their own cash flow is tight, there is an accumulation of 'pent-up' debt in the market place and the whole cycle of making payment slows down. Because of the polarisation of the business community towards smaller businesses with less dependence on their cash flow from the larger businesses, even the pressure on large businesses to pay on time simply will not be enough to support a small business's cash flow.

Banking Relationships

Focusing on the banking relationships with businesses, the banks have their PLCs in order, but the life blood of a business is the supply of the overdraft which is a key financial tool for working capital. If this major source of working capital is only available to 'blue chip' companies, what chance is there for three to four-year-old small businesses, with modest profits and reserves, getting off the ground? Small businesses will chase all the normal sources of finance because the banks refuse and they immediately have a credit and repayment problem. On the Continent very few businesses take out high value, long-term loans. Banks in the UK have a resistance to any working capital which is turned over a number of times a year.

Slow Payment

I asked why UK companies often take longer to pay on any credit term. It was mentioned that many of Intrum's European offices sell, particularly to small businesses, a stamp which they place on all their invoices and statements that states 'Unless this account is paid within the terms agreed, this account will be placed in the hands of Intrum Justitia.' As a company, what they are doing is increasing the awareness of the need for prompt payment. They also issue certificates to businesses which are displayed which read 'This business is protected through Intrum Justitia who are providing debt protection.'

In the UK small businesses do not have the time, the management skills or finances to put in a formal credit policy. That is why Intrum run training courses throughout the year for small firms, in Europe these are called 'Credit Schools'. They are exceptionally simple support mechanisms which set out how to create a credit policy and why there is a need for one. The schools also teach how to monitor sales ledger accounts and collect the debts, and in the final stages what legal actions can be considered if the debt is not paid.

Shop Keeper Culture

Regrettably, in the UK there is still a 'shop keeper culture' – the proprietor has the attitude 'Who do I need to pay?', as if personally looking at the debt to keep the business going. 'What in fact is the minimum that needs to be paid?' Basically it often seems that as long as the bank is happy everyone else can await payment. It was emphasised that there are probably 3.5 million businesses, including sole traders and partnerships, with this mentality trading in the UK.

The ill-educated manager's attitude is still: 'What do I need to do to survive?' And 'What is my list of priorities at the end of the month?' The number of managers who apply for business training is fairly limited, and the colleges are not providing the necessary support and framework of education. The DTI may monitor businesses but Intrum feel that the department does not do enough to support business, including some 'Business Links'.

Approach to Debt Recovery

Intrum's approach to debt recovery is interventional between the supplier and the purchaser. There is pressure on creditors to try and keep as many customers as they can, and despite the poor relationship that can exist between suppliers and customers, there is still a desire to retain those customers at all costs. This is because the cost of getting new customers as a percentage of sales is extremely high. The message now is all about client retention. At some point there is going to be a massive delinquency. For example a business is going to decline because of their credit policy and they will have to cease trading. This is where the relationship needs a 'little bit of a nudge'. Intrum have always taken an ethical approach and with this relationship they can tailor their service to their client's requirements. This method of collection does require their clients to be a little more sophisticated and wiser on how they intend to operate their sales relationships.

Depending on a company's credit terms which can be anything from 7 to 120 days, there can be arrears but customer care is essential to keep a working relationship. Softer letters are still sent to debtors, but the good relationship between buyer and seller is maintained. Obviously Intrum want the debt recovery business but they are there to assist their clients in getting over a particular problem: that of cash flow. Once the client realises that they are heading for a full or partial write-off of a debt, they move into proper debt collection activity, telephoning and sending letters, but at this point the debt could be at the 180 day stage!

Because of the general desire to increase sales there has been a softening of credit scoring for card applicants, particularly in the period between

1995–1997. Credit card policies are more liberal and resources are going into marketing and sales. To spend more on assessment would not be cost effective. For this reason Intrum's volumes are now growing as everything is becoming sales driven. The danger is that credit scoring or credit adjusters are saying 'If we change the score what proportion of debts can we accept?' They then price the product and service accordingly at the front end of the business. As an example of this trend Intrum handled 1.6 million consumer cases in 1996.

Writing Off Debts

Time and time again I have heard of businesses writing off debts because their staff did not have the time, experience and technical knowledge to pursue the debt. For this reason Mary Colorado runs for Intrum a special Debt Surveillance Unit. The unit will continuously monitor the debt and the debtor's circumstances for up to six years. At present this service is only available for individuals, sole traders and partnerships.

There can be particular problems when reviewing this type of case, which may involve divorce settlements and a bank holding a joint agreement on an unsecured loan. A debt lodged with this unit averages about £600. Quite often clients have tried to collect these debts inhouse, and then with debt collection agencies through to litigation, without success. Sometimes if court action has taken place despite it appearing uneconomical to proceed, the debtor has adverse information entered against them which prevents them gaining credit and they get 'fed up' with being chased. But two to three years later the unit discover that they have assets. This type of action is also useful when the debtor constantly avoids payment.

General Collection Policy

Every client is interviewed personally so that the full circumstances of the debt are understood. A tailor-made package is then created for each client. Importantly, no action is ever taken by the collectors without consultation with their customers.

The key factor for the collection teams is whether it is commercially viable to proceed. Their computer systems are highly sophisticated, and the staff who collect the debts are given a three-month training programme after which there is a continuous plan of action to update their knowledge.

For further information on their debt collection schemes contact Intrum Justitia Ltd, Warwick House, Birmingham Road, Stratford-upon-Avon, Warwickshire, CV37 0BP (tel: 01789 415181).

Our Ref.   5867/92450
Date   Tuesday, 15 July 1997
Direct Tel   **01789 412128**

Dear Sirs

Our Client: nytown Merchanting PLC
Outstanding Account £2750.63

We have been instructed by our above named client to recover from you the amount shown.

Despite repeated requests for payment the sum remains outstanding.

Unless we receive payment within three days from today's date, it is our instruction and intention to issue proceedings against you, without further notice.

If such proceedings are necessary, you will become additionally liable for the Court Fees, statutory recoverable costs, and interest at the rate of 8% per cent per annum until payment.

On the entry of judgement, and if the sum remains unpaid you could be subject to enforcement action, and your details entered on the Registry of County Court Judgements, which will affect your credit worthiness in the future.

Please make your cheques payable to our client, or alternatively contact the reference above to arrange for other alternative methods of payment, for example by credit / debit card.

We look forward to hearing from you, and trust further action on our part will be unnecessary.

Yours Faithfully

INTRUM JUSTITIA

When telephoning please ask for G Barron on 01789 412128

Intrum Justitia Limited	Telephone: 01789 412081	Registered in England	Registered Office:
PO Box 35	Telefax: 01789 412077	No. 1918920	Warwick House
Stratford-upon-Avon	Internet http://		Birmingham Road
Warwickshire CV37 0BW	www.intrum.com		Stratford-upon-Avon
			Warks CV37 0BP

Figure 9.1 Sample letter

SOLICITORS' ADVICE

Pritchard, Joyce & Hinds are a firm of solicitors in Beckenham, Kent, specialising in commercial and consumer debt recovery. They also work for debt recovery agencies and have a number of 'take on' debts (debts which other solicitors have not succeeded in recovering).

Keith Lyward, Collections Manager, in an interview, told me that it is sometimes difficult to explain to their clients that the bad debt began when they, the client, took on a new customer. Clients now expect a considerable amount of extra help when reviewing the variety of debt recovery options which are available. Before Keith Lyward or other members of his team take on a client, they always ask what type of service they require. The answer to this question is essential as the client may have already telephoned and written to the debtor, and now demands immediate action. From their experience, once a debtor recieves a letter from a solicitor, the debtor knows that their creditor 'means business'.

From the beginning this firm takes a friendly and approachable attitude to all their clients, and they like all clients to communicate with them on a continuous basis. If a client has many small debts which they consider too small to sue for, providing there is volume it is still worth while negotiating a fee to collect any debt between £10 and £25. On a 'no recovery, no fee' basis the creditors have nothing to lose.

High Court or County Court?

I was surprised to hear from Keith Lyward that some solicitors actually put more actions through the County Court as solicitors costs on process are so low in the High Court where a debt is under £2000, that they have to charge a handling fee. PJ&H like to use the High Court for the speed and efficiency (see Nathan & Company), but they have also overcome the delays in the County Court by using the Summons Production Centre (SPC) in Northampton which is a 'fast track' method of issuing a County Court Summons. Apart from the speed of the issue (which is guaranteed within 48 hours), normally these Summons are issued within 24 hours and posted to debtors the same day. A further advantage for creditors is that the maximum fee for issuing a Writ in the High Court or a Summons in the County Court is £500, whereas a summons issued through the SPC centre costs a maximum of £75. This is a fact that has not been publicised in the Credit Profession. Keith Lyward confirmed that debtors have actually walked through their door on day three with a cheque to cover both the debt and the costs.

PJ&H are one of the very few High Street solicitors who use the SPC system of issuing summons.

Costs

One of the first questions a client always asks is, 'How much is it going to cost?' A volume client may be charged a very nominal sum to collect a debt. It all depends on the number of debts and their complexity. Clients are advised of the fees that will be charged before they agree to accept a debt for collection, and if proceedings are issued clients are advised what costs and interest are being claimed the same day as instructions are sent to the court. A debt for a few hundred pounds may be uneconomical to collect if it is going to be defended and where a solicitor or agent has to attend the hearing. For this reason some clients elect to appear in person. PJ&H issue a guide to help the plaintiffs with the procedures through the County Court, thus reducing the overall cost still further.

History

Pritchard Joyce & Hinds was established in 1982 when a larger local practice split, and three of the partners, with about 20 other staff, took over the Beckenham and Forest Hill offices. They have grown considerably and the Debt Recovery Section now has one of the most advanced computer debt collection systems, supported by six Litigation Solicitors and 13 other administration staff.

To gauge the way their team help their clients to understand debt recovery through the courts, they have written the *Short Guide to Legal Proceedings through the County and High Court*. This is available from Pritchard Joyce & Hinds, Solicitors, St Brides House, 32 High Street, Beckenham, Kent, BR3 1AY (tel: 0181 650 1400).

DEBT RECOVERY THROUGH THE HIGH COURT

In an interview with Nathan & Company, Officers to the Sheriffs of Greater London, Hertfordshire, Surrey and the City of London, they explained that in 85 per cent of Writs of Fi Fa passed to the Sheriffs of Greater London, they gain some form of recovery. This is a far higher recovery rate than through the County Courts.

The history of the Sheriff's Officers is fascinating. The office of Sheriff is pre-Conquest, and it is alleged that it may have been established by the year 992. In those days the Sheriff was the Monarch's representative in the County. It was not just an office for collecting debts, but for collecting fines, executing people, raising armies and taxes. Times have now changed.

Their Tasks and the Barriers

Basically a Sheriff's Officer's role is one of translating a Judgment into action to gain a payment for creditors. One of their immediate problems is that 15–20 per cent of defendants simply disappear or move to another location. More than often Nathan & Co. are not advised by the plaintiff's solicitors that the debtor has another address.

Many companies now purchase large houses or country mansions (because they are cheaper to buy) from where they operate their business. Sheriff's Officers are not allowed to enter private premises but they do have powers of entry in respect of commercial property. It should also be remembered that all debts under the Consumer Credit Act must be actioned through the County Courts.

The judgment creditor has a choice of forum on where to issue proceedings. There are no restrictions in issuing proceedings in the High Court for any amount. But if a creditor decides to issue in the High Court for below £600, he is not able to collect the cost of execution from the defendant. It is also possible that the court will transfer the matter to the County Court.

Most of the credit industry are now issuing proceedings in the County Court because it is cheaper. However, because the transfer value has just been lowered to £1000, as Sheriff's Officers, Nathan & Co can accept these judgments from the County Court for enforcement. The benefit for creditors is that they gain the possibility of High Court enforcement using the Sheriff to collect the debts which is far speedier. There is greater pressure on the debtor, as the registration of the County Court judgment and the Sheriff on their doorstep is more likely to result in a recovery.

The opinion of Claire Sandbrook, the Deputy Under Sheriff of Greater London, is that the credit industry has also not realised the usefulness of the 'transfer up' procedure. For example, if the plaintiff tries to execute in the County Court and their bailiff reports 'Gone Away' or 'No Goods' or 'Debtor Cannot be Found' or quite often, 'Unenforceable – unable to make Contact with the Debtor', the County Court bailiff working the normal hours of 9–5 can do little more. Regrettably for the creditor at this point the methods of enforcement such as Charging Orders, Garnishee, Insolvency or Bankruptcy proceedings just increase the costs for the creditor and take yet more time. Claire Sandbrook and her colleagues are now pioneering a transfer up service to encourage the Credit Industry to make more use of Sheriffs.

One of the advantages when a Sheriff is given a County Court Warrant which has been transferred marked 'Unable to gain access to debtor's premises' against a Limited Company at their commercial premises, or when the office or works is always locked up, is that under the High Court Rules the Sheriff has the right to seek instructions from the creditor's solicitors to break in to the premises, levy, and remove goods or property. The CGA (cannot gain admittance) or a 'no goods' (*nulla bona*) return used to be a basis for bankruptcy but owing to a recent case which has been confirmed by the Court of Appeal, a creditor cannot rely on a return of 'no goods' to present a petition. In the past this method was used by creditors to short-cut the system of issuing a statutory demand. Now the Courts, before accepting a petition, must see evidence that the Sheriff has entered the premises and has not been able to levy.

Fear of Bankruptcy or Insolvency

In some cases where the value of an execution on goods would only raise £300–400, the next step to enforce the judgment is usually to issue a winding-up petition. In this example, if a winding-up petition for a debt of about £8000 is sent to the debtor before it is advertised, the threat of actually becoming insolvent is a key inducement to pay. The debtor, while they may not be worried about losing desks, chairs and filing cabinets, will suddenly 'find' £8000 before the petition is advertised. The judgment debtor is also liable for the costs. Execution is therefore a cheaper solution at the outset because there is no deposit to pay for the insolvency proceedings, whereas for a petition to be presented a deposit has to be raised first.

The 'Trading As' Problem

As there may be at least 900,000 businesses operating from home addresses in the UK, I asked Geoffrey Roberts, Managing Director of Nathan & Co., on which name do they try to enforce the judgment. Mr Roberts stated that everyone had a different opinion of enforcements on individuals 'trading as' or 'known as'. But he is a great believer that proceedings should be taken against the individual.

Foreign Judgments Transferred to the UK

A small percentage of Nathan & Co's judgments are foreign. If someone is going to execute in London on a foreign judgment it means that they have considered it is likely to be a substantial debt, perhaps in the region of £1.5 million. In these cases the job of the Sheriff's Officers is to check the value of the assets. Clients dealing with a multinational company want their debts paid, but they may still want to trade with them. This is a 'Catch 22' situation as there has to be consultation with the creditor's solicitors before the judgment is enforced. The creditor has to realise what the costs implications are, and also whether the asset or assets to which the Sheriff is being directed are free and unencumbered. There is also an added complication that the creditor may still wish to delay the action to collect the debt as they do not wish to lose the trade. However, if a debt is for £1.5 million, how long can a creditor delay taking action?

When the creditor is reviewing this type of decision they will ask Nathan & Co. to obtain further information on a company's asset strength so that a credit assessment decision can be made. Very often it is not until the Sheriff's Officer has physically walked into the debtor's premises, warehouse or site, that they can actually observe and evaluate what stock levels and materials are available to them to seize.

Can You Trade on Credit When a Sheriff Executes?

I was reminded that execution does not prevent continuation of trading. This is a misconception about using Sheriff's Officers or County Court bailiffs. It is possible to continue to trade even if the relationship between the creditor and debtor has got to a point where the Sheriff's Officer is on the doorstep. Even if the supplier reaches this stage in the credit cycle it is still possible and necessary to trade with a debtor.

In the late 1990s it is very difficult to win customers, and every customer that a supplier has, they must try to keep. The Sheriff's Officers approach is therefore not to upset the trading relationship: they are there to enforce the judgment of the Court. It was emphasised that businesses still have sanctions on how to deal with bad payers, such as agreeing to direct debits, or stopping the supply of goods or services. When execution takes place the trading relationship may not have been broken down irreparably. It is only when proceedings are taken to wind up a business, to make the debtor insolvent, that it is time to stop trading.

It is essential for creditors to get under the skin of their customers to decide whether the latter have a temporary cash flow problem, or whether it is a business that is going down fast. In the latter example the best thing to do is to terminate the trading relationship.

For further information on the Sheriff's Officers services, Nathan & Co. (Sheriff's Officers) Ltd can be contacted at 2 Serjeants' Inn, Fleet Street, London EC4Y 1LL (tel: 0171 353 3838).

REGISTER OF COUNTY COURT JUDGMENTS

In an interview Paul Mudge, Chief Executive of Registry Trust (and incidentally at present President of the Institute of Credit Management), confirmed that 1,245,830 County Court Judgments were issued in 1996.

Since 1854 there has been a list in England and Wales of people who have had judgments obtained against them for money they owe. Until 1986 the Register was kept by the Lord Chancellor's Department. Since then it has been kept on its behalf by a non-profit making company – Registry Trust Ltd.

Almost all County Court judgments in England and Wales are registered and since April 1993, all administration orders against individuals. Since 1989, Scottish decrees and Manx judgments have also been registered. (It is understood that discussions are now taking place with the Lord Chancellor's Department and the High Court to see if there is a possibility of Writs also being published by Registry Trust in the future.)

Further information on CCJ registrations from Registry Trust Limited, 173–175 Cleveland Street, London W1P 5PE (tel: 0171 380 0133).

THE DIFFERENCES BETWEEN ENGLISH AND SCOTTISH LAW IN DEBT RECOVERY

In an interview with Mr Jim Nolan of Nolan Macleod he emphasised that readers should realise that there were differences in pre and post judgment procedures when reviewing debt recovery in England and Wales, and Scotland. Mr Nolan has already read the previous on English proceedings and has kindly drafted the following.

Scotland has its own entirely different system of law which, over the past three hundred years, as well as adding important concepts to, has assimilated a great deal of the procedure of, English law.

Immediate Action

Scottish law enables the creditor to take various enforcement or containment steps to recover a debt in order to secure, preserve or even better his position immediately an action is instructed. This gives a creditor suing in Scotland a distinct advantage as in some instances a debt can be secured within hours of raising an action.

Court action to recover debts for any amounts can be commenced in the Court of Session or the Sheriff Court. The Court of Session has recently introduced a fast-track procedure for very large commercial cases. However, 95 per cent of debt cases are raised in the Sheriff Court as the costs are far less and the case is likely to be concluded much quicker than in the Court of Session, where counsel must be employed. Indeed, in terms of the Consumer Credit Act 1974, actions involving 'consumer contracts' *must* be raised in the Sheriff Court where the debtor resides and cannot be raised elsewhere.

Debts under £1500

The court sets a preliminary date between four and six weeks ahead, by which date the debtor must indicate whether he intends to defend the action and, if so, a date for proof (trial) will then be set after a defence has been noted. If no defence is stated, then judgment will be entered against that debtor. The issuing cost is between £6 and £35.

Debts over £1500

The debtor must indicate within three weeks of service of the action whether he intends to defend the case and, if he does, he must state a defence within a further two weeks. Thereafter, pleadings must be adjusted within eight weeks after the preliminary hearing will take place at which the sheriff will normally fix a date for proof (trial). This date is subject to the pressure of business in each Sheriff Court but one would hope to obtain judgment in a defended action in about six months. The issuing cost is £45.

Return of Goods and Deliver Actions

This type of action often used by finance houses is treated as above but one would expect to get interim judgment ordering the delivery of goods and, depending on whether delivery was achieved or not, would move the court to imprison the defender for contempt of court by the deliberate flouting of a court order, and if it was felt that this was not appropriate, to grant judgment for the value of the goods and damages for wrongful detention thereof. The issuing cost is between £35 and £45.

Bankruptcies and Liquidations

In Scotland, interim trustees or provisional liquidators can be appointed on cause shown almost immediately the action is raised. The issuing cost is £57.

Rates of Interest

This is set by the terms of the contract and applies from the date set within the contract. If no such date or terms exist, then the statutory rate of 8 per cent applies from the date of service on the debtor. Interest runs until payment is made.

The basic expenses (excluding issuing costs which are added to the costs) awarded against the debtors in undefended actions as at April 1997 are as follows:

Sum Sued For	Cost
Over £1500	£111.40
Over £250	£55.60
Over £50	£38.50
Under £50	£25.00

These costs rise at around 5 per cent per annum.

Options

a) Before Judgment has been Obtained

There are two options that are competent at the start of the court action and before judgment is obtained, namely Arrestment on the Dependence and Inhibition on the Dependence. An arrestment takes the form of 'catching' funds owed by a third party to the debtor. It is similar to the English garnishee order. Registering an inhibition on the dependence of an action prevents the debtors from passing good title to or giving security over heritable property they may own. They cannot do so without first discharging the inhibition, i.e., clearing the debt in respect of which the inhibition was taken. In Scotland, the creditor is able to carry out a search at any time against any heritable property, ascertaining the owner of the same and usually discovering any equity therein to help decide whether or not to secure the debt by inhibition.

b) After Judgment has been Obtained

Post judgment, the two forms of diligence mentioned above are equally competent and operate in the way described above. Earnings arrestments operate similarly to English attachment of earnings orders. There is no equivalent of the English oral examination apart from within the context of bankruptcy and liquidation proceedings and as these are so much more inexpensive in Scotland, they are used to the same purpose. In Scotland, solicitors instruct sheriff officers (who are the equivalent of English bailiffs) and messengers at arms (who are the equivalent of English High Court sheriff officers) directly and their future remuneration depends on the efficiency and speed with which they carry out their instructions.

The Statutory Demand

This operates the same way as in England and is commonly used to start bankruptcy or liquidation proceedings. Consideration should always be given to instituting sequestration (bankruptcy) proceedings or, in the case of a limited company, having a liquidator appointed. In Scotland in case of personal bankruptcy, if the accountant in bankruptcy has been appointed trustee, all fees thereafter are borne by the government. This does not apply to liquidations. Such actions can be commenced by statutory demand.

There are three main reasons for considering such actions in Scotland:

1. issuing costs are very much less than in England
2. in bankruptcy, the creditor need not bear the cost after the petition has been granted
3. interim trustees or provisional liquidators can be appointed immediately upon presentation of such a petition to preserve any assets.

Further information from J.G. Nolan, Nolan Macleod, Solicitors, Donaldson House, 39 Donaldson Street, Kirkintilloch, Glasgow G66 1XE   tel: 0141 777 6366.

INSOLVENCY SIGNALS

Without knowing any background information on the commercial activities of a company, it is sometimes possible to see warning signs by looking at sets of accounts.

One particular company (Company X) was placed in receivership in December 1984. The company was formed in October 1952 and from the beginning they concentrated on producing high-quality printing for nationally known magazines. The initial share capital was raised from £100 to £300,000. Their last set of audited accounts, for the year ended 30 September 1984, was issued on 14 March 1985.

The auditors qualified their report by stating that the accounts had been prepared on a 'going concern' basis, which assumes that adequate finance would continue to be available to the company and the group, and that no liability would arise under the guarantees in respect of bank borrowing.

In the Chairman's report it states that the directors have entered into a new banking arrangement which was presently subject to continual review. The turnover and operating profit/loss for the three preceding years were as shown in Table 9.1.

A non-trading profit for the year 1984 was finally made when freehold land and buildings were sold.

Table 9.1 Profit/loss accounts for Company X

	Turnover	Operating profit (loss)
1982	15,660,182	(180,586)
1983	12,926,120	(427,183)
1984	11,971,925	(257,585)

By December 1984 the new bankers, in conjunction with a factoring company, had advanced £3 million. Trading conditions were still difficult, so between 1985 and 1986 certain properties were sold and the entire operation was scaled down. In August 1986, one major printing contract was not renewed. This was due to intense competition. The draft figures for 1985 showed:

Turnover: 11,623,642   Operating loss: 1,251,327

On 23 October 1986 at the request of the directors, their new bankers appointed a well-known firm of accountants to act as joint administrative receivers under a fixed and floating charge dated 21 December 1984.

I will now quote from an accountant who was representing individual creditors. His report states that the principal reason for the failure was an increasing loss at one of the sites. When the joint receivers took over, there was more than one option that they could take to protect the business. The receiver had to consider the viability of the business, their customers, pressure from creditors, the workforce and the shareholders. The options available to the receivers were:

1. To see if there was sufficient turnover to keep certain divisions of the group operating;
2. to find purchasers for the various units;
3. to close down the units which would mean a forced sale of the assets;
4. to advertise the businesses for sale.

In the event, the receivers decided that it was far more advantageous for the creditors as a whole to continue to run the printing business, as there would be a better recovery for creditors. The major creditors supported this proposal and this decision stopped customers from presenting counter claims.

By the middle of September 1988, although the operation had again been scaled down, loses were still being made and no buyers had come forward to purchase the site. It was therefore decided by the receivers to discontinue operating the business and sell off the plant and machines. In this particular case the receivers, by not insisting on a forced sale of assets in 1986, managed to sell off machinery for higher values. The unsecured creditors received a dividend of nearly 50 per cent of their debts.

Had creditors purchased a PAS financial analysis report from Syspas Ltd. they would have received the graph shown in Figure 9.2.

Richard Taffler, Chairman of Syspas Ltd. and Professor of Accounting & Finance at the City University Business School, launched his Z Scoring and Prediction of Company Failures project in 1979. His company has had a 99 per cent positive track record of identifying companies as being weak before they actually fail. Syspas also ranks all UK companies against each other by Z scoring and then ranks them on a scale of 1 to 100. The system is not a black

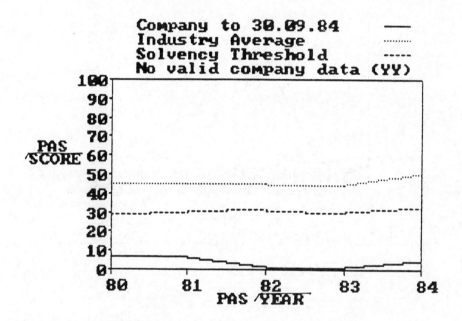

PAS Model: 2 – Unquoted Industrial
Industry: 53 – Publishing & Printing
Latest Year End: 30.09.84

PAS YEAR	PROF MARG	GEAR-ING	FIN. RISK	CRED. POS.	PAS SCORE	Z SCORE	IND PAS
1980	2	1	2	5	8	−3.57	46
1981	5	1	2	1	7	−3.89	45
1982	2	−	2	1	2	−6.09	45
1983	1	−	1	1	1	−8.79	44
1984	2	1	2	1	4	−5.97	50

Risk rating :   5

Figure 9.2 *PAS* financial analysis report

box but it provides a deep insight into a company's financial health. See Figure 9.3 for ASDA Group plc which shows how a company can regain its health.

For further information contact Guenter B. Steinitz, Syspas Ltd., Dyers Hall, 11/13 Dowgate Hill, London EC4R 2SU (tel: 0171 236 1024).

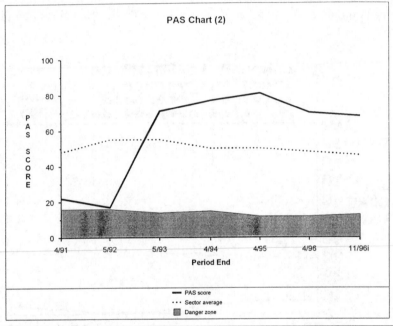

Model 3 - Quoted retail & wholesale

Sector 440 - Retailers & Wholesalers Food

Health rating :A -

Date amended: 17.03.97

Period ends	Retained cashflow	Debt cover	Current funding	Liquidity	PAS Score	Z Score	Sector Average	Rating
4/91	5	--	6	2	22	1.15	48	D
5/92	1	--	8	2	17	0.27	55	E
5/93	5	4	9	4	71	7.31	55	B
4/94	7	3	9	6	77	8.32	50	B+
4/95	7	4	9	6	81	8.41	50	B+
4/96	7	2	9	5	70	6.83	48	B
11/96i	8	1	9	4	68	6.39	46	A -

Retained Cashflow	= Retained cashflow	/ Total liabilities	34%
Debt Cover	= Total debt	/ Quick assets	10%
Current Funding	= Current liabilities	/ Total assets	44%
Liquidity	= Net quick assets1	/ Operating expenses	12%

1 [Quick assets less Current liabilities]

Figure 9.3 ASDA Group PLC, PAS financial analysis report

INSOLVENCY

There comes a time in a collection process when either bankruptcy or liquidation proceedings may have to be considered. However, there may now be a different way of protecting your interest. Before this course of action is commenced, I strongly advise checking that the individual, partnership, limited company or association does have assets which are available to you, the creditor. There are two problems for creditors in general.

Debenture Holders

If a debenture holder has a fixed charge on an asset in the business, this charge will have a prior claim even before the claims of the Crown and other preferential claimants (see below). The debenture holders who have floating charges have prior claims on any assets covered by the floating charges once the preferential claims and expenses have been paid. It is at this point that the poor, unsecured creditors may have the possibility of a percentage of any assets that can be realised. It can be seen that if any suppliers can substantiate their Reservation of Title claims, it would put them in a far stronger position if the goods have not been sold by the insolvent business (see Chapter 1, Reservation of Title).

I have deliberately highlighted these facts first, because I am constantly disturbed to hear that many suppliers still believe that if they take proceedings to wind up a business they will be paid. The Insolvency Act 1986 and Company Directors Disqualification Act 1986 serve to strengthen certain procedures which may curb some dishonourable practices. However, when a business fails there is normally very little, if anything, left for creditors. The new procedures under Voluntary Arrangements may in future give creditors a higher dividend, particularly if action can be taken early enough by or on behalf of insolvent businesses. The problem for creditors is that they cannot take the initial steps to initiate the procedure for a voluntary arrangement. The creditor can only suggest to the debtor or company that this may be the best course of action to take (see Interview with Malcolm Cork).

Preferential Claims

Schedule 6 of the Insolvency Act 1986, states the following categories of preferential debts:

- Amounts due to the Inland Revenue only in respect of PAYE and sub-contractors' deductions. Other tax liabilities do not have preferential status.

- Amounts due to the Customs and Excise in respect of VAT, car tax, betting and bingo duty. VAT is preferential for a period of six months before the relevant date, whereas for the other Crown preferential claims, the period that can be claimed is 12 months.
- Amounts due to the DSS in respect of social security contributions.
- Contributions due to the occupational pension schemes.
- Remuneration of Employees under the Employment Rights Act 1996. The new Preferential Claims include Land Fill Tax, Beer Duty, Lottery Duty, Insurance Premium Tax and Air Passenger Tax.

Malcolm Cork Interview

In an interview Malcolm Cork, a Senior Partner of Moore Stephens Booth White, London, confirmed that since July 1995 when Moore Stephens merged with Booth White & Co., the specialist insolvency firm, the combined strength of accounting consultancy and insolvency work was of great assistance when businesses have an urgent problem. Both the merged firms have a long history – Booth White had been established for over 125 years and Moore Stephens for over 90 years. The combined firm has 11 partners who specialise in insolvency. Their head office is at 1, Snow Hill, London EC1 2ED (tel: 0171 334 0334). They also have six branch offices.

In reviewing the new insolvency procedures since the Insolvency Act 1986, Malcolm Cork thought that the use of Administrative Receiverships had waned. Administrative Orders have never been particularly popular, and Voluntary Arrangements are still being used sparingly, and are still to come through.

Since my original interview in 1989, I was told that his firm are still resuscitators, and that trade creditors still have some influence on a potential insolvency situation. He emphasised that banks are now more reticent in appointing receivers, and that they do so as a last resort.

Administration orders – which are often commenced at the request of directors themselves – really mean that Moore Stevens Booth White are now acting as debt counsellors. In a vast majority of cases, while unsecured creditors may not receive their payment in full, they do in fact receive a better return than if there had been a complete 'close down' of the business. There is now the protection and continuity of the businesses, which can continue to trade in the future. This is of benefit to everyone concerned with the individual business. Not only the creditors, but also the actual debtor and their employees gain some security.

Initially, when the new Insolvency Act became law, it was felt that the banking institutions took a very jaundiced view of administration orders, but latterly the banks appear to recognise the necessity for this type of possible rescue. Government departments such as the Inland Revenue and the VAT authorities are also supporting the Act. The Official Receiver's Offices are now aware of the advantages of Voluntary Arrangements and are currently very keen to use them. Changes in insolvency training are still needed. Often insolvency practitioners were fully-skilled in the procedures for winding up companies, but when it came to the day-to-day routine of running a business they were lacking in that experience.

What is Insolvency?

A company can be insolvent but it may not be a terminal problem. There may be a lack of liquidity but this does not always mean the death of a business. 'Insolvency is the lack of ability of the business to be liquid.' There is a vast difference between an insolvency and an arrangement that will in the end create a better return for the creditors.

When looking at a company, consider whether it is insolvent and what the options are. Quite often granting credit or ceasing trading is a decision which has to be taken quickly. Finance companies need to know whether there is any chance of their loans being repaid. An insolvency specialist will look at the whole spectrum of possibilities to protect an ailing business.

Turning to the basic legislation, the Insolvency Act 1986, has superseded the Bankruptcy Act 1914. The earlier companies acts were consolidated into the Companies Act 1985. Many sections of this were repealed or amended when the two principal current statutes – the Insolvency Act 1986 and the Company Directors Disqualification Act 1986 – were brought in.

THE INSOLVENCY ACT 1986

New Options

Since the introduction of the Insolvency Act 1986, several new options are now available to debtors and creditors. When financial difficulties occur one of the following options may be the best way to reduce the final write off. I am being negative, as normally there are exceptionally small dividends for un-secured creditors when an insolvency occurs. No two insolvencies are ever the same. However, the speed at which a secured creditor can act often means that by the time the general body of creditors realise that the company they are supplying has difficulties – the business has failed.

The only way that credit granters can safeguard these 'surprise' insolvencies is to constantly update the history file on their customers and watch the sales ledger for signals which may indicate operational and financial problems.

Corporate Voluntary Arrangements

One of the changes in the Insolvency Act 1986, is that now a voluntary arrangement can be made with the agreement of creditors. Sections 1 and 2 of the Act set out the way in which the directors of a limited company contact a licensed insolvency practitioner to review whether a moratorium or a composition is practical. It should be remembered that a composition is a form of compromise which means that creditors are offered something different from what is claimed or due.

An arrangement is a method of rearranging the payments to creditors, often over a longer period. Under both the voluntary arrangement for limited companies and individuals the management of the business is not taken over. Under the Insolvency Rules 1.3 the nominee has to investigate the 23 matters set out in these rules. The nominee must include them in the proposal which must be reported to the Court within 28 days of receiving notice of the proposal from the directors. The proposal, to quote Moore Stevens Booth White, must be 'comprehensive, indeed exhaustive'. Once the court agree to the proposal, a meeting of creditors is called to consider the proposal. Creditors must receive at least 14 days notice for the meeting and at the same time receive a copy of the proposal, and a statement of affairs which has been prepared by the directors. If it is a directors' proposal, then the nominee must report to the court on the proposal. Any scheme agreed at the meeting must have the approval of the unsecured creditors. However, there must be a majority of 75 per cent in value of those creditors voting either personally or by proxy. (No proposal can be approved which varies the rights of a preferential creditor, unless that creditor agrees.)

If the scheme is approved at the meeting, the nominee becomes the supervisor. There is also provision in the rules for a creditor to apply to the Court if they think their position has been unduly prejudiced by the arrangement. The supervisor must send an abstract of the receipts and payments every 12 months to the Court, the Registrar of Companies, the company, the creditors, the members (if appropriate) and the auditors (if the company is not in liquidation).

Individual Voluntary Arrangements

The process for individuals is, in principle, more or less the same as for limited companies except that the nominee applies to the court for an interim order. This order protects the individual's estate while the scheme is being assembled. The nominee must report to the court within 14 days of the interim order to say whether he or she feels that a meeting of creditors should be convened to consider the proposal. There is a register of voluntary arrangements which is available for public inspection at:

Registrar of Voluntary Arrangements, DTI Insolvency Service Headquarters, 12th Floor, Commercial Union House, 22 Martineau Square,
Birmingham, B2 4UZ.

Administration Order

Before the Insolvency Act 1986, there was often only one course of action that
banks and other secured chargeholders could take when a business had severe
financial problems. They would call in a receiver. Under the old legislation a
receiver and manager did try, wherever possible, to keep the business, or part
of it, going and to sell it as a going concern. The result of these actions was
that, in many cases, secured chargeholders received some or all of the funds
that they had advanced from the assets which the receiver and manager had
been able to sell. The unsecured creditors in many cases did not receive any
dividend.

These situations may still continue, but under the new legislation, a committee of creditors may be formed, which ensures that the major creditors
receive information from the administrative receiver. VAT bad debt relief can
also be obtained without creditors having to wait until the company goes into
liquidation.

The Administrator

The Insolvency Act 1986, introduced the new office of an 'administrator', who
can be appointed by the company or creditors, unlike the old Act, where it
depended on the debenture holder to appoint a receiver. The procedure is
that a company's directors or their creditors may apply for an administration
order by presenting a petition to the court. Under Section 8 of the Act, the
Court has to be satisfied that the company is, or is likely to become, unable to
pay its debts (as per section 123 of the Act). A key phrase under Section
8(3)(d) is that it would be a more advantageous realisation of the company's
assets than by a winding up. The petition to the court must be accompanied by
an independent report on the company's affairs, such report normally being
by an insolvency practitioner. Notice of the petition must be given to any
debenture holders who have the power to stop the procedure by appointing
an administrative receiver or a creditor having issued a petition to wind up a
company. The administrator, unlike a supervisor in a voluntary arrangement,
is given full power to manage and reorganise the business. The advantage of
an administration order is that, although the company may be insolvent, a
greater dividend for creditors may be realised. This particular idea didn't
seem to catch on – so its benefits are still dubious.

It still remains to be seen how effective this scheme is in protecting the assets of an ailing company. Between the presentation of the petition and the actual hearing date, no enforcement of any security and no executions on goods or other assets can take place. Winding up petitions can be presented, but action cannot be taken until the court actually decide whether to grant an administration order. If the order is granted, an administrator has three months to provide a copy of his proposals to the creditors and the Registrar of Companies and to make it available to the shareholders. The court can agree to an extension.

Immediately the appointment is made notice of it must be advertised in the *London Gazette* and a newspaper.

Within 21 days (or any extended period) of the request to them for it, the administrator should receive a statement of affairs from the officers of the company. Most importantly, the creditors must be advised of the appointment within 28 days. The administrator must call a meeting of creditors to approve the proposals within the above three-month period. If the proposals are approved the creditors may appoint a committee of between three and five. This has the power to request that the administrator give them details of his or her actions.

All invoices, orders for goods, or business letters must state that an administrator has been appointed. Under the Act, creditors and members of the company are given a certain amount of protection as, if they consider that the administrator is acting prejudicially to their interest, they may apply to the court for relief.

Liquidations – the Other Alternatives

Limited companies can still be wound up by their members or by the creditors through a voluntary liquidation. A members' voluntary liquidation can take place if the directors issue a declaration of solvency to the effect that they have made a full inquiry into the company's affairs and that they have formed the opinion that the company will be able to pay its debts in full, together with interest, within a period not exceeding 12 months (Section 89(1), Insolvency Act 1986).

Under the same Act there is now provision for calling a meeting of creditors within 28 days from the date at which the liquidator formed the opinion that the company could not pay its debts within the period stated in the directors' declaration. Creditors have to be given at least seven days notice of the meeting of creditors. A statement of affairs and other financial information must be verified by affidavit to the liquidator. For detailed requirements see Section 95, Insolvency Act 1986. Once the meeting takes place, the creditors have the opportunity of electing their own choice of liquidator, and the winding up then follows the same course as a creditor's voluntary liquidation.

Creditors' Voluntary Liquidation

This does not mean that in a voluntary liquidation creditors will be paid their debts in full. It simply means that the company took the action to place themselves into liquidation, instead of waiting for a creditor to petition to the court for the company to be wound up. The procedure for winding up an insolvent company under a Creditors' Voluntary Liquidation is initiated by the directors.

The only people that can place a company into voluntary liquidation are the shareholders. The shareholders must be given 14 days notice of an EGM (Extraordinary General Meeting), at which time they can pass the resolution placing the company into liquidation. They must on the same day hold a creditors' meeting.

Following the older legislation additional rules have been made. To stop the assets being sold before the creditors' meeting, the liquidator is not allowed to sell any property or goods (other than those which are perishable or will immediately diminish in value), unless he or she has the agreement of the court (Section 166). The notice of the creditors' meeting, which must be sent no less than seven days before the meeting, must include proxy forms and give details of:

- the name and address of an insolvency practitioner who will provide creditors, free of charge, with details concerning the company's affairs;
- the location near the company's principal place of business, where, in the last two business days before the meeting of creditors, a list of creditors' names and addresses will be available for inspection free of charge (Section 98).

The meeting of creditors must be held between the hours of 10.00am and 4.00pm. Creditors at the meeting may nominate their own liquidator. A statement of affairs verified by the directors must show details of the company's:

- assets, debts and liabilities;
- names and addresses of creditors, and the securities held by them;
- the dates when securities were given.

The detailed requirements are noted under Section 99 of the Insolvency Act 1986. Creditors must have submitted their proof of debt and proxy form before the meeting to be able to vote at the meeting of creditors.

Resolutions at the meeting are passed by a majority in value – not number – of those voting in person or by proxy. This means that the large creditors have a greater control on who is actually appointed liquidator. At their meeting the creditors can appoint a liquidation committee of not less than three and not more than five of their number (Section 101). If the creditors do not object, up to five shareholders may join the committee.

To conclude, if there are any assets that are available for unsecured creditors it is far better to try to arrange for a Creditors' Voluntary Liquidation, as the Department of Trade and Industry fees are substantially less than those charged in a compulsory winding up.

Compulsory Liquidations

Any creditor, under the Insolvency Act 1986, can send to a debtor the new statutory demand under Section 123 of the Act (Section 221 if the debtor company is an unregistered company). The demand requires the debtor to pay the debt within 21 days, and must be posted to or served at the registered office of the company. The demand actually states that if the debtor wishes to avoid a winding up petition, they must pay the debt within the 21-day period.

The issuing of this statutory demand sometimes stirs the debtor into paying. It should be remembered, to quote Steve Hill of Coopers & Lybrand that 'in a compulsory winding up you can write your debt off on day one'. The tiniest dividends are paid to creditors. If there is any surplus, one of the largest beneficiaries is the Department of Trade and Industry, who charge a 15 per cent fee on the first £50,000 that is realised.

However, if a petition is then presented, the initial cost would be in the region of £700. A deposit of £500 plus a court fee of £50 is also required, to cover the Official Receiver's costs. This is where a pre-suing report can indicate whether taking proceedings would be cost effective. If it appears that only the VAT content of the invoices will be reclaimable, then a careful calculation must be made. For example, a £5000 invoice includes £652 VAT, therefore, if winding up proceedings are being considered, a far higher outstanding debt is required so that costs are not swallowed up by VAT refund.

Under Section 123(2) of the Act, a company is also deemed unable to pay its debts if it is proved to the satisfaction of the Court that the value of the company's assets is less than the amount of its liabilities, taking into account its contingent and prospective liabilities.

The Petition

A debt of £750 must be owed for a petition to be presented to the Court. This can be done by one creditor or a group of creditors. Sections 122 and 123 of the Act cover the various grounds. Under Section 122(b) a company which has been registered as a public limited company may be wound up if it has not

Form 4.1

Rule 4.5

Statutory Demand under section 123(1)(a) or 221(1)(a) of the Insolvency Act 1986

> **Warning**
> - This is an **important** document. This demand must be dealt with **within 21 days** after its service upon the company or a winding-up order could be made in respect of the company.
> - Please read the demand and notes carefully.

Notes for Creditor
- If the creditor is entitled to the debt by way of assignment, details of the original creditor and any intermediary assignees should be given in part B on page 3.
- If the amount of debt includes interest not previously notified to the company as included in its liability, details should be given, including the grounds upon which interest is charged. The amount of interest must be shown separately.
- Any other charge accruing due from time to time may be claimed. The amount or rate of the charge must be identified and the grounds on which it is claimed must be stated.
- In either case the amount claimed must be limited to that which has accrued due at the date of the demand.
- If signatory of the demand is a solicitor or other agent of the creditor the name of his/her firm should be given.

Demand

To _____

Address _____

_____

This demand is served on you by the creditor:

Name _____

Address _____

_____

The creditor claims that the company owes the sum of £_____ , full particulars of which are set out on page 2.

The creditor demands that the company do pay the above debt or secure or compound for it to the creditor's satisfaction.

Signature of individual _____

Name _____
(BLOCK LETTERS)

Date _____

*Position with or relationship to creditor _____

_____

*Delete if signed by the creditor himself

*I am authorised to make this demand on the creditor's behalf.

Address _____

_____

Tel. No. _____   Ref. _____

N.B. The person making this demand must complete the whole of this page, page 2 and parts A and B (as applicable) on page 3.

Figure 9.4 Statutory demand, Section 123, Insolvency Act 1986

been issued with a certificate covering the share minimum allotment requirements (under Section 117 of the Companies Act 1985) and more than a year has expired since it was so registered (see Chapter 3, Public Limited Companies). The petitioning creditor can apply for an order for a provisional liquidator. This may be done to safeguard any assets which may be in danger even before the court has granted a winding up petition. If the petition is granted by the court, a copy of the order is forwarded to the official receiver, the company and the Registrar of Companies.

Under Section 132(1)(a) and (b) of the Insolvency Act, it is the duty of the official receiver to investigate the causes of the failure, if the company has failed, and the promotion, formation, business dealings and affairs of the company. The official receiver may then report these findings to the court if he thinks fit. Unlike in a voluntary liquidation, in a compulsory liquidation, creditors are required to submit proof of debt forms.

Within 12 weeks of the winding up order the official receiver must decide whether he will summon meetings of the company's shareholders and creditors for the purpose of choosing a liquidator. He must, however, summon such meetings if he is requested to do so by one quarter in value of the creditors. An order also stops proceedings being taken against the company, except by leave of the court.

Directors' Responsibility

Where it can be seen that wrongful trading (as defined in Section 214 of the Insolvency Act) was carried out, the directors or past directors may have to make a contribution to the company's assets, if the court consider that the person responsible knew, or ought to have concluded, that there was no reasonable prospect that the company would avoid going into insolvent liquidation. The questions to be asked, where any limited company appears to have been insolvent for a considerable period, are:

1. Are there grounds for alleging wrongful trading?
2. Have the directors any personal assets?
3. What are the chances of a successful action, which will produce a payment for creditors in general?

Each case must be considered separately. For example, a successful test case for wrongful trading was heard in March 1989. The problem for the creditors was that the legal costs totalled £90,000, and the two directors were jointly and severally liable to contribute £75,000 from their personal assets. This payment was passed to the liquidator. The case highlighted the fact that the company carried on trading when it was insolvent. The directors' defence, that the accounts were late in being produced, was no excuse, as they knew that their sales had been down on the previous year.

It may seem that with the Company Directors Disqualification Act 1986, and the Fraudulent and Wrongful Trading section in the Insolvency Act 1986 that you, the credit granter, are safeguarded. I am inclined to disagree, as there are a large number of cases which never get to court. Liquidators, administrative receivers and administrators are required to submit a report to the Secretary of State if they believe that the conduct of directors makes them unfit to be concerned with the management of a company. The actual number disqualified is very small. The index which shows these directors can be viewed at Companies House in Cardiff. Malcolm Cork, in reviewing some of these wrongful trading cases, stated that there are two key questions that directors must answer to prove wrongdoing:

- Did you trade the company recklessly?
- Did you run the company when you knew it was insolvent and you knew there was no likelihood of money being paid out to the creditors, or in other words, did you accept credit not knowing how you were going to repay it?

False Optimism by Directors, Partners and Sole Traders

Malcolm Cork confirmed that with CVAs and IVAs the existing management were often far too confident about their expected turnover and profits, and they sometimes gave over-optimistic projections on cost cutting. Consequently these businesses failed, with little possibility of a dividend for creditors.

There are also few of these arrangements as it appears that credit managers in general still do not tend to adopt a rescue culture attitude. If they thought about saving their customers rather than issuing a Writ, they would gain more in the long run.

Bankruptcy

One or more creditors can present a bankruptcy petition if the sum involved is £750 or more. There are other methods of service of a statutory demand, besides personal service on the debtor. Rule 6.3(a) of the Insolvency Act 1986 indicates what should be done, for example, if the debtor has absconded or is keeping out of the way with a view to avoiding service.

The personal assets of an individual may be seized, but it is important first to investigate who actually owns the property. Property which is held in trust by the debtor for others cannot be sold. Equipment, tools and even the vehicle used by the bankrupt to earn a living are excluded, and the same applies to the furniture, bedding, clothing, household equipment and provisions necessary for the basic domestic needs of the bankrupt and his family.

Although future legislation may again change the balance, due to wrongful trading and the requirement of the Company Directors Disqualification Act 1986, many more 'business managers' may decide to become unincorporated and revert to being sole traders. With the change of Government in May 1997 there are now strong indications that the New Labour administration will be far tougher in disqualifying directors for fraudulent or wrongful trading.

Another View of Insolvency

Will Company Voluntary Arrangements be reformed to make them more workable? This was a question that Steve Hill, insolvency partner at Coopers & Lybrand, thought was an important reform. There have been two ministerial statements but no legislation has yet been placed before Parliament, and with a new administration the policy may now change. In Steve Hill's opinion there is a growing tendency for honest debtors and directors to seek help when they get into difficulties. There is more recognition now that liquidation or bankruptcy are not the only options. Provided that the debtor takes immediate action, sometimes a company can be saved. For instance, a firm of accountancy practitioners bought premises in the 1990s during the property boom. During the recession interest rates climbed, property prices plummeted and a decent business collapsed. A Voluntary Arrangement was arranged for the partners and the business merged with another firm of accountants.

Voluntary Arrangements are increasingly popular for professional firms because of the risk of losing their professional status. This method of arrangement enables them to continue to work in their own fields. Many solicitors in the High Street who have been squeezed on conveyancing have also had to be rescued. This is not to say that every business is rescuable. There are businesses which have reached the end of their life cycle and the kindest thing one can do is to give them a decent burial.

There now appears to be a social recognition that there is much less stigma attached to failure. In a perfect world debtors would realise that their business was coming to its end, they would shut up the shop and pay off the creditors. But we do not live in a perfect world. We live in an ever more complex commercial environment. There are substantial costs, for instance, in laying off a workforce. Businesses which are solvent on a normal trading basis can become insolvent solely for the reason that they are closing down.

One of the continuing problems for tenants is the seemingly inalienable right of landlords to put pressure on their tenants, hence upwards only rent reviews with many 25 year leases. Businesses can fail just because landlords are demanding too much for rent. Then if a business fails in say 6 years the landlord can demand the other ninteeen years' rent. These are a few of the reasons which put certain creditors in a privileged position as against the ordinary creditor and why in a typical trade insolvency the average creditor will get nothing. It is not because the debtor is a rogue or the insolvency practitioner is too expensive, it is because we have too many laws which put certain creditors in an absolutely privileged position.

Because for good social reasons the employee has this protection, the meagre funds that are available in the insolvency are paid to the employees. The average trade creditor often gets no dividend and loses a customer. What does this mean for the average credit manager? In Steve Hill's opinion, 'You cannot live in the modern world without credit, so all you can do is manage credit as best as you can'. Incidentally, in concluding the interview, Steve, without wishing to advertise, confirmed that insolvency advice costs as little as £69 an hour, and if someone has a problem the initial meeting is free. His firm do not charge until they are confident that they can help an ailing business. For further information contact Mr Steve Hill, Insolvency Partner, Coopers & Lybrand, Plumtree Court, London EC4A 4HT. Telephone no. 0171 606 7700.

SUMMARY

When considering taking proceedings, the time involved, costs incurred and whether a debt recovery agency or instructing solicitor is your best option are the points that must be borne in mind before a collection decision can be made.

- In the event of non-payment, do you wish to retain the customer?
- Have they any assets?
- Is it worth taking proceedings considering the size of the debt?
- Do your staff realise the cost and variety of legal proceedings available?
- Remember that collection proceedings in Scotland are different from those in England, Wales and Northern Ireland.

Further Reading

The following publications will help readers to appreciate the intricacies of insolvency legislation.
  '*An Outline of Insolvency Procedures*' by Patrick Hartigan FCCA FIPA FSPI MICM.

Bulletin, which reports on current insolvency cases and aspects of insolvency law, and the *Weekly Insolvency Gazette*. All the above are published by Moore Stephens Booth White, available from Mr P. Hartigan, Moore Stephens Booth White, 3/5 Rickmansworth Road, Watford, Herts WD1 7JH.

Phoenix, the business recovery and insolvency journal of Coopers & Lybrand.

Insolvency in brief, Choices for troubled companies and several other booklets on related topics, all published by Coopers & Lybrand, Plumtree Court, London EC4A 4HT.

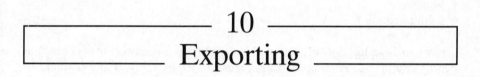

10
Exporting

THE RIGHT ATTITUDE AND RISK TAKING

Large profits can still be made when exporting. But I am sure that some UK exporters in the past have thrown up their hands in disgust after their first overseas order became a nightmare. To quote one trader 'Everything seemed to go wrong.' In fact, their attitude to overseas selling was that as their home sales were not being maintained, it was logical to export. The increased sales would help their profit margins and clear stocks which were not moving. How wrong they were!

Since 1990, with companies re-engineering, restructuring and demerging, credit staff are now often required to take on the task of export manager and/ or shipping manager. You may also ask why should credit control staff still have to consider the many areas outside the payment terms.

With the competition from overseas companies setting up in the UK, our domestic market is being constantly attacked. Therefore it would seem sensible to consider exporting. By exporting, profit margins can sometimes be far higher than in the home market because unit costs can be lower for longer production runs. However, quoting Ian Campbell, the Director General of the Institute of Export, the prospective exporter may need to ask 'Should I really export?' For some companies selling to an export marketing company might be an easier option. There is only one stumbling block. Selling overseas is rather like watching a horse jump in the Grand National. There are many hurdles to cross before the sale is converted into an actual shipment and the transaction converted into a payment. The fundamental reason why so many transactions in overseas trade end in failure is that the following factors are not carefully considered well before accepting an order:

- Government regulations
- Legal requirements

- Financing and payment terms
- Political/economic/commercial risks
- Transportation
- Documentation
- Local customs/consumer preferences
- Distance
- Language
- Communication.

Thorough investigation of all these areas may seem almost impossible, but export intelligence is all about desk research. Regrettably, if any segment of marketing or any of the other aspects is not reviewed, even if an order is taken it could become a total loss. But by working through a check list the above factors can be reviewed and profitable sales can be made.

The initial desk research must be carried out to ascertain whether the product or service is marketable in a certain country. The exporter must also consider the competition in the local market and overseas competitors. But just as important are the UK exporters who are already supplying in that country. This competition is intense.

The Risks

With some 240 countries overseas in which it is possible to sell, there will always be some risks of non-payment unless detailed research is carried out. For instance the World Bank, in their 'Global Development Finance' report published in March 1997, stated that since 1980, 60 countries had had to reschedule their sovereign or official debts. One of these actually had to reschedule eleven times and the majority for more than three times. Some of the above countries have also had to reschedule their commercial debts but the list is not exactly the same. Therefore it can be seen that at any one time a large percentage of the countries in the world may be insolvent! To help readers reviewing the risk, Dun & Bradstreet's *International Risks & Payment Review*, published monthly, gives a concise update on payments and economic and political conditions. To highlight insolvencies in Europe, Creditreform's list of insolvencies demonstrates the risk of business failures (see Table 10.1).

The European Union – a Warning

About 60 per cent of all our exports are sold to the European Union and since 1992 more countries have joined the EU. It was agreed in July 1997 that the following countries would be joining within the next three years: Poland, the

Table 10.1 Insolvencies in Europe 1995–1996

Countries	Absolute		Changes in %
	1995	1996	
Austria	4994	5600	12.1
Belgium	7157	7400	3.4
Denmark	2621	1900	−27.5
Finland	5234	4900	−6.4
France	59,503	59,900	0.7
Germany	28,785	33,000	14.6
Great Britain	43,484	42,900	−1.3
Greece	1395	1500	7.5
Ireland	693	670	−3.3
Italy	16,016	15,600	−2.6
Luxembourg	320	390	21.9
Netherlands	5874	5600	−4.2
Norway	3899	3800	−2.5
Spain	1345	1100	−18.2
Sweden	12,585	12,200	−3.1
Switzerland	9761	10,200	4.5
Total	203,639	206,660	1.5

Czech Republic, Slovenia, Hungary, Estonia and Cyprus. This will add about another 50 million consumers to the Community.

When the UK decided to join the EU in 1972 the attitude of the Government was that selling to Europe would be as easy as selling in Birmingham, Cardiff or Edinburgh. A potential market of over 300 million consumers was on our doorstep. In theory this was correct, but every country in Europe has its own character, which can vary from one district to another. Customers and social aspects must always be studied. For instance, do not try to use the same agent for both Spain and Portugal! Be careful which language you use when considering selling in Belgium. It is imperative to review a country's background and history in order to appreciate why each nation is so different from the others.

There are a number of new regulations which must also be understood when selling to the EC. For example the fairly complex packaging regulations in Germany are a problem. Agency law, distribution of goods and exclusive purchasing agreements all have to be studied for all the EC countries.

The World Market

One quick way to review our share of the world market is to obtain a copy of the *Export Times'* survey which shows, in descending order, the value of sales, percentage changes and the export/import balance and ratios on 200 countries (see Further Reading for details).

Speaking broadly, if a product or service is good and the price realistic I can almost guarantee that a buyer in one of the 240 countries will agree to transact, provided that all the requirements set out below have been reviewed.

Hidden Cost

Can a profit be made after allowing for the competition in the trade? I ask this question first as there is a vast amount of hidden costs which, when added together, can greatly increase the basic price of the product or service before any profit margin is calculated. The marketing research and administration charges, if they are considered at the planning stage, will mean that a real profit is made when the final price structure is agreed. Additional costs which do not normally occur in the home market are documentation charges for certification, inspection fees, translation costs, bank charges, health and safety certificates and extra packaging.

Talking to exporters who are successful, they all confirm that if the product is exactly right for the individual market, and if it is competitively priced and delivery is made at the stated date, there is absolutely no bar to selling. However, with the intense global competition of the 1990s, often a lower price or longer credit terms will clinch a deal.

I will now try to guide readers through the initial stages.

Where Do You Start?

Depending on your product or service, you must check to see whether certain items can be exported. You may need an export licence (and there are several types); you may even need a licence to communicate, for example, with Iraq. Check with the DTI's Export Control Organisation, 6th Floor, 66–74 Victoria Street, London SW1E 6SW (tel: 0171 215 8070). They or other Government Offices will be able to advise whether the products need prior approval under the Strategic Export Controls. For example as at July 1997, the UN has trade sanctions on selling to Angola, Iraq, Libya, Rwanda and Somalia.

There are rules about military equipment, nuclear-related goods, dual use goods designed for civil use but which could be used for military purposes, chemical weapons equipment and certain microorganisms, biological equipment and technology, as well as many other sectors.

There are still certain tariff restrictions, exchange control regulations and health and safety requirements that must be observed.

Pre-inspection of Goods

Many countries throughout the world, especially if they are short of Foreign Exchange, require goods to be pre-inspected for quality before dispatch and sales documents examined for a price comparison. Do not underestimate the potential problems when pre-inspection is required.

MAJOR RISKS

In reviewing the country, you may not like their politics, but if they have a good reputation for payments and they do honour their contracts, this should be included on a check list for a country evaluation. A second problem that has to be considered is that a country's economy may be exceptionally strong but, due to political uncertainty, contracts could be interrupted and payments dry up. This is an instance where credit insurance (insurance of debt) could be considered, (see Chapter 11, Credit Insurance).

The commercial risk of non-payment has to be evaluated from two different standpoints. Can the individual buyer actually pay, and what is their record? Secondly, the buyer may be able to pay, but there are exchange control regulations in that country which will preclude a payment. For example, traders who sold to Turkey years ago are still awaiting settlement. The uninsured commercial debts incurred in Nigeria in 1980 have had to be converted into promissory notes. The final repayment was due in the year 2010! With the oil price now more stable there is no reason why UK exporters should not consider this market. However, the current political scene is not hopeful: in 1987, Nigeria was our 26th largest market, with sales of £482 million, whereas in 1996 they ranked 43rd, with sales of £200 million.

Credit Limits and Payment Terms

Marketing and carrying out research for style, preference and customer requirements is obviously essential (see page 204 for marketing research). But unless the exporter has a unique product or service which is in tremendous demand, it is likely, with intense competition, that the buyer will be able to force the seller to give either longer credit or a lower price or both and even dictate which currency they will trade in! Within the last five years many countries have been able to produce products which are cheaper due to far lower labour costs and worldwide lowering of the price of raw materials.

Many export transactions become total losses because the exporter does not ask the fundamental questions 'Who is the actual buyer and what is their track record and are they solvent?'

In reviewing the commercial, economic and political risks the following points should be considered:

1. Can the buyer pay the entire transaction in full or on the proposed terms and what is the maximum term that can be extended?
2. Is the buyer already paying the suggested sums to other exporters or traders in their own country or are they exceeding the terms?
3. Are there any economic problems, such as a shortage of foreign exchange, which will automatically delay payment?
4. If credit insurance is being considered or a policy is already in force, will the underwriters be able to give up-to-date information?
5. In considering the proposed transaction, is it worthwhile making a far lower profit (provided that you have calculated all the export costs) to get your toe in the door for repeat business?

Payment Methods

Once a strategy has been agreed on the length of credit for a particular customer and once the country's economy has been studied, it is then possible to decide on which payment method or combination of methods can be used.

Payment methods throughout the world are gradually changing. The NCM and Institute of Export commissioned their fifth *Survey of International Services* which was published in July 1997. In it they mentioned that there was an increase of up to 91 per cent in the number of exporters who were selling to Europe on open terms, whereas in Latin America 45 per cent of exporters used letters of credit compared to 63 per cent in the 1996 survey.

Payment Method According to Risk

Credit has often been described as 'confidence, trust and belief in your customer's ability to pay at a definite future date for goods supplied today'. Once you have this confidence the following methods can be used which will give a greater or lesser degree of security for payment and at the same time increase or reduce the control over the goods being despatched.

Open Terms

Where there are no exchange control regulations and there has been a history of prompt payment between buyer and seller, 'open terms' or open account is a perfectly satisfactory way of trading. Open terms reduce bank and documentary charges.

Cash Against Order

In some countries exchange control regulations require the Central Bank to give permission before the shipment can be sent.

Cash Against Documents

Cash against documents (CAD) terms are widely used in Europe and where there is confidence in banks. This method is simple. The export documentation is consigned to the bank with exact instructions that the documents are not to be released to the importer or their agent until payment is transferred to the exporter. A sight draft (Bill of Exchange) is not required.

Letters of Credit (L/Cs)

Warning. Letters of Credit are complex; the validity of the credit may be an exceptionally short period and it may be impossible to ship the goods in that short time. The principal questions that must be answered is 'Are the terms workable?'

Always re-read credits, the clauses can be a minefield. Amendments and extensions can be obtained but they are expensive and who would pay the costs? There are many types of Letters of Credit and the cost of raising each type is different, depending on the security of payment.

Under all Letters of Credit there is a doctrine of strict compliance. Banks only see the documents so that if there are discrepancies the credit will be rejected. It is estimated in the UK that perhaps 70 per cent of all credits are rejected by banks on presentation because of mistakes in documentation. Most international banks follow the ICC (International Chamber of Commerce) UCP 500 rules which all exporters who use L/Cs should study. The most secure credit is an ILC (Irrevocable Letter of Credit). This type cannot be cancelled or amended without the agreement of the exporter or importer. Delays in payment can occur when the importer's opening bank has insufficient funds available. Again it depends on the credit status and reputation of the importer's bank.

A further type of credit is the Unconfirmed Irrevocable Letter of Credit. Unlike an ILC, the advising bank in the exporter's country has no obligation to pay the exporter. When reading this type of credit, advising banks will often add the words, 'This credit does not bear our confirmation.' Incidentally there is the Standby Letter of Credit which is not a credit in the real sense but a bank guarantee, that if the buyer does not pay to terms, the exporter can apply to the bank for payment.

Finally, not all banks are financially strong. It was reported in 1997 that some 300 Russian banks may still be insolvent. There is also a vast number of banks in the USA, some of which are very small!

Prospecting Your Products and Services

Once you can confirm that there are no restrictions barring you from exporting to certain countries, you can then carry out the market and country research. Most of the world's countries or areas are covered by about 80 desk officers at the Department of Trade & Industry, Kingsgate House, 66–74 Victoria Street, London, SW1E 6SW. These desk officers specialise in specific countries and special sectors. They deal with enquiries from traders and at the same time liaise with our 222 posts which cover the 189 countries throughout the world with which we have diplomatic relations.

From experience, I can confirm that these desk officers have an enormous amount of information and are very experienced and helpful. They are still able to supply a limited amount of information free of charge, for example, Market menus for the 80 key countries (see Using Government Sources, page 205), but for most other country publications there are now charges.

The same desk officers can be contacted through the Government Offices and Business Links which are located throughout the UK. A number of Chambers of Commerce have links with the 230 'Business Links' which employ 63 Export Development Counsellors (see Chambers of Commerce, page 206).

The New Administration and Export Policy

With the new Labour administration appointed in May 1997 it is too early to see what changes in Government assisted schemes will affect exporters. However, as at July 1997, Margaret Beckett, the President of the Board of Trade, launched an 'Export Forum' to review the effectiveness of the official support for the many Government services for helping exporters. So far sources close to the Minister have stated that previous export schemes which were successful under the previous Government will continue. For example, the DTI's 200 'Export Promoters' who have been seconded from industry have a wealth of knowledge on individual markets and sectors and will probably be retained.

EXPORTING TO FRANCE

With the narrow strip of water that separates England and France, readers may feel that exporting to France would be comparatively simple. However, firstly the language barrier must be considered. An official of the French Desk Exports to Europe Branch, DTI, emphasised that some knowledge of French was considered to be essential if selling to France is being contemplated.

UK sales to France in 1996 were £17 billion and France is our third largest export market. More traders were trying to enter the market as the strength of the pound made selling to many countries in the world more difficult. There is plenty of help available from our DTI French desk officers. The British Embassy in Paris has many officers working in the commercial section, and locally engaged commercial officers work at our Consulates-General in Bordeaux, Lyon, Marseilles and Lille and are available to help UK exporters. Their knowledge of local conditions is most valuable. Trade Missions to France are still popular; this may be because of interest resulting from the Channel Tunnel and the European single market. Their *Market Menu on France* gives a list of information and literature which is available free of charge, plus the *Country Profiles and Reports* which are chargeable. The menu also lists the addresses and telephone and fax numbers of our Embassy and the four Consulates General Offices and the information and tailor made services which they can supply through their Commercial Offices (see Desk Research – Using Government Sources, page 205).

The French Desk also supplies a Trade Brief. This is a simple overview of the opportunities that exist for UK exporters and information on imports/ exports and basic notes on trading.

A catalogue of all the Export Publications is available from the DTI Export Publications Orderline, Admail 528, London SW1 8YT (tel: 0171 510 0171).

The Language Barrier

Living on an island, we have never found it easy to master other languages. Taylor and Partners employ 2400 translators who are trained to understand commercial transactions. Certain translators also specialise in legal, medical, engineering, chemical and many other segments of industry. Taylors also carry out typesetting, proof-reading and a full colour printing service. With the single market it is still essential that UK exporters' communications are understood, and Taylors can supply overseas nationals to help traders use their international sales department.

Further information from Taylor & Partners Translators Limited, PO Box 59, Winchester, Hampshire, SO23 8XL (tel: 01962 779798 Fax: 01962 779669 Compuserve: 10 0045.600@compuserve.com).

HOW DO YOU MARKET A PRODUCT OR SERVICE?

Every country has their individual character and style. In countries such as the USA, India, China and Nigeria, the physical areas are so large that consideration must be given to the exact area you are trying to sell to. This is where the desk research will enable you to save wasted time and costs on useless prospecting.

Question one to be considered: Is it advisable to sell direct or is an agent required? This is a critical legal point because in certain Middle Eastern countries, for instance, there are stringent requirements. Agents already appointed, for example, may have exclusive rights. To illustrate how to overcome this problem, the Committee for Middle East Trade (COMET) have published a superb 80-page guide to selecting, appointing and working with agents in the Middle Eastern markets. It is priced £15 and can be purchased from The Committee for Middle East Trade, 33 Bury Street, London, SW1Y 6AX.

Business Failures

A different approach to credit assessment has to be made since the 1990s collapse of the Soviet Union, the worldwide privatisation of nationalised industries and the establishment of entirely new countries. Among these countries are the Czech Republic and Slovakia, and the independent control of a number of other countries, for example Uzbekistan and Kazakhstan. There may be less information on the track record of newly-established businesses.

One international credit insurer confirmed that they use up to 175 credit bureaux and agencies to research businesses throughout the world.

Many initial marketing techniques may seem impossible to unravel, but help is at hand. I will use France, the USA and the Middle East as examples in this chapter. Much of this information can be relayed via satellite fax and computer links, but there are five principal sources: government departments, Chambers of Commerce, Business Links, trade associations and commercial marketing companies.

In exporting it is unusual for one source to have all the vital market facts. It is better to use every available source. My reason for being so insistent is that, unless the product is unique in Western Europe, I estimate that for every item sold there are ten competitors in each country. Consequently, all the market intelligence has to be gathered to evaluate whether exporting will be a gamble or a profitable venture.

DESK RESEARCH – USING GOVERNMENT SOURCES

The Department of Trade and Industry, through their Export Market Information Centre Library, has a comprehensive collection of overseas statistics, trade directories and development plans. Much of the material is on microfiche and on data bases. The library is open five and a half days a week for personal users and short enquiries can be referred by telephone. Before researching it is essential to check your product code. Because different countries use various product classification codes, it is advisable to check all known reference numbers before starting on research.

From January 1989, the Association of British Chambers of Commerce undertook to manage the Export Market Research Scheme (EMRS) on behalf of the Joint Directorate of the FCO and DTI (Foreign & Commonwealth Office and Department of Trade & Industry). Through the Chambers of Commerce in the Association, their members can carry out export market research so that companies can be helped to reach sound decisions on whether to export to new markets and how to introduce a new product or service.

Through more than 50 Chambers of Commerce who have approved status they also manage the Lexas National Languages for the export Campaign which was launched in 1993 to provide accredited independent consultants who understand how languages and cultures operate in the business world. There is also a subsidy of up to £650 for a business language report. The purpose of this scheme is to encourage companies to export by providing financial assistance so that 'commissioned research is based on sound methods'. The scheme also provides for independent professional export marketing research advice. When companies are carrying out 'in house' research for the first time up to half of the essential travel costs and interpreter's fees, plus a daily allowance towards hotel and other costs may be allowed. This scheme does now cover the European Community countries. However, under this marketing and research scheme, up to half the cost of employing professional consultants will be paid, up to £20,000 per project. If market research publications have to be obtained, one-third of the cost is refunded. For trade association and commissioned research for members, up to three-quarters of the cost is refundable.

Through the local regional officers or the desk officers at Victoria Street, essential information on the commercial activities and opportunities can be funnelled through the commercial staff in the embassies.

In the past there has been criticism of the Export Intelligence Service which advised British exporters of opportunities for specific sales. Again, the reason why some exporters have not used this method of finding markets is that the description of their own product or service was not sufficiently detailed. In January 1989 the DTI announced that they would continue to funnel the export enquiries from their commercial officers. These export leads are now marketed by Prelink Ltd, Export House, Wembley Hill Road, Wembley, Middlesex H49 8BU. This is a company which specialises in providing a computerised desk-top information and trading network. It is understood that nearly 15,000 UK exporters use the EIS scheme to find new buyers.

Embassies, Consulates General and Trade Offices

In 1997 there was a new approach to helping exporters to gain new and increased markets. By using the Market Information Enquiry Service (MIES) commercial staff will investigate the potential for selling a particular product or service. The Representative Service (ERS) is available to help exporters identify the best agents or distributors. The cost of these services starts at £100 for four hours research and rises to about £1200 for 24–48 hours work. There is also a range of other services to support exporters before they visit or when visiting a market.

I interviewed some of our commercial officers and locally engaged staff who have visited the UK, and found that they are totally focused on selling. They know their territories and the competition in the market place. Their attitude is now totally different from the old days, when commercial duties were a burden that had to be carried out.

CHAMBERS OF COMMERCE

For the first time in about 200 years of UK Chamber of Commerce history, the Association of British Chambers of Commerce is now developing a quality assured consistent business support network. As at June 1997 there were some 53 approved chambers which provided a comprehensive international trade service. In 1996 these chambers organised over 1170 trade missions to more than 80 countries, generating about £500 million of follow-up business. Here I will report on specific chambers which only deal with a certain country or area. These are the American, French and Arab British Chambers of Commerce. With the vast number of problems in exporting I think it is suicidal to try to sell abroad without the assistance of a major chamber.

The London Chamber of Commerce & Industry

The London Chamber of Commerce & Industry is a major organiser of selling and buying missions for its 3500 members. It is estimated that 70 per cent of their members who are owners of businesses trade internationally.

The Chamber is particularly good at arranging receptions for inward delegations where they can introduce UK exporters to new markets. Often after an export mission returns there will be a 'report back' briefing. Fifty seminars, conferences and workshops are run each year. They have a team of 37 who are employed exclusively to deal with international trade, customs and trade procedures, exchange control, EU affairs and linguistics. Through their committee structure there are 100 active market and trade specialists who serve on the many advisory committees.

The Chamber runs London's only Euro Info Centre and will be opening a second centre in Westminster. They will have links with 250 Euro Info Centres throughout the European Union and can introduce potential business partners through the BRE (*Bureau de Rapprochement des Enterprises*). Their library, with a reading section, is well stocked with a large number of directories and overseas market information. Their new computer network is now in place and the instalment of the library management system will be completed in early 1998.

All the staff are particularly helpful and have built up years of experience. The London Chamber is one of the Association of British Chambers of Commerce Approved Chambers. The Chamber produces an annual reference book for exporters, *Export Handbook*, and a bi-monthly bulletin, *International Trade Matters*. They also sell papers on Commercial Agency and Customs and Practice for Documentary Credits.

Further information from The London Chamber of Commerce, 33 Queen Street, London EC4R 1AP (tel: 0171 248 4444).

Birmingham Chamber of Commerce

The Birmingham Chamber of Commerce was formed in 1783 and they have over 5000 members. This Chamber has not only a superb export division but the European Business Centre is attached to their headquarters. These centres create two-way communication on products and services provided by medium and small businesses. The single market now means that companies need to know about community policies, funding and grants, standardisation of VAT, employment law and the all-important competition policy. Through a computer link to Brussels, they are also able to access the following databanks: the European Community Laws (CELEX); Scientific and Technical Research Programmes (EXBS); Financial Development Projects (PABLI); Principal Community Acts and Official Publications (SCAD), and Tenders for Public Works (TED). In the *Birmingham Venture* newsletter, a number of overseas and European companies are seeking joint-venture or technology transfer agreements. Companies in the UK can be introduced through the Business Cooperation Centre in Brussels.

Other Specialised Chambers

The French Chamber of Commerce in Great Britain was established in 1883 to promote Franco-British trade and develop business contacts. In 1996, France was our third biggest export market with sales of £17 billion. Our imports were £17.7 billion. The Chamber has over 600 members. With the lowering of trade frontiers, the French government has invested millions of francs in training their schoolchildren to become linguists. Looking at their new members, who have joined the Chamber from both sides of the Channel, it is obvious that many major companies are now starting marketing to increase their volume sales. This is actually a warning to those who feel chambers are not necessary. The Chamber's magazine, *INFO*, is clear and concise and the feature articles do reflect a wish to give pure technical information. Editions normally feature specialised subjects such as tourism, communication and transport. These seminars on sector trading are highly professional and the workshops on the differences between the English and French legal systems are particularly good. Traders attending any of these meetings would immediately be able to begin to understand the differences in selling and the cultural differences that are separated by such a narrow strip of water. They are an exceptionally friendly and helpful Chamber.

Further information from *Chambre de Commerce Francaise de Grande-Bretagne*, Knightsbridge House, 197 Knightsbridge, London, SW7 1RB (tel: 0171 304 4040).

The Arab-British Chamber of Commerce

The Arab-British Chamber of Commerce has commercial contacts with all 20 Arab League countries. Sir Geoffrey Howe, the former Foreign Secretary, when he opened their beautifully restored building in Belgrave Square, stated that 'The importance of the Chamber's work is evident from the scale of trade.' He confirmed that the efforts of their staff are appreciated by the many British firms which are actively trading with the Arab world. This chamber is superbly organised and in my opinion is one of the finest in this country. With a staff of about 60 it is the largest in Europe. Their membership is about 500.

Although trade with the Middle East has declined over the past six years, it is still vitally important to have up-to-date information on the different regulations and social attitudes which are totally different from country to country.

The technical and country seminars that the Chamber runs are of an exceptionally high standard; their speakers are normally the most knowledgeable in their field. A full report is sent to all members who attend these briefings.

They publish a weekly *Trade Information Bulletin* for their members which gives a long list of export and import opportunities. Their bi-monthly

magazine *Arab British Trade* includes in-depth country reviews and a list of forthcoming conferences and exhibitions. When they review a sector of industry it will include a list of research papers and publications.

Translation

The Chamber has a first class technical translation unit which specialises in commercial, technical, medical and financial texts. Their language courses are especially designed for general and business purposes. A few phrases of Arabic and a little cultural awareness can make all the difference in creating the right relationship when trading with Arab clients.

Visas

Visas for members can be obtained far more quickly than by using normal channels. Many of their staff have been in the Diplomatic Service, therefore they have exceptionally good liaison with all the Arab League embassies.

Documentation

The Certification and Documentation department handles the certificates of origin, commercial invoices and arranges for legalisation by all the Arab embassies who require these procedures. Finally, their library is well stocked with commercial and business books and a vast number of newspapers and periodicals in English and Arabic.

Further information from the Arab British Chamber of Commerce, 6 Belgrave Square, London, SW1X 8PH (tel: 0171 235 4363).

The American Chamber of Commerce

For anyone wishing to export or import, this Chamber is a must. It has an entirely different character from any other that I have visited. It was established in 1916, it has 1000 members, and their 30 directors also serve on some of the biggest blue chip companies in the UK.

The USA is our second biggest export market with over £9.7 billion sales in 1996. It may seem easy to trade because they speak English, but it is definitely not so. In the past some of the biggest claims for non-payment have been submitted to the Export Credits Guarantee Department (ECGD) because the background to the buyer had not been fully examined. The Chamber, being physically so near to the American Embassy, has exceptionally good liaison with the Minister of Commercial Affairs. This department has a large staff. Through a computer link, companies can be put in touch with others who wish to buy and sell. A foreign buyer programme targets all the major trade shows in the USA. The Chamber can introduce exporters and importers via their computer link to the 60 chambers of commerce in America. They also have links with the worldwide trade centres, and 76 AMCHAMS.

Lunches

At their monthly lunches they invite major government and company executives to give short addresses. Quite often their comments are not reported in the national press, but their presentation is printed in the Chamber's monthly publication, *Atlantic*. Although this magazine reads rather like an in-flight giveaway, now and again there is an article which gives solid technical trading advice. 'Fundamentally, we get people together', was how Robert Brunck, their Director General, summed up their function.

Further information from the American Chamber of Commerce (United Kingdom), 75 Brook Street, London, W1Y 2EB (tel: 0171 493 0381).

The Middle East Association

The Association was founded in 1961 to promote trade between the UK and the Middle East, i.e. all Arab countries as well as Iran and Turkey. The Association's staff have considerable experience in Middle East markets, having spent many years working in and/or exporting to these markets.

The Association's Director General, Mr Brian Constant, lived for many years in the area and recently retired from Lloyds Bank where he was responsible for trade and project finance for all Middle East markets. Mr Rex Brown, the Secretary, joined the Association in 1992 following a full career in British Petroleum. His last post was Area Coordinator, Middle East. The Director of Trade Relations is Mr Paul Rhodes, who has 20 years of experience of business development across the region in the telecommunications sector. The other staff member is Mr Lawrie Walker, a retired member of the Diplomatic service who has 25 years of service in the Middle East and was in charge of the British Embassy commercial sections in Bahrain, Iraq, Libya, Kuwait and Turkey.

The Association organises seminars, discussion group meetings, working lunches and so on. Speakers include British Ambassadors and Commercial counsellors from our Middle East Embassies, businessmen with direct experience of the market and visiting Ministers and senior officials from overseas Governments. The Association also sponsors and organises DTI supported trade missions to Middle East markets as well as UK participation at some trade exhibitions in the region.

Further information from the Middle East Association, Bury House, 33 Bury Street, St. James's, London SW1Y 6AW (tel: 0171 839 2137).

The International Chamber of Commerce

The International Chamber of Commerce (ICC) was founded in 1919 by business leaders to try and get the world's economy moving. The movement has always been totally independent of any government. This body's sole purpose is to make it easier to do business internationally. The original members were drawn from the UK, the USA and Europe. It has now 7000 members drawn from over 130 countries. The ICC is the only business organisation which has 'first category' consultative status with the United Nations and the other UN agencies. Apart from collecting information on trading and international investment they are now deeply involved in trying to protect the environment. The ICC has five key objectives:

1. It promotes open trading based on free and fair competition.
2. It seeks the maximum freedom of movement across frontiers of goods, services, investment and information.
3. It stands for free enterprise and the market economy.
4. It believes in self-regulation by responsible businesses.
5. It promotes the idea that trade, investment and the transfer of technology should be encouraged and that there should be a fair return and security to those providing capital, expertise and technical know-how from one country to another.

Through its specialist commissions it formulates and promotes the following elements of international trade:

• Air transport	Intellectual property
• Arbitration	International banking
• Competition law	International commercial practice
• Energy	Maritime transport
• Environment	Marketing
• Financial services	Taxation
• Insurance	Telecommunications and IT
	Trade policy.

Through its exceptionally thorough method of setting rules for worldwide trade a large number of rules and guides have been issued. I consider that these publications are 'Bibles' for conducting trade and receiving payments. By following these rules, exporters will greatly reduce the possibility of discrepancies. This can be done provided that the salesforce and export and credit department staff understand the terminology in the guides that describe the workings of the rules.

I will highlight just a few of their 88 publications, which are available in seven languages. The *Incoterms* publication, no. 460 (1990 edition) is the universally recognised set of definitions for international trading. For instance, many terms such as *ex works, named place, CIF, COF* and *FOB* can be misinterpreted. If buyers, sellers and the banks quote *Incoterms* 1990 when they draw up their contracts, these misunderstandings will be reduced.

Trading Shipping Terms or Terms of Delivery

Many export transactions are delayed, costs increased and losses made when both exporter and importer misunderstand commonly used terms in different countries. ICC's *Incoterms 1990* has been revised to incorporate the increasing use of EDI (Electronic Data Interchange) transactions.

There are 13 trading terms which the ICC has grouped into four basically different categories. For example, in Group E, EXW Ex Works named place, the seller makes the goods available to the buyer at the seller's own premises. The guide also shows who has responsibility for licences, carriage and insurance and when the delivery and transfer of risks between seller and buyer takes place.

To illustrate the risks when exporting I have seen enormous costly disputes because an American importer's definition of a term included a freight charge that it thought the UK exporter would pay. If the words *ex works* (Southampton) had been added, both parties would have understood what their obligations were. In the *Incoterm* 460 publication, not only are the meanings of the terms between the buyer and seller given but it also highlights what both parties must do to enable the contractual term to work. If readers find the above terms difficult, an exceptionally well-illustrated *Guide to Incoterms* no. 461 has been issued. This is a first-class teaching aid as the terms are shown in picture-diagram form. Some of the international transport, customs and insurance certificates are shown.

To reduce the complexity of terminology when translating foreign contracts ICC has introduced a new glossary of nearly 1500 technical words. The English term is translated into German, Spanish, French and Italian, which are followed by indices for each language.

The ICC guide no. 500, *Uniform Customs and Practice for Documentary Credits*, is an essential publication for any exporter who receives letters of credit. The *Uniform Rules for Collection*, no. 522, is a tremendous aid in understanding how banks apply the rules in collections.

The *ICC Guide to Export/Import Basics* no. 543 will help businesses to understand the legal, financial and transport aspects of international trade. It also refers to *Incoterms 1990*, UCP 500 and the ICC Rules for Arbitration.

Further information from ICC United Kingdom, 14–15 Belgrave Square, London SW1X 8PS (tel: 0171 823 2811).

The Institute of Export

The Institute of Export was formed in 1935 as a professional association for those engaged in overseas trade and international export practice and management. Its education unit administers its examinations and a number of courses are run throughout the year on the theory and practice of exporting. The Institute's official journal *Export Today* keeps exporters up to date with current developments and advises members on the activities in the UK branch network.

Further information from The Institute of Export, Export House, 64 Clifton Street, London, EC2A 4HB (tel: 0171 247 9812).

THE SIMPLER TRADE PROCEDURES BOARD (SITPRO)

Documentation

Inability to understand and process export documentation is one of the major headaches for any trader. However, there is an enormous amount of help and assistance available. Exporters will be able to sleep at night if they follow precise international rules.

The management of many companies suddenly announce that they will start exporting. They do not, however, give any thought to the technicalities and cost in time involved. Neither do they realise that it is necessary to give their staff training in understanding the highly complex series of transactions which combine to make a profitable sale.

The Simpler Trade Procedures Board (SITPRO) was formed in 1970 to guide, stimulate and assist the rationalisation of international trade procedures and documentation. The Board is financially supported by the Department of Trade and Industry. The members of their Policy and Advisory groups come from many fields, for example, the Association of Bankers, the major clearers, export agents, Customs and Excise, the International Chamber of Commerce, port and freight authorities, trade associations and represesntatives of major trading companies.

One of SITPRO's aims is to help exporters to produce clear and concise documentation so that the contract details that appear on the paperwork can be understood by all the parties involved in an overseas transaction. This is particularly important for SMEs who wish to become active exporters. SITPRO is trying to reduce the procedural barriers as far as possible and to make them as similar to and as simple as their domestic equivalent.

Publications to Help Exporters

With the exceptionally high rejection rate of Letters of Credit, SITPRO's three *Guides and Checklists* (for importers, exporters and sales executives) will help traders to reduce errors. They are written in an easy to follow, non-technical language. The set of three is priced £12.50. Their *Export Guide* is a new export foundation kit which takes exporters through the procedures and methods of exporting, from planning to getting paid. This is priced £17.50. Their *Top Form 2* is a guide to the UK aligned export forms. It contains examples and explains the range of export documentation that is available.

SITPRO also produce the following factsheets:

General Export Factsheets	*Payment Factsheets*
General export	EU Cross Border Payments
SITPRO & the UN aligned system	UCP 500
Single Market	Credit Insurance
Temporary Export from the UK	Getting Paid
Completion Guide for Dangerous Goods Notes	Financing Your Exports in the Short Term
Rates Standard Shipping Notes	Reducing Letter of Credit Rejection
Guidance Notes on Exporting for Small and Medium Size Enterprises	The Internet & International Payments
Country Factsheets (28 in total)	

Payments

The other aims of SITPRO are to improve the speed of transmission of documents and reduce the payment delays between the importers, banks and the beneficiaries. They have developed a range of documentation systems to suit any size or type of exporting company. All the systems are fully compatible with each other and all their documents are drafted to international standards (the UN layout key). Only certain licensed computer software houses, are allowed to sell their systems.

Further information from SITPRO, 151 Buckingham Palace Road, London SW1 9SS (tel: 0171 215 0825).

MARITIME FRAUD

The International Maritime Bureau (IMB) is an intelligence gathering organisation which helps businesses, shippers and cargo carriers to identify and investigate criminal and fraudulent transactions. Ships which change their names in the night, fraudulent letters of credit and counterfeit components are some of the problems which they investigate. *Commercial Crime International* and a fortnightly *Confidential Bulletin to Members* give dramatic information which is of the utmost importance to traders. For example a suicide of a bank's president, piracy and default of shipping companies can be highlighted.

Much of the Bureau's time is taken up in authenticating documents for banks before negotiation. They have developed a data bank on individuals and companies throughout the world who have defaulted on payments and where there is a record of malpractice or fraud.

Mr P. Mukundan, an IBM director, warned traders to check their cargo insurance as all policies now exclude cover if ship owners become insolvent. In 1997 the greatest risks were the fleets of cargo carriers of the former Soviet Union and Eastern Bloc.

IMB is a division of the International Chamber of Commerce.

Further information from ICC International Maritime Bureau, Maritime House, Linton Road, Barking, Essex, IG11 8HG (tel: 0181 591 3000).

RULES AND REGULATIONS: 'EVERYTHING YOU NEED TO KNOW'

A guide which no exporter should be without is *Croner's Reference Book for Exporters*. Mr U.C.H. Croner, who studied law at the Berlin University in 1933, continued his studies in Switzerland where he obtained his LL.D with a thesis on liability insurance in railroad transportation. He came to England in 1938 and when the Second World War commenced he had the brilliant idea of publishing a regular news-sheet to keep shippers advised of the then-current regulations. In 1941 a *Shippers' Overseas Correspondence*, printed in English and Spanish, was published – this was the birth of Croner's Guide. The Guide, which now runs to hundreds of pages, keeps UK exporters up to date on the regulations in this country and the importing country's regulations. Under a subscription service each month a set of amendment sheets plus a summary sheet of changes is issued. Apart from the amendments an *Export Digest* is issued which highlights major international trading news.

This Guide is set out like an encyclopaedia, starting with a definition of export terms, then the control regulations and prohibitions list of products are highlighted in some detail. A schedule of goods and countries which cannot be supplied, plus the CN (Combined Nomenclature) reference numbers are included. The outward and inward customs procedures which includes customs entries, the simplified clearance procedures, transit and transhipment requirements, SAD requirement and the EEC Community Transit system are also covered.

Under *Export Finance*, the Guide clearly shows where to find detailed information. At the same time it describes the differences between the payment terms and the way in which the exporter's security may change by using, for instance, a usance draft or a confirmed letter of credit. There is a short section on protesting bills of exchange which is often missed in other text books.

In the next section, marine and war risks insurance and the clauses which are included are covered. Information on postal requirements, certificates of origin and where to obtain them is helpful for first time exporters. If readers are confused on the differences between a Bill of Lading and a Short Term Sea Waybill they will find the answer under 82K. Commonwealth preference for customs duties, invoice forms and dangerous goods requirements are described. Many an exporter encounters problems where the VAT rates and sales are complex. The format of these notes is particularly clear.

Country Information

This is the major section of the Guide. The individual country guides give in the simplest way all the documentary requirements when importing into a country. Over 150 countries are listed and the information includes: public holidays, import restrictions and a vast amount of information on commercial invoices and the vital pre-shipment inspection. As an example, reproduced in Figure 10.1 is part of a country sheet that relates to Denmark.

Finally, to show the number of worldwide regulation changes that can take place in one month, Croner's, in the summary sheet for July 1997, listed four changes in Export Controls, a change of name for Zaire, total updates for Greece, Hungary, Mali, Oman, Poland and South Africa.

It can be seen from these few notes that exporters do need to be helped to keep up to date with the worldwide importation requirements. Once a transaction is delayed, not only can there be severe additional fees that have to be borne by the exporter but also the all-important profit margin on the sale can be totally lost.

APRIL, 1997   DENMARK

Constitutional monarchy in NW Europe consisting of peninsula of Jutland, the two islands of Zealand and Funen and a number of smaller islands and **Greenland.** One of the OECD countries. Member of the European Union (EU) and the European Economic Area (EEA). **Capital:** Copenhagen. **Population:** 5.2 million. **Principal Ports:** Aalborg, Aarhus, Copenhagen, Esbjerg.

TERRITORY also includes the **Faroe Islands** who like Greenland are **NOT** members of EU.

LANGUAGES: Danish. English widely understood.

WEIGHTS AND MEASURES: Metric system.

ELECTRICITY SUPPLY: 220/380v. 50 cycles AC.

CURRENCY: 1 Krone = 100 Ore.

EXCHANGE RATE: 10.51 Kroner = £1 Sterling (fluctuating rate).

INTERNATIONAL DIALLING CODE: 00 45.

TIME: 1 hour ahead of GMT (1 hour ahead of BST).

PUBLIC HOLIDAYS: Jan. 1; Mar. 27, 28, 31; April 25; May 8, 19; June 5; Dec. 24, 25, 26.

EMBASSY (COMMERCIAL SECTION): 55 Sloane Street, London SW1X 9SR (Tel: 0171-333 0200, Fax: 0171-333 0270); open 9.00–4.30, closed Sats. Consulate-General at Edinburgh-Leith. Consulates at Belfast, Birmingham, Bristol, Cardiff, Gibraltar, Glasgow, Harwich, Hull, Jersey, Liverpool, Manchester, Newcastle, North Shields, St. Helier. Vice-Consulates at most ports and industrial centres.

BRITISH EMBASSY: Kastelsvej 36/38/40, DK2100 Copenhagen O (Tel: (45) 35264600, Fax: (45)35431400).

CHAMBER OF COMMERCE: Det Danske Handelskammer (Danish Chamber of Commerce) Borsen (Royal Exchange) DK 1217 Copenhagen K. Tel: 33950500; Telex: 19520 CHACOM OK; Fax: 33152266

BUSINESS ORGANISATION: British Import Union, Borsen, 1217 Copenhagen K.

FISCAL/CUSTOMS AUTHORITY: Ostbanegade 123, 2100 Copenhagen O.

TRADE STATISTICS (INTRASTAT) AUTHORITY: Danmarks Statistik, Sejrogade 11, Postboks 2550, 2100 Copenhagen Q.

NATIONAL CODES: VAT and Excise: DK; **Statistics:** DK.

COMPOSITION OF VAT NO: 8 digits in 4 groups of 2. Number must be preceded by national code.

VAT: Mervaerdiafgift.

VAT REGISTRATION LIMIT: DK 20,000 (£2000 (aproximately)) annual turnover.

VAT CERTIFICATE ISSUED ON REGISTRATION: Yes

VAT REGISTRATION NO. ISSUED FOR VAT PURPOSES ONLY: No. Integrated fiscal number was introduced on 1.5.90.

STANDARD RATE OF VAT: 25%. No reduced rate. Zero rate: minimal coverage.

VAT MONTHLY RETURNS TO BE USED: By repayment traders and bad payers, otherwise quarterly.

Figure 10.1 Extracts from the country information section of *Croner's Reference Book for Exporters* (*continued over*)

DENMARK   APRIL, 1997

IMPORT RESTRICTIONS: Most goods may be freely imported from all sources. I/L are required for certain textiles, kitchen and tableware of non-EU origin.

EXCHANGE CONTROL: None.

BILLS OF LADING/CONTRACT OF CARRIAGE: No special regulations. B/L, when required, may be made out "to order".

CONSULAR INVOICES: None.

CERTIFICATES OF ORIGIN: For Hong Kong goods and wines and spirits only. No special form. See also **EU Forms** below.

COMMERCIAL INVOICES: Show customers's VAT registration number. There is no requirement for the commercial invoice to accompany consignments in intra-EU trade.

EC FORMS: Community Transit documents for intra trade are only required in certain situations (see pages 36m/36n). EU preferential rates of duty can be claimed for goods going to the Faroe Islands. An EUR1 Movement Certificate is therefore required for goods valued over £4830 going to the Faroe Islands. For consignments below that value, exporters can use an invoice declaration (see page 36k for example of format). As an alternative to the invoice declaration, exporters can use EUR2 until 31 December 1997. **Facsimile signatures** not allowed. (See also **Certificates of Origin.**)

SPECIAL CERTIFICATES: Certificates of health are required for plants and certain foodstuffs. A veterinary certificate is required for livestock. A certificate of age may be required for spirits.

CONSULAR FEES: None.

MARKING OF GOODS: Certain goods must bear an indication of the country of origin, and certain others must be marked simply as foreign goods.

PACKING MATERIAL: No restrictions, but a sanitary certificate required if hay or straw is used for shipments to the Faroe Islands.

MARKING OF CASES: No special regulations, but if gross weight exceeds one ton the weight must be shown.

SHIPPING ARRANGEMENT: There are many services operating from the UK to Denmark and references should be made to Lloyd's Loading List. There are also direct road, rail and groupage services.

AIR FREIGHT: Foregoing regulations apply. Services from the UK: **All-cargo:** SAS; Lufthansa. Other services: Aer Lingus; Aeroflot; British Airways; BMA; Dan Air; JAL.

POSTAL PARCELS: Foregoing regulations apply except that SAD forms are **not** required, EC yellow label (C. 1130) required for goods **not** in free circulation. Customs declaration: (see page 59). Customs declaration form not required if goods are in free circulation in the EU.

APRIL, 1997   DENMARK (2)

SAMPLES: Samples of n.c.v. are admitted duty-free. All other samples are admitted against deposit or bond provided they are re-exported within six months.

BANKS: Amaqerbanken, Danmarks Nationallbank, Den Danske Bank, Unibank A/S; Standard Chartered Bank.

DUTIES: Assessed at specific rates or ad valorem on the c.i.f. value. EU (including UK) goods enter duty-free. EU preferential tariff treatment granted on goods from certain countries. Tariff is based on the Harmonised System (HS) (see page 131).

UK REGULATIONS: Export Licences required for goods in the Prohibition List (see Page 13). **Customs Pre-Entry** necessary for goods exported under licence (other than Open General Licence), or otherwise under Customs control (see page 34q).

Croner's Reference Book for Exporters costs £312.63 and this includes a year's update. For subsequent year updates, the cost is £237.88. A subscription for this publication can be obtained from:

Croner Publications Ltd, Croner House, London Road, Kingston upon Thames, Surrey, KT2 6SR (tel: 0181 547 3333).

Croner's Europe Guide

Croner's Europe comprises two loose-leaf volumes which aim to keep businesses in the UK informed of EU legislation. Although particularly relevant to those trading across borders, much of the information is also relevant to non-exporting companies as EU law now has immediate and far-reaching effects in employment, health and safety and consumer-related areas.

Volume I includes a summary and commentary of policy areas such as harmonisation of standards, company law, indirect taxation, transport, research and development, employment law, health and safety, environment and consumer law. Details of the implementation of legislation in the UK and other member states are included where possible, and there is a comprehensive further information section giving contact details of helpful bodies and institutions. Of particular use to those trading in Europe is a section on the drafting of commercial agreements to comply with competition law and guidance on marketing and advertising in the single European market.

Each month the amendment service includes the Brussels Update pages which give a synopsis of the recent developments in key policy areas and notes the reactions of major pan-European associations such as UNICE, the European employer's federation. There is also a new section called the Commission Work Programme which tracks the progress of proposed legislation, summarising the key points, reporting on the passage of the proposals through the legislative process and giving full bibliographic details for each relevant document.

A subscription for *Croner's Europe* can be obtained from Croner Publications Ltd, Croner House, London Road, Kingston upon Thames, Surrey, KT2 6SR (tel: 0181 547 3333).

WHICH CURRENCY?

When considering bank charges, losses as well as profits can be made as variances, as the rate of exchange differences will dramatically alter profit margins. Depending on the country to which goods or services are being invoiced, it is far more sensible to first review whether the invoice is going to be quoted in sterling or a different currency. Hard currencies such as US dollars, French francs, Deutsche Marks or yen can be purchased 'forward' through a bank. This means that the exporter can calculate before the contract has been finalised the exact value in sterling of the converted transaction. It is dangerous to agree to accept a currency which is not freely convertible.

Here are two examples where exporters did not research the convertibility of currencies. An exporter of freezing equipment to Iceland did not realise that the only time in the year when Icelandic kronas are convertible is in October and November. This is when their cod is exported to Greece. The trader did finally manage to sell the currency but due to delays and the discounting of the currency an actual loss on the export sale was made. In the second case an exporter who could not arrange for the Nigerian nira to be converted into sterling actually used the nira balance in a different way. The company arranged for a sales conference to take place in Nigeria so that the credit balance could be used.

This, of course, is not the way to export profitably, but it does help to reduce the loss. I have also heard of companies who have these types of problems reverting to crisis techniques, and selling their debts for as little as 10 per cent of the actual value of the contract. To guard against an economic factor, credit insurance is most valuable.

There are three publications which highlight payment delays. Dun & Bradstreet's *International Risk and Payment Review* surveys the payment position on over 100 countries.

Euromoney Project and Trade Finance, published monthly, reports on a more detailed schedule of delayed payments, credit insurance, cover availability, overseas projects, banking and finance. Euromoney also publish *FX Manager*, a journal of currency forecasting and risk management.

Information from Euromoney Publications, Nestor House, Playhouse Yard, London, EC4V 5EX (tel: 0171 779 8999).

Foreign collection information is also published in National Westminster Bank's *International Trade Bulletin*, published monthly.

Foreign Exchange Exposure

In reviewing the money markets over the last ten years, countless countries have had their currencies raided by international speculators. Exporters should first contact their bankers for a currency review. In the previous edition of this book it was mentioned that when a company agrees to a contract in a currency other than sterling there is an automatic risk that their profit margin could be attacked.

Many UK companies still seem to think that any adverse movement in the rate of exchange could not be protected. The export profitability could evaporate if companies do not take a forward contract. This type of contract enables a trader to buy a specific amount of currency at a predetermined rate on a specific future maturity date.

Through using HEXAGON the Desktop Electronic Banking System of HSBC Trade Services not only can the spot rate be checked 365 days a year, 24 hours a day, but also international payments can be transferred and amendments to documentary credits can be carried out. All the electronic messages are translated into UN/EDIFACT format.

Further information can be obtained from HSBC Trade Services, London International Branch (tel: 0171 260 9232).

SUMMARY

There are many, many more areas to consider when exporting as regulations and government restrictions are different in most countries of the world. However, profits can still be made if diligent research and marketing is carried out.

- Have you studied the economic, political and commercial risks of the relevant country?
- Are there any licensing requirements?
- Can your product or service be sold in as many as possible of the 240 countries?
- Do you know where to go for research and is there enough profit margin to pay for it?
- Do you understand the payment terms and documentation?

11
Credit Insurance – Why Insure?

Most businesses insure their premises, plant and machinery, stock, and automatically take cover for fire, accident and often consider loss of profits cover. It therefore seems sensible to consider credit insurance (insurance of debts) to guard against a sudden loss. Credit insurance has to be paid for, so the profit margin of a business wishing to gain cover must be studied. Between the period 1995 and 1997 premium rates have dropped due to competition and the strength of the economy. But as at July 1997 market indications are that the rates that an inexperienced trader may have to pay are 1 per cent premium on insured turnover (an experienced trader could pay between 0.3–0.4 per cent or even lower depending on the sector or risks involved). It is wishful thinking to believe that even our domestic market is safe: economic cycles now move far quicker, and the 'boom and bust' economy may now be a feature of world trading which will not disappear.

Reviewing our overseas trade there are always political events, changes of government, financial crises and even climatic changes that can completely change a safe market into a high risk area, or a total write off (see Chapter 9 for UK failures and Chapter 10 for major country business failures).

MAJOR INSURERS

Since this book was first published in 1990 there have been major developments in the credit insurance market. The Government's export insurer has privatised the short-term (under 180-day) terms to NCM Credit Insurance Ltd who also now cover the UK domestic market (see interview below). Trade Indemnity plc, the UK insurer which also covers overseas sales, has merged with a French company (also see below). The Government insurer for exports, ECGD, are still covering the 'long and large' major contract and project business where credit terms are anything from two years upwards. Other insurers such as Coface LBF (French), AIG (UK) Ltd (American), Hermes Credit Services Ltd (German), Namur (Belgian) – which has merged with an American company – and Sun Alliance Financial Risks Ltd are all very active in the credit insurance market.

NCM Credit Insurance Ltd

To understand NCM's underwriting policy and to show how creditors can reduce their fear and anxiety when their debts are insured, I interviewed the following personnel. Terry Bridgeman, Director of Group Risk Management, Julie Barton and Mrs Teresa Fox, both Senior Managers, Claims Underwriting & Recoveries, Mel Bailey, Manager Special Risks, and Julia Kidd who is a specialist on insolvency all agreed to talk to me.

Underwriting Policy

When NCM purchased the short-term business from ECGD in 1991, one of the first decisions they made was to integrate the computer systems of the Dutch NCM and the British credit insurance systems. Their computer operation is now a world leading system which has already integrated the databases of Holland, Denmark, Sweden and the UK. The Group underwriting system enables them to issue policy documents in nine different languages and issue credit limits and premium invoices in up to 16 different languages. Their programme team have already built in the ECU, so policy holders will have an extra choice if they require it when monetary union is finally introduced.

By creating a global information system they now know their total exposure on any single organisation and claims experiences. The databases of groups, not just buyers, have been combined, because their buyer in the UK may be a customer of their other companies operating globally. Their database is huge, containing about 6 million records, and in the UK alone there are about 1.8 million records.

The greatest change that has taken place in underwriting policy has been to create centres of intelligence, so that underwriting takes place at the closest point to where the buyer and the risks lie. In this way the maximum information is available to underwriters including trade associations, press reports and local news etc.

Reviewing the UK scene there are now more multiple credit limits in this country. This may be because all the customers that sell in that sector are applying for limits. Many limits are higher than they were five years ago, possibly due to the many mergers that have taken place.

Claims and Recoveries

NCM will consider any market in the world where their customers wish to sell. With newly emerging markets they may require an indemnity of perhaps 50–75 per cent depending on the risks. Mel Bailey, Manager of the Special Risks section, stated that they were always willing to consider a rescheduling of a debt. For example, their intensive care unit last year helped an airline-related business to survive, when the financing by the parent company of the buyer was suddenly withdrawn. There were insufficient funds to keep the buyer operating, but there was still a need to obtain new finance. What this unit did was to maintain NCM's support by continuing their insurance cover and at the same time minimising their risk and secure payment. Many hours were spent in negotiating with the customer and the buyer. Orders were still being gained by the buyer within the Receivership. An agreement was made that secured NCM's debts by having a separate account set up in their name, and this gave them sufficient comfort to continue covering shipments.

This unit can often support an ailing business by first talking to the suppliers, then considering whether the subject company is a viable concern. Their basic philosophy is to allow a company in trouble to 'trade out' of the problem within a reasonable time span. Customers are still required under the policy clauses to notify them within 90 days of a potential loss, but quite often their underwriter's information sources will have some clues that there is a financial or political problem.

Wrongful Trading

Although the law in the UK allows the attachment of a director's personal assets if 'wrongful trading' can be proved by the Court, it is almost impossible to take action. Julia Kidd stated that proving the directors 'know or should have known that they were insolvent' is difficult. NCM's policy is to get the directors to make an offer of payment. The reason for this is that the Courts are not strong enough, and this type of action can cost £50,000 minimum. However, if they think there is going to be a benefit, even if the directors cannot be struck off, provided that the debt is more than £750 they would wind up the company, especially if the director is a director of numerous companies. Presenting a case for fraudulent trading is far easier, and they emphasised that although there has not been a rise in 'long firm' fraud, they have noticed quite a number of cases in Germany.

Types of Policy

From the time when NCM was privatised in 1991 their sales management realised that they needed to develop their services for the smaller business. As a result the new improved Compact (on-line) Mark 11 Policy has been launched for businesses with sales of up to £3 million, although if a business finds that this policy suits them the underwriters will be happy to cover up to £5 million. There is no minimum turnover figure and customers can choose to insure UK or export sales or have combined cover. Unlike the previous version, overseas political risk cover is available. Importantly, if the policy holder only requires two buyers to be insured, a policy can be raised.

The Domestic Policy covers sales within the UK for protracted default or the buyer becoming insolvent.

The Commercial Risks Policy covers sales in the UK and the rest of the OECD, but unlike the International Policy, political risks are not covered.

The International Policy can cover sales in the UK and to any overseas country. It covers the trader against commercial and political risks overseas. Incidentally, the political risks cover for exporters of British beef was particularly useful in 1996 when truckers held up consignments in France.

The Global Policy is particularly useful when a multinational company is switching production from one country to another.

Information

Apart from the Country Reports that NCM issue to their customers, there is another great advantage if a policy is raised. Policy holders do not have to pay the £6000 registration and installation fee to be able to use the NCM Profound on-line information service. In my opinion this makes it an exceptional information service. Apart from business and competitor analysis there are over 40,000 full text market research reports, and when the item appears on the screen the cost is noted so that the customer knows exactly how much the report will cost.

For further information on NCM's services contact NCM Credit Insurance Limited, 3 Harbour Drive, Capital Waterside, Cardiff CF1 6TZ (tel: 01222 824000).

Export Credits Guarantee Department

ECGD is a very different organisation from when I last reviewed their ac tivities in 1989. ECGD, the Government export credit agency, was establishec in 1919 to assist British traders to adapt to new trading conditions. In 199:

they sold their short term, under two year (non-capital goods) business to NCM Credit Insurance Ltd, the private insurer. They are now a proactive insurer and have a more flexible approach, including covering a range of credit lines for SMEs. They still issue guarantees for 'long and large' project finance business where payment terms are spread over a number of years. Their Buyer Credit Finance scheme helps exporters especially when the buyer, often an overseas government, will only pay stage payments on a major project. The amount of the contract usually has to be £5 million, but normally they are much larger. The credit repayment period must be at least two years and a minimum of 15 per cent of the contract value must be paid to the exporter prior to the commencement of the credit period. Their lines of credit can finance contracts as low as $25,000 where the exporter who is selling capital and project goods or services is paid by the UK Bank. Finance provided to the borrower will normally be between two and five years.

ECGD list their lines of credit by country, the UK and overseas banks, and value in their quarterly *Newsletter*. Their *Newsletter* also summarises cover available throughout the world, giving the Underwriters' names and telephone numbers.

ECGD still raise policies for Bond Risk Cover, as unfair calling of bonds is still a risk in a number of countries. The 'Tender to Contract, Forward Exchange Supplement' is also available to cover exporters against the risk of exchange movements while tendering for major overseas contracts.

Further information from ECGD, PO Box 2200, 2 Exchange Tower Harbour, Exchange Square, London E14 9GS (tel: 0171 512 7000).

Trade Indemnity plc; EULER Trade Indemnity (from 9 March 1998)

Trade Indemnity (TI) started writing credit insurance in 1918. In the early 1980s, ECGD's lack of flexibility led them to believe that their domestic policy holders needed extra protection when selling abroad, so they introduced political risks cover in 1984. In this short period, from 1984 to 1989, approximately 20 per cent of ECGD's short-term business had been captured. TI's insured export and international turnover is now over £17 billion per annum.

In May 1996 Trade Indemnity were acquired by Compagnie Financiere SFAC and in November 1996 the group changed their name to the EULER. This is now the holding company for a number of credit insurers including SFAC (France), COBAC (Benelux), ACI (North America) and SIAC (Italy).

In 1992 TI introduced a Multi-market Policy for businesses who principally sell in the UK, but who are also exporting to EU and OECD countries. Under this policy up to 25 key markets can be covered. Buyer insolvency and extended non-payment cover is available with a negotiable cover of between 80 and 85 per cent. This type of policy now represents about 38 per cent of their business. In 1997 they introduced a World Markets policy, combining commercial and political risk cover for UK and export trade under the umbrella of one single policy.

In reviewing political risk cover (a government action that stops a commercial transaction), policy holders are still adding this endorsement when trading with Italy and Greece. I was reminded that Western Europe is very different from Eastern Europe. Although some countries in the former Soviet bloc are getting stronger, for example, Poland, Czech Republic and Hungary, Bulgaria and Romania have been declining economically.

Trade Indemnity, in common with other insurers, are concerned about the apparently low take up of credit insurance in the UK, with between only 7 and 10 per cent of businesses buying cover. They are working to open up credit insurance to SMEs as information technology is reducing the costs. Their Suretrade policy covers UK trade for companies with turnover up to £3 million.

For an exporter who has a turnover of between £750,000 and £5 million there is the Export Builder Policy which was launched in 1995. Eighty markets can be covered, and a 90 per cent insolvency, protracted default and political risk cover is available. This is a 'simple, affordable policy' but it is designed for an experienced exporter.

On-line System

TI has been offering their Creditstream on-line policy management system since 1993. Policy holders can link their office PC to TI's database and can make credit limit applications, check the status of claims submitted and report overdue accounts, thus avoiding long telephone calls or writing fax requests. I was also advised that most of the clearing banks have a modified version so that they can act as a joint policy holder on the policy. This system helps them in their decision making when advancing funds to support sales and expansion. Enhancements to the system were launched at the Credit 97 exhibition in April 1997 whereby users can access Trade Indemnity's 'First Source' system and can ask for credit opinions up to £10,000 as a possible alternative to bank reports.

Risk Management Department

TI have also developed a team of risk analysts who have banking experience. They work in conjunction with TI's underwriters to investigate the financial health of companies, monitoring them on a regular basis regardless of size, taking particular account of the pressure they may be under due to economic conditions.

Insolvency

In the previous edition of this book I quoted a definition of insolvency from Charles McCartan who has now retired from TI, but his thoughts on insolvency are still relevant when poor management, overtrading, and boom and bust trade cycles occur. He stated that insolvency is the inability of companies to meet their liabilities as they fall due. In his view it was characterised not by lack of assets but by their wrong disposition within the company. For example, if all a company's cash is tied up in, for example, finished goods which cannot be sold, the company is liquid in a sense, but it is also illiquid, as the assets are wrongly disposed. This is often a contributory factor to insolvency. Credit insurers often have a problem when, if a specialist product is not supplied and the customer is placed on stop, this situation can create an insolvency.

Trade Indemnity have seen companies which look close to collapse but they know that if cover is cancelled, this action could precipitate it. Their concern is to help restore financial well-being. They do this by meeting the buyer and his banks to see how the risks all round can be reduced and supplies maintained. Failures can be averted by helping to support suppliers and bringing companies back to health.

For further information on Trade Indemnity plc contact 1, Canada Square, London, E14 5DX (tel: 0171 739 4311).

Coface LBF

Coface LBF is a major world-wide insurer with turnover of FF2860 million in 1996. They acquired London Bridge Finance in 1993 who had been involved in debt protection since 1959.

Coface perhaps differs from other insurers as they are keen to take on small as well as large business. There is no minimum sales figure that is required to be insured for either UK or overseas sales. On exports, their policy holders can choose which countries they need to insure against political risks.

Their back-up service for information is extensive as they have 200 sources of credit information, much of which is on-line. They also own a number of credit bureaux throughout the world. Therefore when a customer takes out a policy, if they have buyers who are in arrears, once collection action is being considered, Coface will take over, collect the debt and pay the legal expenses.

They have just two policies. The 'Open Trader Policy' which can cover sales in the UK and overseas and political risk is included. The second policy, the

'Top Trader', can cover the non-payment of accounts above an agreed level. Overseas countries in the OECD group can also be included.

Further information from Coface LBF, 15 Appold Street, London EC2A 2DL (tel: 0171 325 7500).

CMR Intrum Justitia, A Credit Insurance Management Service

'People do not recognise the risks in the UK; there is still a lack of understanding on how they can protect themselves against bad debts. There are two reasons: the costs, and a perception that prospective clients feel that the insurer will not be able to underwrite the client's customers.' Many businesses also feel that they know their customers so there is a reluctance to insure. Most of the companies with a turnover of under £1 million are run by salesmen. The accounting function takes second place, credit insurance is a hindrance for them in selling, and they do not employ a credit controller!

In an interview Christian Hoy, Managing Director of CMR Intrum Justitia, confirmed that the above views on credit insurance were held by many managers in the UK. Mr Hoy showed how risky it is to hope that one will get paid by enumerating the value of additional sales that have to be gained to cover an uninsured debt (see Table 11.1).

Many small companies who do not employ a specialist to oversee a credit insurance policy sign a contract with CMR Intrum who hold a Managed Policy with NCM Credit Insurance Ltd. The work that CMR Intrum do is to support their clients by taking away all the complications of running a policy. A prospective client's buyers can be vetted for credit limits within two or three days, and payment terms can be agreed on up to 180 day terms.

The Routine

Once a sales invoice is raised the client sends it to CMR Intrum so that a credit limit can be raised and it is declared. They also make sure that declarations are made and premiums are paid. CMR Intrum do not send out

Table 11.1 Additional sales required to clear bad debt

Bad debt (£)	Profit margin (%)	Lost profit (£)	Additional sales required to break even (£)
10,000	5	500	190,000
10,000	10	1000	90,000
10,000	15	1500	56,600
10,000	20	2000	40,000

their clients' invoices but they do monitor and follow up any arrears if a client has no-one to run their sales ledger. If there is a claim or a debt recovery problem the client hands the whole action over to the policy administrator who would negotiate the claim, whether it be in the UK or overseas, with NCM. To help credit personnel and students to understand how a policy can work to their advantage, here is an actual case study.

Our client, Aristo Fabrics Limited, manufactures knitted fabrics and had been established for less than one year when they were approached by their local Chamber of Commerce to respond to an enquiry that had emanated from France.

Aristo Fabrics Limited applied to us for an initial credit limit of £10,000 which after investigation was duly approved. The goods were supplied and payment was subsequently received. Shortly afterwards the buyer placed a further order of £20,000 for which again we agreed the credit limit.

Just before the goods were despatched the buyer placed further orders which increased the total indebtedness to over £35,000. In view of the pressures to meet the buyer's ever-increasing demands our client failed to apply for an increased limit. He was therefore horrified to receive our notification later that week withdrawing the limit as we had learned of the buyer's insolvency.

It transpired that our client believed that due to the source of the enquiry there was a legitimacy to the order and that the buyer's credit-worthiness was 'undoubted'. Fortunately, by having taken out the initial cover Aristo Fabric's debt was greatly reduced and was bearable, though not without pain. Had the full debt been taken by our client it is almost certain that they would not be here today and enjoying the success of a thriving knitted fabrics manufacturer.

To give an indication of premium rates, for businesses with turnover of £1 million the premium rate could be as low as £5000 which could include debt recovery. For further information contact Mr Christian Hoy, CMR Intrum Justitia Ltd, Equitable House, Lyon Road, Harrow, Middlesex HA1 2EW (tel: 0181 863 7648).

SUMMARY

Unexpected bad debt could easily force a company into having to cease trading. Premium rates for insuring a debt are coming down, therefore if a business has a sufficient profit margin, credit insurance not only protects bad debts but also helps the business to obtain cheaper finance from its bankers.

- Do you need credit insurance?
- Is the insurer experienced and do they pay claims without delay?
- If selling overseas, do you need political cover?
- Can you obtain cover for what you want if it is not necessarily for the whole turnover of your business?

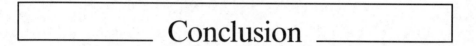

Conclusion

SUCCESS AND FAILURE – FREE OF CHARGE TRANSACTIONS

Commercial and industrial businesses in the UK advance about three times more unsecured credit to their customers than the major clearing banks. Without credit, a vast amount of profitable business would be lost. By increasing credit assessment and monitoring their customers in a more thorough way, perhaps some of the businesses could have reduced their past losses.

Trade cycles over the last 20 years seem to be developing quicker. With the possibility of the UK joining the EMU in the near future, further dramatic changes could affect employment and business expansion.

Dun & Bradstreet, in their survey of 372,871 establishments in 1995, found that the average profit before tax was 5.5 per cent. Why is this important? Because in 1996, which is considered to be the year when we climbed out of the recession, there were 24,306 Bankruptcy Orders and 13,902 Compulsory and Creditors Voluntary Liquidations in England, Wales and Scotland.

My review of some of the insolvency procedures serves to illustrate just how small the dividend may be when a business becomes insolvent.

Many businesses increase their profits annually by successfully using credit as a marketing tool. They are also able to administer their sales ledger so that they accept only a small commercial risk. A small commercial risk is not a gamble. Selling by credit is to increase profit.

Further Reading

For the study of assessment and collection techniques and the organisation of the sales ledger credit control department the following are recommended:

Credit Management Handbook, Burt Edwards (fourth edition), Gower Press, 1997, £55.

This is a superb book which in its 468 pages reviews many of the credit procedures which would be equally useful for personnel working in large or small companies, for home and overseas trading. The 13 experts who contribute to the book are indeed specialists in their field. The editor of the book, Burt Edwards, has had over 36 years experience in credit and treasury work; he has also written *Getting Paid for Exports* and is joint author of *Credit Insurance* with Dick Briggs.

Credit Management, R.N.V. Bass (third edition), Stanley Thornes (Publishers) Ltd., 1991.

Dick Bass is a first class credit manager who believes in thorough planning of all activities. His sections on credit policy and cash flow planning are particularly good. There is also a section covering export risk assessment where balance sheet terms in 12 languages are listed.

Management of Trade Credit, T.G. Hudson and J. Butterworth (third edition), Gower Press, 1984, £35.

This text book, which is in its third edition, is a well-produced guide to trade and industrial credit which covers all the main areas of assessment and collection routines. It does not go into great detail, but the assessment chapter will help credit staff to understand the way in which ledger records can be used to review credit limits.

Directors' Personal Liabilities – A Complete Guide to Boardroom Practice, E.A.S. Hutchinson (fourth edition), Institute of Directors, 1988, £7.95.

Credit Management – The Key to Profitable Trading, ed. Michael A. Barry, John Wiley and Sons Ltd, 1997, £42.50.

The following books will assist readers in their export research:

Export Credit, Herbert Edwards, now published by Gower Press, new edition, *Getting Paid for Exports*, £35, January 1990.

This is a comprehensive guide to the credit management of UK exports. There are many checklists and information sources which do not appear in any other text book on credit.

Schmitthoff's Export Trade, Prof. Clive M. Schmitthoff, Stevens (eighth edition), tenth edition due to be published 1998, £40.

This is without doubt the finest book on the law and practice of international trade that has ever been written. This is another exporter's bible; I would never try to export without having this book to hand.

The Bankers Almanac For readers who need to know the exact addresses of international banks in the UK and worldwide, plus the corresponding banks and their agents. This four-volume annual guide can save exporters thousands of pounds when trying to trace payments.

Finance of International Trade, Alastair Watson – Institute of Bankers.

How to understand the financing of international trade, foreign exchange and documentary credits.

Handbook of International Credit Management, ed. Brian Clark, Gower Press, second edition.

Brian Clark, who has had over 40 years experience of international trade, has assembled many contributors, all of whom are experts in their field.

Readers who would like a detailed review of underwriting principles should read:

Credit Insurance – how to reduce the risks of trade credits, Dick Briggs and Burt Edwards (Woodhead-Faulkner Limited), £40 (currently out of print).

This is the first book to be published in the UK exclusively devoted to credit insurance.

Magazines and Journals

Export

Export Today, the official journal of the Institute of Export – monthly
Export Trade, published by Setform – monthly
Export Times, published by Nexus Media Ltd – monthly
Overseas Trade, published by the DTI – monthly

United Kingdom

Credit Management Bulletin, published by Croners – fortnightly
Credit Control, published by House of Words Ltd – monthly

FT Fraud Report, published monthly, covers current fraud news reports in the UK and overseas.

Index